MILTON STUDIES

XXXIX

MILTON STUDIES

XXXIX ❦ Edited by
Albert C. Labriola

UNIVERSITY OF PITTSBURGH PRESS

MILTON STUDIES

is published annually by the University of Pittsburgh Press as a forum for Milton scholarship and criticism. Articles submitted for publication may be biographical; they may interpret some aspect of Milton's writings; or they may define literary, intellectual, or historical contexts—by studying the work of his contemporaries, the traditions which affected his thought and art, contemporary political and religious movements, his influence on other writers, or the history of critical response to his work.

Manuscripts should be upwards of 3,000 words in length and should conform to *The Chicago Manual of Style*. Manuscripts and editorial correspondence should be addressed to Albert C. Labriola, Department of English, Duquesne Unviersity, Pittsburgh, Pa., 15282–1703. Manuscripts should be accompanied by a self-addressed envelope and sufficient unattached postage.

Milton Studies does not review books.

Within the United States, *Milton Studies* may be ordered from the University of Pittsburgh Press, c/o CUP Services, Box 6525, Ithaca, N.Y., 14851, 607–277–2211.

Published by the University of Pittsburgh Press, Pittsburgh, Pa. 15261

Published by the University of Pittsburgh Press, Pittsburgh, Pa. 15261

ISBN 0-8229-4130-9

ISSN 0076-8820

CONTENTS

MILTON STUDIES

XXXIX

NO MARCHIONESS BUT A QUEEN: MILTON'S EPITAPH FOR JANE PAULET

Kate Gartner Frost

DESPITE RECENT OVERUSE, the term "marginalization" seems to apply very well to Milton's *Epitaph on the Marchioness of Winchester*, for this important early piece has apparently not been deemed all that important to Milton studies.[1] Here and there in surveys of Milton's minor works, a sentence or two will be devoted to its conventionality, or to its adherence to early-seventeenth-century (especially Jonsonian) models, or to its place in the development of Milton's metrics.[2] Occasionally there is an offhand evaluation: "an unequal and, on the whole, not very good poem"; "technically interesting"; "self-conscious . . . and rich in courtly extravagance."[3] Until recently the single critical effort devoted to the *Epitaph*, Gayle Wilson's four-page effort of 1974, attempted to make a case only for rhetorical structure.[4] In 1999 Louis Schwartz examined the poem in the light of seventeenth-century childbed mortality.[5]

Such neglect is, to some extent, understandable. The poem's subject, after all, is a young woman who did little more than marry, bear children, and die in the attempt. Its supposed intent, a currying of favor or patronage, was soon to be abandoned by the author in favor of a larger discourse. Nevertheless, *An Epitaph on the Marchioness of Winchester* does not leave Jane Paulet to languish in the shadow of her pale progenitors and the conjunctives of her birth and marriage. Nor can it be relegated to mere academic exercise or attempted preferment. Rather, the poem affirms Paulet's personal identity, separated, even exalted, from her male-designated position in society. Its text and structure witness the movement of a woman from the earthly bonds of marriage and childbirth to a spiritual eminence effected by her own virtue.

The critical devaluation of Milton's *Epitaph* arises from a series of perceived problems that stem from Jane Paulet's traditionally engendered passivity, with the few readers who have noted them laying them at the door of Milton's youthful experimentation or inexperience.[6] These begin in the poem's *exordium* (1–14), where normal elegiac conventions are undermined, and manifest themselves threefold in its *divisio* (15–46), effectively creating a kind of collapse in authenticity. I would maintain, however, that the matter of these first six periods is systematically undercut, both linguistically and

1

structurally, by the final full period of lines 47–74. In effect the poem breaks into two parts, the second outweighing, even obviating, the concerns of the first in a subtextual progression that stresses Jane Paulet's ultimate moral agency. I propose here an overview of the poem that will throw light simultaneously on the subject of the *Epitaph* and its possible recipient, stressing its movement from passivity to agency and, more particularly, the role played by the *conclusio* in undermining the preceding *exordium* and *divisio*.

I support my thesis with a reading of the *Epitaph* in the light of premodern Augustinian poetics,[7] a task which entails skills and habits rather different from those generally employed by the modern reader. My reading takes Milton's poem as more than casually structured, and it mandates that one subordinate the habit of deriving primary meaning from sequential textual order to the act of pursuing a comprehensive overview of the work. This is primarily an intellectual process: Augustine had referred all material beauty to the rational order of the universe, the means to its perception lying not, he says in *De vera religione*, "by the eye of the flesh or by any bodily sense, but by the [mind]."[8] The world of Augustinian poetics ideally was ordered by reason. The artist's task was not to impose an individual and thus particular and to some degree irrational order on his creation but rather to reveal to his audience the inherently logical order of the cosmos, thus turning its gaze to the Creator and eliciting admiration for the skill with which the artifact was constructed.

Such a reading entails a detached consideration of the poem's structural subtexts as well as a close examination of its language. Taking into account not just the confines of a single genre, the reader aims to examine the work in the entire—in terms of the circumstances and milieu of its writing and of the formal and aesthetic expectations that its maker sought to satisfy.[9] In carrying out such a reading, this essay will examine the limina that underlie the discursive fabric of Milton's *Epitaph*, acknowledging those that are ratified by that fabric. It aims to 1) confront the ramifications of historical context in the poem, 2) examine the critical problem of its supposed bifurcation, 3) explore its arithmetical substructure—which entails discussing its underlying arithmology, and 4) attempt a careful reading of its discursive surface, that is, literal referents, theme and image, typological references, and rhetorical strategies.[10]

My application of Augustinian poetics assumes an intentionally authored work that asks to be understood on its own terms before being released into the sometimes chaotic world of modern criticism.[11] However, the modern reader unfortified by the work of careful and creative literary historians is at a disadvantage unless she is willing to add to her skills techniques of reading that aim at revealing the potential full meaning of the work. Its parts must be viewed in the light of the whole and the implications of the whole brought to bear on each of its parts. This process may put that reader—accustomed to scanning the semantic line discursively as primary activity—at a bit of a loss. But improved evaluative skills will reveal new criteria for coherence in the complex process of relating part to whole. The result is a less fragmented reading, its perceptions less fettered to theoretical bias and the subjective instant and, one hopes, more given to meditative, rational study.

HISTORICAL CONTEXT

An Epitaph on the Marchioness of Winchester is a conventional example of seventeenth-century epideictic verse, and any serious attempt at understanding its place in the century's and in Milton's canon must first elucidate its occasion and historical import. On 15 April 1631, the twenty-three-year-old Marchioness of Winchester lay dying. The young poet who was to write her epitaph was then approaching his twenty-third birthday and his final year at Cambridge. Merritt Hughes reminds us that "although Milton's twenty-third birthday fell on December 9, 1631, his practice in dating his poems . . . suggests a time early in that year as the date of [Sonnet 7]."[12] It was a period of rich productivity for Milton; to it have been assigned variously the Hobson poems, *Song: On May Morning,* Sonnet 7, *On Shakespeare,* and (debatedly) *L'Allegro* and *Il Penseroso.*[13] Before him lay *Lycidas* and, more important for Jane Paulet's epitaph, behind him lay *On the Morning of Christ's Nativity. An Epitaph on the Marchioness of Winchester* was composed probably during the summer term of 1631 and first printed in the 1645 *Poems.* Most of the poems of the period bear the trappings of academe, or at least are directed at an academic audience. Following convention, the poem would seem to be intended for the family of the Marchioness, perhaps for the marquess himself. (John Shawcross points out that "Milton's connection with aristocratic and titled people continue[d] throughout his life, despite his political views and position.")[14]

If this is indeed the intended audience, as some scholars speculate, then Milton can be seen as currying favor in, for him, an unexpected direction, for the Winchesters were conspicuous among the old Catholic aristocracy. Under missionary influence of the Seminarists and Jesuits, English Catholicism, frequently distinguished by the gentle background of its adherents, was re-created during the last three decades of Elizabeth's reign, particularly in the North. Families of the old Catholic aristocracy sent their sons abroad to be trained for the priesthood, whence they returned on the dangerous English Mission. They passed in disguise through the countryside, sheltered in a secret network of recusant country houses, of which Basing House, seat of the Winchesters, was one. The Catholic establishment, targeted by both the English Reformation and the Council of Trent, attempted to survive on its own terms, which proved its undoing. A stubborn independence, because it mandated separation from even the most conservative elements of the Established Church and perpetuated a continuum of pre-Tridentine doctrine and practice, doomed it to impotent isolation. Dennis Flynn's recent study *John Donne and the Ancient Catholic Nobility,* although it focuses on a somewhat earlier period, vividly sets forth the conditions under which such families, in this case the Heywoods, Donne's maternal connections, attempted to survive. Such conditions prevailed for—and often ruined—some prominent families: the Percys, Stanleys, Brownes, and, of course, the Paulets, who sought to remain faithful to the old religion and who participated in the often perilous intrigue which the attempt mandated.[15]

I propose, however, that Milton was casting his eye in a direction more congruent with his growing Protestant radicalism and that he had occasion to proceed in that direction. In 1616 at the king's behest the duke of Buckingham, after a closely contested election, was made chancellor of Cambridge (a perceived insult to Parliament, which was then in the process of impeaching him). His first act was to incorporate Archbishop Laud as a doctor of the university. The latter immediately began to meddle with the university's religious status, mandating conformity, in order "that both universities may receive the same rule, go on the same way, and so be the happy mother of piety and union through the Church."[16] Cambridge Arminians seized the opportunity. Royal patronage ensured that headships of colleges fell to those whose friends pressed hardest at court, and the Arminians were advanced, happy to pay the price: they preached obedience, defended royal policy and royal taxes, denounced English Parliaments and Scottish rebels, and, occupying secular office, they voted for secular justice. These college heads, representing "as yet a small academic party," wasted no time setting reform in motion, concentrating on the conversion of university scholars, so that soon one might hear "sermons very shocking to good Protestant ears" and see the Anglican service performed in baroque elegance with elaborate organ music and swinging censers.[17] Peterhouse led with its splendidly refurbished architecture, fittings, and liturgical embellishments, and undergraduates from other colleges resorted there "to learn or practise popery." The Arminian faction gained in numbers, bringing increasing pressure to bear on the Puritan strongholds of Emmanuel, Corpus Christi, and Sidney Sussex, for whom the situation threatened to become a new despotism.[18]

The fight was on, and Milton was at Christ's to witness part of it. With the battle lines drawn as they can be only in academe, Laud, who saw the universities as seminaries essential in building a right-thinking clergy, gave the conflict its major impetus with announcement of an ecclesiastical visitation. The university resisted, led by Vice Chancellor Beale, who actually secretly supported Laud. But bitter infighting took its toll, and annual election of the vice chancellor made for on-again, off-again support of the Arminian cause. The assassination of Buckingham in 1629 signalled an end to the matter, for he was succeeded as chancellor by Earl Holland, who "did nothing to enforce uniformity, and resisted . . . Laud's claim to visit the university as metropolitan"—inaction and action which certainly would have met with the young Milton's approval. John Shawcross has reminded us that even though Milton came to be associated with what is loosely labelled Puritanism, we should not forget that he was educated toward a career in what would have been Anglicanism, until he was "church-outed."[19] His course of study at Cambridge was ministerial, and his signing the Subscription Books in 1629 (and again 1632) indicates that his vocational intent had not yet altered.[20] Unfortunately, we have no direct evidence of Milton's participation in the melee, since his immediate activities during the period are difficult to chart, although from mid-April 1630 to the beginning of 1631, when the plague closed the university, he was at his father's home. But that he was in the middle of negotiating his personal, religious, and political loyalties seems probable. Although the *Epitaph* seems at first to bear no relation to this negotiation, an examination of its historical context alongside of its structure I think will prove a different case.

The subject of Milton's *Epitaph,* Jane Paulet née Savage (1607–1631), was the eldest daughter of Thomas, Viscount Savage. Her maternal grandfather was Earl Rivers. The family, rooted in the old Catholic faith, remained devoted to the queen, with her father serving as Henrietta Maria's chancellor and her mother as a lady of the queen's bedchamber. At the age of fifteen Jane was wed to a scion of the old Catholic aristocracy, John Paulet, Lord St. John, of Basing House, Hampshire. Her first son, Charles, was born seven years later in 1629, the year his father became fifth marquess of Winchester. Her death in 1631 likely resulted from blood poisoning, which also carried off her second, stillborn child. According to a letter from her sister, the duchess of Buckingham, to her father, dated 16 April 1631, the Marchioness "was delivered before shee died of a deed boye."[21] Sparse contemporary witness to her existence indicates that she was of literary bent (some of her poetry seems to have been translated into Spanish),[22] and most references (like the elegies penned by Jonson, Davenant, and the Roman Catholic Walter Colman) conventionally recount her grace and beauty.[23]

One account of her death, in a letter of John Pory to Sir Thomas Puckering, provides intriguing information: "The Lady Marquess of Winchester, daughter to the Lord Viscount Savage, had an imposthume upon her cheek lanced; the humour fell down into her throat, and quickly despatched her, being big with child, whose death is lamented as well in respect of other her virtues, as that she was inclining to become a protestant."[24] This is a rather odd comment about a young woman so strongly yoked to the Catholic cause. Her parents continued faithful to the queen, her brother eventually turned his back on the earldom to become a Jesuit, and her husband was to be known as "the great loyalist" for his endurance of the famous two-year siege of his seat at Basing House by Parliamentary forces, forcibly dragged from its burning wreckage where he had sworn to die rather than surrender. For such a young woman (she was a month from her twenty-fourth birthday at the time of her death) to move toward Protestantism would be a painful and perhaps risky affair. But if her inclination were true, or perceived as true by the young Milton, then in his twenty-third year, meditating on the exigencies of time and fate, then this is an interesting context for Milton's composition of the *Epitaph* and presentation of the Marchioness. Although there has been some supposition that the *Epitaph* was composed for a collection of verses supposedly made in her honor at Cambridge, no such collection is extant and, indeed, its initial existence is dubious.[25] Hence Milton's connection with the Marchioness is slender and without much substantive support: they shared an arithmetical age and, possibly, a rejection of traditional religious orientation—he of the Church of England moving toward a more radical reformed faith, she of Roman Catholicism toward Protestantism. At present there is not much to go on.

Another possible connection has been noted by the poet's biographer William Riley Parker, who perceives the link between the Marchioness and Milton's Helicon, "the banks of *Came*," to be her kinsman Henry Rich, Earl Holland, Chancellor of Cambridge University from 1629 to 1649.[26] The Marchioness was a Rich on her mother's side: Elizabeth Darcy was the eldest daughter of Thomas, third Lord Darcy, first Earl Rivers, the grandson of Frances Rich, sister to Robert, second Baron Rich (1537–1581), grandfather of Holland.

This kinship Jane Paulet herself ratified in a letter to Holland, circa 1630, where she states that she has "ever found him a worthy friend and kinsman."[27] Son of Penelope Rich, Sidney's Stella, he was a handsome, rising courtier, favored by James I, gentleman of the bedchamber to Prince Charles, and eventually the surrogate wooer of Henrietta Maria. In 1624 he was made Earl Holland, largely through his currying of favor with Buckingham. But Holland seems to have been a not very successful timeserver in a period that demanded extremely adept timeserving. Like the Savages, he was of the queen's party, but by 1642 he had allied himself with Parliament and then reverted to the king in the Second Civil War, for which diversion of loyalty he paid with his

Chart I: The Jane Paulet-Henry Holland Connection

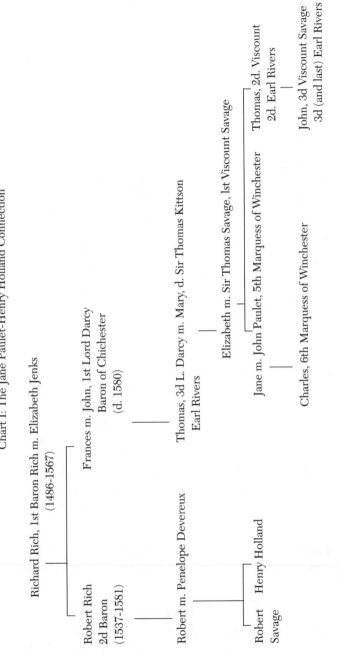

handsome head in 1649.[28] Clarendon had no good opinion of the Earl: "He was a very well-bred man, and a fine gentleman in good times: but too much desired to enjoy ease and plenty when the king could have neither, and did think poverty the most insupportable evil that could befall any man in this world."[29] Regardless of his later unfortunate political footwork, at the time of the composition of the *Epitaph* he was, in his connections to the Marchioness, in his Protestantism, in his opposition to Laud, and in his lax administration of religious conformity at the University, a very possible recipient of Milton's verses. Moreover, at the time of the poem's inclusion in the 1645 edition, Holland was a Parliament man, while the marquess was confined in the Tower of London for treason.

To stop here is truly to relinquish both the Marchioness and her epitaph to the margin. It is to see her solely as a woman defined by her birth, her male connections, and her biology: "The Marchioness is of noble origin . . . , she is known for her virtuous, gentle disposition . . . , she is more than devout . . . , lastly, she meets her death in childbirth, that is, in the accomplishment of her duty as a Christian spouse."[30] Moreover, her image is "the sum total of all motherly and wifely qualities that we find throughout the Sonnets. The 'deification' of woman, mentioned in respect to Sonnets X and XIV, is already present in this epitaph, since the last lines depict her, not as an earthly noblewoman but as a Queen in heaven."[31] In effect, Jane Paulet has been reduced to an antiquated (if fecund) sonnet lady, by Milton's time a creaky bore. If this characterization is accurate, the critical silence that surrounds this poem is perhaps justified. Milton's male chauvinism is demonstrated once again. Wilson's article—until very recently the sole critical examination of the poem — explores the structure of the *Epitaph* but presents the Marchioness merely as an extension of her male lineage. Wilson emphasizes the topos of descent upon which the poet draws to win his audience (presumably her husband and family): "By means of these associations, her importance in a hierarchical society is enhanced, and the sense of loss stemming from the death of such a highly placed member of society is heightened. Her descent then is the chief source of 'her praise.' "[32] Her deeds are confined to marriage and the production of progeny. If this status, achieved by birth and marriage, is the sum total of Jane Paulet's accomplishments, then the *Epitaph* must be perceived as mendaciously conventional and deeply flawed. But examination of the poem's bifurcated structure and complex subtexts disproves such summary judgement.

BIFURCATION

The *Epitaph* first appeared in the 1645 *Poems,* where, taking up some four pages, it follows *At a solemn Musick* and is followed in turn by *Song. On May morning.* It exists as well in British Museum, MS Sloane 1446, 37v–38r, which contains a variant that will be discussed further on. I wish first to address the matter of complete stops, particularly the stop at line 10, which will be a point of debate in this essay. There is no extant holograph manuscript of any of the poems earlier than 1637, and the copy for the 1645 was likely prepared by an amanuensis.[33] Even the most pristine authorial copy would have been at times treated rudely by the printer, in this case Ruth Raworth. In his edition of the *Epitaph,* John Shawcross has changed the 1645 full stop of line 10 to a comma, citing as his rationale: "I use a comma because the strong stop—particularly a period—separates the thoughts and I think they should not be. The word 'Yet' in l. 11 is a contrastive continuance of the thought."[34] Shawcross arrives at this editorial decision with the Sloane MS variant in mind. This manuscript, in a scribal hand, omits lines from the 1645 text and substitutes for lines 15–24:

> Seven times had the yearly star
> In every sign set up his car,
> Since for her they did request
> The God that sits at marriage feast,
> When first the early matrons run
> To Greet her of her lovely Son.[35]

The author is identified as "Jo Milton of Chr. Coll Cambr." and the title reads: "On the Marchioness of Winchester whoe died in childbedd. Ap. 15. 1631."[36] Lines 15–16 and 19–22 of the 1645 version are missing. Noting that the passage "fits neatly into the whole" and contains the information that Jane Paulet's first child was born seven years after her marriage, Parker accepts the Sloane variant as possibly an early draft bearing Milton's revisions, although he admits that it may be "a careful bit of meddling by an informed person who thought to improve Milton's lines," a not unknown practice.[37] In general, editors have disregarded the Sloane variant: H. F. Fletcher excludes it entirely, and the Columbia editors deny it any significance. Pointing to its sparse punctuation, Shawcross suggests that "what was published was revised after 1631 and 1645 (probably closer to the later date), and a transcription in any case by one or more hands. . . . Milton was not the one who penned the copytext."[38] Parker suggests that the MS variant contains an accurate piece of biographical information not in the 1645 version, and that the Sloane version represents an authentic early draft allowed to circulate.[39] Since we have no examples of Milton's punctuation dated before 1637, the point may be moot, although Mindele Treip has maintained that "direct indications that Milton cared about punctuation and had evolved distinctive practices concerning its use are to be found in extant autograph manuscripts of his early poems."[40] I must agree with Emma Roth-Schwartz, who takes issue with Shawcross's emendation, primarily on aesthetic grounds: "The period after 'death' indicates a most rhetorically appropriate long pause which coincides with the end of the sentence. . . . I think the strong stop at the end of l. 10 is metrically justifiable."[41] My own acceptance of this pointing reflects my perception of the poem's structure.

The first evidence of bifurcation in the *Epitaph* stems from its rhetorical arrangement in the sections commemorating Jane Paulet's life and death. The first, consisting of the *exordium* and *divisio,* dealing with her time on earth, comprises twenty-three couplets with full stops at lines six, ten, and fourteen and employing third person narrative and implied second person address (22). The second, the *conclusio* (47–74), manifesting only one final stop and employing direct address, consists of twenty-eight lines (or fourteen couplets). When these two are set off against each other, some thematic elements of the poem take on new and vibrant importance, revealing the obvious bows to convention that inaugurate its first part only to be undercut by its second. The *Epitaph* opens with the traditional identification of the subject in terms of her male connections: she is "honoured Wife" to Winchester, daughter to a viscount, heir to her baronial grandfather. Her own identity is viewed as an addendum to these distinctions: "Besides what her virtues fair added to her noble birth." Despite the traditional recording of the deceased's familial connections—this is, after all, an epitaph—the poem's first period seems rather like overkill. In the opening of the structural section at line 47, however, all such pretensions to familial honors have disappeared: she is simply "Lady"—according to the *Oxford English Dictionary* a term traditionally applied to a queen, especially to the ancient queens of what we call Wessex, of which Winchester is a chief seat.[42] Also conventional is the subject of a life cut short that might have been more lengthy had the subject's merits been considered: "Yet had the number of her days / Been as complete as was her praise, / Nature and fate had had no strife / In giving limit to her life" (11–14). The Marchioness here passively accepts limitation. But the juxtaposed second section awards her an active role denied by the first: "That to give the world increase, / Short'ned hast thy own life's lease" (51–52). This emphasis, it seems to me, encourages the reader to reexamine the "virtues fair" of the first section as moral agents. Indeed, upon such reconsideration, it is possible to identify in the poem's early lines a subtext of accountability, weighing, and measuring—although the measure is short (deliberately I think to enforce its contrast with the perfect measure of the poem's last twenty-eight lines). Hence, although both sections begin with images of the grave, the first implies descent, death, darkness, short measure, while the second moves to the topoi of ascent, new life, light, and perfection. Milton has held the traditional "stuff" of the epitaph up to scrutiny and found it wanting for Jane Paulet.

The effect of undermining holds especially for the poem's mythological excursions. The first, beginning at line fifteen (Jane Paulet's age at her marriage), presents Hymen, god of marriage. Called to the Marchioness's wedding feast, he bears a sputtering torch and, in his garland, a bud of cypress. Milton, as all his editors point out, derives this image from Ovid's account of the wedding feast of Orpheus, doubly yoking death and poesie. A further antithesis shows up in the second section, where the fatal garland gives way to the flowers and bays and the "perfect moan" of Helicon. Such an antithesis occurs as well in the replacement of Lucina, goddess of childbed, by Atropos in the next full period. The conflation of childbirth and death is echoed in the second section by the introduction of Rachel, who, like the Marchioness, after seven years of barrenness produced a first illustrious son and gave up her life in the bearing of a second. (Milton had dealt with Jacob in 1624 in *A Paraphrase on Psalm 114*, but without emphasis on Rachel or his marriages.) Both "through pangs [fly] to felicity."

If these antithetical conjunctions between the poem's parts hold, then the third rather odd period, the horticultural simile in the *divisio,* takes on new and startling meaning. Literally, it reads as follows: A slip of winter pink, taken for a root cutting, watered by a spring shower and hence beginning to grow in its rooting bed, is thoughtlessly picked by a country fellow.[43] The flower droops its head sideways, and the drops of dew that adorn it foreshadow the tears that will be shed at its funeral. The simile, which had been forecast in *On the Death of a Fair Infant Dying of a Cough,* presents certain problems. It does not follow the mythological continuum which precedes it, and its referents are obscure and, in at least one instance, confusing. It begins with the conjunction "So." But what is the referent? The entire thirty-four lines preceding? Or the mythological episodes on Jane Paulet's marriage and childbirth? Who is the "slip"—the Marchioness or her stillborn child? Who is the "swain"? And why is Winter, leading her "carnation train," female, a unique gender designation in Milton and generally a rare usage in the Renaissance?

Let us look at possible parallels or antitheses in the second section. In Paradise (it seems to be Dante's Paradise) the Marchioness, now a "bright Saint," sits next to Rachel who is "much like [her] . . . in story," with a likely pun on the last word. (The use of "story/storey" as floor or level dates, according to the *OED,* at least to 1400. An instance almost exactly contemporaneous with the *Epitaph* is provided by Donne in a sermon on Isaiah 7:14 for Christmas 1624: "But though thou be but a Tabernacle of Earth, God shall raise thee peece by peece, into a spirituall building; And after one Story of Creation, and another of Vocation, and another of Sanctification, he shall bring thee up, to meete thy selfe, in the bosome of thy God."[44]) Milton has been selective in his description of Rachel: she is a Syrian, a shepherdess, her barrenness is emphasized, she has borne the "highly favor'd" Joseph, her husband has served for her, and like the Marchioness she is raised in status (one remembers that, although she was Jacob's favorite, Rachel was second wife). The figure expresses similar but antithetical concerns: the unheedy swain "crop[s]," that is, deflowers, the slip, which is being rescued from winter damage through rooting in a new bed. Rachel leaves Syria and her father's house (stealing his household idols) for Jacob; Rachel sits in glory, the blossom droops sideways on a dying bed.

I should like to suggest the following reading for the simile: the Marchioness, daughter of the old Catholic aristocracy, is in the process of transplantation from Catholicism ("Winter's . . . carnation train") to the new soil and vernal showers of Protestantism. (Conversion of a Catholic heiress to a great house would be a triumph in a period when each side sought to add stars to its crown. The greatest success came through the conversion of prominent individuals: intellectuals were wooed in universities, men of influence at royal courts—Buckingham himself was besieged in 1622 by Catholic missionaries but proved constant. In Catholic Europe young aristocrats on the grand tour with their tutors found themselves courted by urbane cardinals, entertained by the colleges of their nations, guided round the city by compatriots of the old persuasion.[45]) Like Rachel, the Marchioness flees her father's house and renders useless his gods. But unlike Rachel, who is "serv'd" by her husband (a phrase with sexual implications), the Marchioness is "crop[ped]" and "pluck't," with associations of ungentle wooing. The pearls of dew she wears are heraldic as well as poetic: in heraldry pearls are small white or silver balls set on a coronet; to "wear" is to display on one's shield. (The blazon of the marquess of Winchester featured a falcon, its neck encircled by such a coronet.) On earth these pearls fall from her coronet as tears for her funeral. In Paradise her coronet becomes a crown.

This interpretation implies that the marquess himself is the uncouth swain. The young Milton may well have made such an identfication, given Paulet's religion and politics in 1631. The association seems even more likely when one remembers that in 1645, still smoky from the ruins of Basing House, he languished in the Tower charged by Parliament with treason.[46] The siege continued from August 1643 to 16 October 1645. Winchester was committed to the Tower on 18 October. The 1645 Poems had been registered twelve days earlier.

If the poem delivers a subtle insult to Winchester, it likely pays compliment to Jane's kinsman, Earl Holland, for its opening line identifies the Marchioness's "rich Marble."[47] I would like to suggest that the *Epitaph* may indeed have been directed at Holland and that there probably was no collection of verses. Milton may have been currying favor, but the *Epitaph* was directed at a far more promising object than the Catholic and Royalist Winchester.

ARCHITECTONIC STRUCTURE

That Milton, like many of his contemporaries, fashioned arithmetical substructures in his poetry has in recent years been the subject of diminishing debate and increasing critical scrutiny. Such practice has been demonstrated both in *Paradise Lost* and in various of the minor poems.[48] I would like to suggest that the periodic construction in the *Epitaph* reflects the long tradition of Augustinian poetics that came to a final efflorescence in the seventeenth century. This practice promoted spatial and arithmetical constructions that emulated the harmony of natural form. For the premodern reader, however, natural form posited a premodern Nature, with its harmony expressed in number, ratio, and musical proportion that contrasted the multiplicity and hence mutability of created things and the unity and constancy of the Divine. The balancing of these subtextual parts—or their deliberate imbalance—provided meaning which could reinforce or undermine the primary text. For modern readers this process may seem creatively restricting, even intellectually subtle. I quote here Donne biographer Dennis Flynn: "Our idea of poetry tends to be associative rather than logical, working more by metonymy than by synecdoche, [while] in Donne's time beauty was a function of design and structure rather than in the eye of the beholder."[49] In her recent exposition of Augustinian poetics, Maren-Sofie Røstvig points to the various loci that laid its foundation in mandating the equation between beauty and an order arranged by number or proportion. The result is a didactive, regenerative poetics in which the reader is led from the multiplicity of the material text through a contemplation of numerical proportion to the mind of God. In effect, the reader, fallen and mutable, can be regenerated by means of the imposition of order, moving from *res creatae* to God the source of all concord (*omnis concordiae caput*).[50]

The poem's construction is, like its linear text, syncritical. In his aforementioned study Wilson envisioned the *Epitaph* as divided into an *exordium* expounding Jane Paulet's age and the credentials of her birth (1–14), a *divisio* developing her praise (15–46), and a *conclusio* in the form of an *exclamatio* that reveals the poet's stance toward subject and occasion (47–74), a division which I accept.[51]

Chart II: AN EPITAPH ON THE MARCHIONESS OF WINCHESTER

John Milton. *Complete Poems and Major Prose,* ed. Merritt Y. Hughes (New York: The Odyssey Press, 1957)

Exordium

I

This rich Marble doth inter
The honor'd Wife ofWinchester,
A Viscount's daughter, An Earl's heir,
Besides what her virtues fair
Added to her noble birth,
More than she could own from Earth.

II

Summers three times eight save one
She had told; alas too soon,
After so short time of breath,
To house with darkness, and with death. 10

III

Yet had the number of her days
Been as complete as was her praise,
Nature and fate had had no strife
In giving limit to her life.

Divisio

IV

Her high birth, and her graces sweet,
Quickly found a lover meet;
The Virgin choir for her request
The God that sits at marriage feast;
He at their invoking came
But with a scarce-well-lighted flame; 20
And in his Garland as he stood,
Ye might discern a Cypress bud.

V

Once had the early Matrons run
To greet her of a lovely son,
And now with second hope she goes,
And calls Lucina to her throes;
But whether by mischance or blame
Atropos for Lucina came,
And with remorseless cruelty,
Spoil'd at once both fruit and tree: 30
The hapless Babe before his birth
Had burial, yet not laid in earth,
And the languisht Mother's Womb
Was not long a living Tomb.

VI

So have I seen some tender slip
Sav'd with care from Winter's nip,
The pride of her carnation train,
Pluck't up by some unheedy swain,
Who only thought to crop the flow'r
New shot up from vernal show'r; 40
But the fair blossom hangs the head
Sideways as on a dying bed,
And those Pearls of dew she wears,
Prove to be presaging tears
Which the sad morn had let fall
On her hast'ning funeral.

Conclusio

VII

Gentle Lady, may thy grave
Peace and quiet ever have:
After this thy travail sore
Sweet rest seize thee evermore, 50
That to give the world increase,
Short'ned hast thy own life's lease;
Here, besides the sorrowing
That thy noble House doth bring,
Here be tears of perfect moan
Wept for thee in Helicon,
And some Flowers and some Bays
For thy Hearse to strew the ways,
Sent thee from the banks of Came,
Devoted to thy virtuous name; 60
Whilst thou, bright Saint, high sitt'st in glory,
Next her much like to thee in story,
That fair Syrian Shepherdess,
Who after years of barrenness
To him that serv'd for her before,
And at her next birth, much like to thee,
Through pangs fled to felicity,
Far within the bosom bright
Of blazing Majesty and Light; 70
There with thee, new welcome Saint,
Like fortunes may her soul acquaint,
With thee there clad in radiant sheen,
No Marchioness, but now a Queen.

His analysis points to a textual substructure based on the poem's verse paragraphs: three full stops each in the *exordium* and the *divisio*, with the *conclusio* forming one long period. In effect, the poem contains seven periodic units. While this in itself is not substantial evidence of an arithmetical subtext, the sevenfold division, so common in the era, suggests that the *Epitaph* may be drawing structurally on the hexaemeral tradition, as Milton was to do later in *Paradise Lost.*[52] This, I contend, is the case. Moreover, the poem's two halves mandate separate prosodic consideration: that is, the first half demands that the lines be read as couplets, the second as single lines, reflecting the traditional 2:1 ratio of multiplicity: unity.

Exordium: The *exordium* contains fourteen lines, with three full stops. Lines 1–6 identify the Marchioness in conventional terms by her aristocratic descent, her rise in station through marriage, her virtues; lines 7–10 address, again in conventional terms, the sum of her short life; lines 11–14 weigh her short life against her virtues. The total of fourteen lines delineates the years of her virginal estate.

Divisio: The sixteen lines of the *divisio* also contain three full stops. Lines 15–22 begin with Jane Paulet's marriage at age fifteen and end with her having reached the age of twenty-two, when she bore her first son Charles, the future marquess. This period presents the first of a series of three reversed processions, in this case, an epithalamic procession that exhibits a pattern of abrupt reversal. The second full period, lines 23–34, begins with her age at death and presents the ill-fated matronal procession. Finally, the third period, lines 35–46, contains the horticultural simile that has puzzled the poem's commentators, presenting the Marchioness in a seasonal procession, "Winter's . . . carnation train," reversed by her bedding and deadly defloration by the "unheedy swain."

Conclusio: This twenty-eight line period moves directly from the Marchioness in life to the Marchioness in death, or rather, eternal life, from conventional to hyperbolic discourse, from narrative and second person address to direct address, from emphasis on descent to ascent, from earthly imperfect short time to the perfection of eternity. These lines, considered singly as steps, reflect her ascent to a perfect life in Paradise: twenty-eight is not only a female number in its association with the lunar cycle but also a perfect number in that it forms the sum of its aliquot parts $(1 + 2 + 4 + 7 + 14)$ and virtuous in that it hits the mean.[53] Viewed as a perfect triangular number, it symbolizes the perfection of eternity toward which the soul yearns and was traditionally employed for funeral verses.[54] If the twenty-eight-line verse paragraph of the *conclusio* asks to be considered as a single entity, then the six paragraphs of the *exordium* and the *divisio* demand consideration in their multiplicity, which may, by the way, account for the apparent thematic fragmentation of the procession episodes. Moreover, this pattern sets off the *conclusio* against the *exordium* and *divisio*, weighing the life of the Marchioness in eternity against her life on earth. Such weighing off is reflected in the poem's arithmetical structure, since the forty-six lines of *exordium* and *divisio* can be considered as twenty-three couplets—twenty-three a traditional number of short time and, in a witty finesse, the age of the Marchioness and of Milton.

The poem's development as panegyric mirrors this balance. The conventions for the panegyric, as set forth in Cicero's *De Partitione Oratoria* (a work with which Milton professes himself familiar in his *Artis Logicae*), concern themselves with three classes of goods: external, bodily, and intellectual (*externis, corporis, animi*). Praise of the first began with family, then fortune and estate, appearance as an indication of virtue, and, finally, achievements, these delineated either chronologically or, more especially, by classification of virtues. Says Cicero:

Consequently all the resources of panegyric and reprehension will be adopted from these divisions of the virtues and vices; but in the whole fabric of the speech the greatest attention is to be focused on the quality of a person's breeding and upbringing and education and character; and on any important or startling occurrence that a man has encountered, especially if this can appear to be due to the intervention of providence; . . . and these same topics of research will be drawn on to supply the causes and results and consequences of things. Nor yet will it be proper to pass over in silence the death of those persons whose life is going to be praised, in case of there being something noticeable either in the nature certainly of their death itself or in the events that follow after death.[55]

Milton's *Epitaph* follows these conventions, but my contention that it displays a bifurcated argument demands further support. That support can be found in at least one contemporary source, *The Arte or Crafte of Rhethoryke* of Leonard Cox, and in Milton's own *Artis Logicae*. Cox, in his discussion of the "oration Demonstrative," places Cicero's biographical mandate and his catalog of virtues in the oration's narration, this followed by either a confirmation or a confutation.[56] Chapter 12 of *Artis Logicae*, "*De Diversis*," identifies such a bifurcated argument as a "dissentany" (*dissentaneo*): "dissentany arguments are equally manifested with relation to one another; each is equally argued by the other; yet by their dissent they more evidently appear" ("*Sunt autem dissentanea inter se æque manifesta alterumque ab altero aequaliter arguitur; tametsi sua dissensione clarious eluescant*").[57] The juxtaposition of the Marchioness in life and in death results in what Cox calls a "contention," with the second half commenting adversely on the first.[58] Hence the poem's structure can be said to reflect its arithmetical and spatial underpinnings.

TEXTUAL READING

If such a spatial reading is to hold, it must be supported by the primary discursive text as well as by the verbal subtext. A reading based primarily on structural aspects of the poem—such as arithmetical units—is generally no reading at all but often a whimsical pattern of play on the part of an overly ingenious reader. Architectonic substructures must be validated by their integral relation to the literal text, whether it be one of ratification or subversion. Such can be done with *An Epitaph on the Marchioness of Winchester*, as a close reading of the poem's language will prove.

Exordium: The first full period of the *exordium* is patently conventional, with its elegiac address and its ticking off of epitaph conventions: address to the reader, birth, lineage, marriage, rank, and references to Jane Paulet's beauty and virtue. On closer look, these conventions are undercut within the linguistic subtext. In the first line of an epitaph one expects an identifying name, something like "Here lies X." But the first line of this epitaph undercuts the name of Winchester with "this rich Marble," a possible, and if one accepts Earl Holland as the designate, a likely pun on the name of the Rich family. Moreover, the contrasting patterns of earthly descent, first by lineage and then to the grave, are set off against patterns of earthly ascent in rank by marriage. Finally, the conventional bow to Paulet's "virtues fair," while it has generally been held to refer to her chaste beauty, reverberates more strongly when one recognizes that "virtue" in the seventeenth century could refer also to "efficacy of a moral nature, influence working for good upon human life or conduct," and "fair" could mean not only comely but also "free from moral stain" (*OED*). Hence the poem's first paragraph weighs her moral efficacy against what the Marchioness "could own from Earth"—whether that be from worldly circumstance or from her own marital and maternal body.

The second period also commands the reader to consider conventions of the epitaph: age, life unseasonably cut off, and death as a final abode. Its first line calls attention to numbers, its second to counting, its third to short time. It ends in darkness.

The third period, with its opening "Yet," commands the reader not only to consider but also to accept the traditional imbalance between the life worth great praise and the life cut short. Its display of the conflict between nature and fate forecasts the unequal contest in the divisio between Lucina and Atropos. We are reminded again of Jane Paulet's age: "the number of her days"—a delicate opposition, I think, of their sunlight to the darkness that ends the preceding period. But their radiance is "[in]complete" and thus no match.

Divisio: The *divisio* also presents three periods, and here Milton undermines conventions: each presents a hopeful, even a joyful, procession that is abruptly reversed. They move from reader address to the mode of narrative fiction, drawing on three seemingly disparate sources: New Testament parable, classical myth, and horticultural simile. The first of these is a kind of reversed epithalamion,[59] which conflates the mythical figures of Hymen, Orpheus, and Christ. The "Virgin choir" expecting "the God that sits at marriage feast" who comes with "scarce-well-lighted flame" is reminiscent of the parable of the wise and foolish virgins and is drawn from Ovid's account of the wedding of Orpheus—a natural association since the two were typologically conflated. Alexander Ross gives a seventeenth-century version of this conflation:

Christ is the true Orpheus who by the sweetnes and force of his Evangelicall musick caused the Gentiles who before were stocks and stones in knowledge, and no bettter then beasts in religion to follow after him: it was he onely who went downe to hell, to recover the Church his spowse who had lost her selfe by running away from Aristeus, even goodnesse it selfe, and delighting her selfe among the grasse and flowres of pleasure, was stung by that old serpent the Devill. What was in vaine attempted by Orpheus, was truly performed by our Saviour, for he alone hath delivered our soules from the nethermost hell; and at last was he turne with whips, and thornes, and piercd with nailes and a speare upon the crosse for our transgressions.[60]

But the God who comes is not Christ but a gloomy Hymen whose cypress bud delicately forecasts the horticultural imagery of the sixth period.

The third period of the *divisio,* also couched in the narrative, opens with a procession of the "early Matrons," which, if we accept the *OED,* can refer to married female saints as well as to those women who in their midwifery assisted the Marchioness at her first confinement. Interestingly, they "greet" her—a word with two distinct connotations: the sense of "to offer congratulations" (as Spenser used it, although he does not use a verb with the preposition "of," i.e., on account of), and the opposite sense of "to weep, cry, lament, grieve." This procession is not just reversed, but abandoned altogether: the Marchioness "with second hope" alone calls on Lucina, goddess of childbirth, and the result is not the "lovely son" of her first pregnancy, but "throes," with the overtone not just of birth but also of the pangs of death. Answering to her call is not a minor nature deity like Lucina but actually one of the Fates, and the words associated with her are grim: "mischance," "blame," "remorseless cruelty." The period concludes with references to the entombment of the stillborn child in terms of "fruit," "tree," and "earth," a forecasting of the horticultural simile that follows.

The horticultural simile has puzzled some among the few critics who have addressed Milton's *Epitaph,* including Cleanth Brooks:

When this image is joined to the poignant flowers passage, there is produced an effect of chilling pathos which is not duplicated elsewhere in Milton's poetry. But the poet must pay a price for this effect. The flower passage, so exquisitely tender when considered by itself, in context serves primarily to mitigate the pain caused by the representation of the Marchioness as a living tomb. The genuine emotion excited by the flower sequence does not produce a catharsis; it merely neutralizes the horror induced by the preceding figure.[61]

This too presents a failed procession: the Marchioness becomes a "tender slip" in the retinue of a female Winter, who, although the Marchioness is "the pride" of her retinue, will "nip" (in horticulture, as a noun, a severe check to vegetation caused by cold; as a verb, to strip or make bare by pinching, or to check growth by pinching off buds or shoots). But the very act of saving the slip for spring rebirth results in its destruction, for it is heedlessly uprooted by a "swain" who intended only to crop the flower. Much of the botanical imagery in this section has sexual overtones: reference to the bed, cropping the flower, and the associations with "pluck't up" (to pull or tear asunder, to raze, to demolish). Can the country lout be identified with the marquess? I think so: the heraldic references in this verse paragraph are particularly interesting. "Carnation" was a known pun for "coronation," bringing to mind the heraldic associations that I have examined above. Hence the Marchioness is the pride of Winter's train, reference I think to the Roman Church and the Old Catholic aristocracy. If the swain is equated with Winchester, then Milton strengthens the accusation by himself entering the poem in this passage ("So have I seen"). The section ends by echoing the motifs of short time and death that have permeated both *exordium* and *divisio:* "hast'ning funeral."

Viewed as a unit, the *exordium* and *divisio* present two obvious short time numbers: the twenty-three couplets and the six periods that traditionally reflect the futility of this world and the preparation for the eternal sabbath. (John Rumrich points to "the odd locution of 'three times eight less one' mimicked in the repeating pattern of two regular octosyllabic lines followed by a truncated seven-syllable line. Milton used that truncated line often in his tetrameter-couplet writings, e.g., *L'Allegro* and *Il Penseroso,* also in Comus's early speech. . . . This is a metrical variation that he had been experimenting with around this time, and it seems likely that he would have taken advantage of it for his numerological architectonic in this poem").[62] In addition, the division of the six periods into three in which conventions are subverted and three in which processions are aborted points simultaneously to the futility of conventional grief and the incapacity of human ceremony to thwart darkness and death.

Conclusio: The final segment moves abruptly from implied second person address and narrative discourse into direct address and apostrophe. If the *exordium* and *divisio* emphasize descent, both in lineage and in movement to the grave, the *conclusio* focuses on ascent. This section divides thematically into halves: the first (47–60) concerns the farewell to earth, opening at the grave, and in nearly every line suffering ("travail sore"), mourning ("tears," "moan," "wept"), or earth, generally in terms of place ("here," "*Helicon*," "banks of *Came*," "world"), position ("noble house," "name"), property ("seize,"[63] "lease") or nature ("banks," "Floweres," "Bays"). The second half (61–74) presents radical change: in the first line the Marchioness "sitt'st in glory," and the lines following are replete with the language of light: "bosom bright," "blazing Majesty and Light," "radiant sheen." In particular, the twice spoken "here" of the first half, becomes the single "there" of the second.

Of great interest in this portion of the *conclusio* is Milton's extended comparison of the Marchioness to Rachel. James Holly Hanford has pointed out that this is Milton's first reference to Dante, and examination of Cantos 22–32 of the *Paradiso* yields much food for thought.[64] In Dante's Mystical Rose, Rachel sits third in the line of the Virgin, just below Eve, heading the line of Hebrew women who believed in Christ to come and who were mothers of the Old Testament children of God. She is enthroned in the half of the Rose whose petals are filled with the Old Testament saints; the other half awaits the New Testament saints—one of them the "new welcome Saint" Jane, another, immediately to Rachel's right, Beatrice the psychopomp. While most of the comments on the poem's prosody concentrate on its use of the Jonsonian funerary four-stress iambic line with initial unstressed syllable in heptasyllabic lines, only Parker has noted the set of feminine rimes at the beginning of the Rachel analogy (61–62).[65] But Parker has not noticed that they are extrasyllabic: as the Marchioness ascends above the eighth sphere to her place in the Empyrean, the feminine lines expand to nine syllables. This device indicates that Milton's early metrical practice was more complex than has been assumed. Certainly he rejected the traditional elegiac distich employed by Sidney and Spenser: a rimed couplet, dactylic hexameter followed by a dactylic pentameter. Perhaps one should look rather to the broad range of sixteenth-century elegiac poetry. I suggest a double connection here: like Rachel, Jane Paulet is a mother of a godly son who, were he to follow her into the New Covenant of Puritanism, would be like Joseph, a savior of his family.

Like Beatrice—and incidentally, like Lycidas, the "genius of the shore"—Jane can also serve as psychopomp to those who will follow her to a reformed Beatific Vision.

The two halves: Jane Paulet achieves sanctity not only by virtue of her maternity but also because of her moral efficacy. Bearing this out is the progression of titles accorded her by the *Epitaph,* which begins in the *exordium* and *divisio* with "Wife," "daughter," "heir," and "Mother," and moves up in the *conclusio* to "Lady," "Saint," and, finally, "Queen." Although both sections open at the grave, there the similarity ends. Jane Paulet as wife, daughter, heir, gives way to Jane Paulet, "Lady." Jane in life has had virtues added to her name, but she dies "to give the world increase." Where in the *exordium* she has endured the "limit to her life" given by fate, she now has through her own agency "short'ned . . . life's lease." "House," a passive verbal in the first section, becomes a nominal governing a transitive verb. In the first, virtue is set aside, in the second, sorrow. A Lucina is replaced by an Atropos who is replaced in turn by a triumphant Rachel, who climbs the mystic ladder of Jacob, "that serv'd for her." The Marchioness, one remembers, was "pluck't up" by that "unheedy swain." She languishes "on a dying bed," while Rachel flies "through pangs . . . to felicity." The wife of Winchester wore armorial pearls, but now she is "clad in radiant sheen." Finally, Jane Paulet, exalted by her own moral efficacy, is no longer a Marchioness, "but now a Queen."

❧

In his epitaph on Jane Paulet, Milton does not conventionally leave the lady to languish in the margins. Quite the contrary, he manages to praise her moral and spiritual efficacy beyond her traditional biological role at the same time as he pays her the compliment of his own considerable poetic skill. However, a reading of the *Epitaph* that ignores the poem's subtexts confirms the image of Milton the misogynist (or at least the male chauvinist) and leaves Jane Paulet, as usual, stranded on the sideline. While I cannot deny to him the proclivities of his time, it seems to me that the Milton of the *Epitaph* allows a greater role for female autonomy than one might expect, at least in the light of recent gender criticism. This essay cannot consider practically the flowering of Milton's poetry that surrounds the *Epitaph,* but when, for example, one compares the eulogized figures of Lycidas and the Marchioness, one notes a distinct difference: this lies in the efficacy of the subject. Both Lycidas and the Marchioness are raised to the heavens: Lycidas becomes, through his position in heaven, the genius of the shore; the Marchioness, raised from baronial coronet to heavenly crown, attains to a commanding position: a shepherdess (one remembers her poetry) like Rachel and a queen. In Jane

Paulet is acknowledged an agency, an efficacy that pervades the subtext of the poem from its inception. Her rising to the "story" of Rachel (and one remembers that Dante awards Rachel a position in the contemplative seventh heaven of Saturn), although occasioned by her marriage and death in childbirth, has been effected by the agency of her own virtue. She has achieved stature on earth by descent, beginning the poem as "honored Wife"—in seventeenth-century heraldry "honored" was synonymous with "crowned." But the poem ends at her second marriage feast, where she is crowned by virtue of her own progression to that feast, not because of the identity conferred by the first, temporal marriage. She is indeed more than Marchioness: in the final union of the soul with Christ, darkly mirrored on earth by her union with John Paulet, she is raised far above earthly rank, whether it be the fourth order of viscount, the third of earl, the second of marquess, to the first and final order of celestial queen.[66]

In conclusion, I hope I have shown that, although a discursive reading of the *Epitaph* may overlook these matters, a reading that recognizes the poem's formal strategies reveals an artifact mature, complex, and intentionally structured, one which draws on the *visibilia* of mundane time to approach the *invisibilia* of eternity. In this sense Milton plays *alter deus*, a role familiar in Augustinian poetics. But Milton refines this role, in effect sharing it with the Marchioness. Jane Paulet née Savage becomes a rich co-creator of the poem and, I venture, like Beatrice and Rachel a kind of psychopomp. So considered, *An Epitaph on the Marchioness of Winchester* is no misogynistic verse experiment but rather a revealing demonstration of a poetics to which Milton adhered early in his career and of gifts he would continue to develop and enrich.

University of Texas at Austin

NOTES

I am grateful to Professor John P. Rumrich for his reading of this essay and his cogent suggestions for its improvement. I thank as well Professor Rosa A. Eberly, who also read an early copy, for her sound rhetorical advice. The text of this essay was retrieved from almost certain computer death by Laura Kramarsky, in whose debt I remain.

1. The poem has been discussed briefly by Michael West, "The *Consolatio* in Milton's Funeral Elegies," *HLQ* 34 (1971): 233–49, in the light of its Christian expression and as a step toward *Lycidas.*

2. Michael F. Moloney, "The Prosody of Milton's *Epitaph, L'Allegro,* and *Il Penseroso,*" *MLN* 71 (1957): 174–78.

3. J. B. Leishman, *Milton's Minor Poems* (London, 1969), 87.

4. Gayle E. Wilson, "Decorum and Milton's 'Epitaph on the Marchioness of Winchester,'" *MQ* 8 (1974): 11–14. West, "The *Consolatio* in Milton's Funeral Elegies," 241.

5. "'Scarce-well-lighted flame': Milton's 'Epitaph on the Marchioness of Winchester' and the Representation of Maternal Mortality in the Seventeenth-Century Epitaph," in *"All in All": Unity, Diversity, and the Miltonic Perspective*, ed. Charles W. Durham and Kristin A. Pruitt (Selinsgrove, 1999), 200–23.

6. Ants Oras, "Metre and Chronology in Milton's 'Epitaph on the Marchioness of Winchester,' 'L'Allegro,' and 'Il Penseroso,'" *Notes & Queries (N&Q)* 140 (1953): 333.

7. The growth in awareness of premodern Augustinian poetics has been slow, and a major statement of theory, history, and practice is yet to be written. In the meanwhile, the most succinct account is to be found in Maren-Sofie Røstvig, *Configurations: A Topomorphical Approach to Renaissance Poetry* (Oslo, 1994).

8. Augustine, *Of True Religion* (Chicago, 1959), trans. J. H. S. Burleigh, 52.

9. Kate Gartner Frost, *Holy Delight: Typology, Numerology, and Autobiography in Donne's "Devotions Upon Emergent Occasions"* (Princeton, 1990), 95.

10. Alistair Fowler, in *Triumphal Forms: Structural Patterns in Elizabethan Poetry* (Cambridge, 1970), 1–2, proposes criteria for arithmetical studies, among which are listed "internal consistency of the perceived pattern." Fowler's mandates hold for all architectonic criticism; unless demonstratively consistent with the discursive linear text, subtextual readings, albeit sometimes enticing and ingenious, are doubtful at best.

11. John T. Shawcross, *Intentionality and the New Traditionalism: Some Liminal Means to Literary Revisionism* (University Park, 1991).

12. *John Milton: Complete Poems and Major Prose*, ed. Merritt Hughes (Indianapolis, 1957), 76. Quotations of the *Epitaph* are from this edition unless otherwise noted. (Milton may have been following the lead of Sidney here in employing twenty-three as a coming-of-age year, and it is notable that his model is *Astrophil and Stella* 23.) Milton was likely considering the *Epitaph* when he composed Sonnet 7 (or vice versa); the two share numerical and textual ("bud," "blossom") concerns.

13. Ants Oras, "Metre and Chronology in Milton's 'Epitaph on the Marchioness of Winchester,' 'L'Allegro,' and 'Il Penseroso,'" 332–33.

14. John Shawcross, in *John Milton: The Self and the World* (Lexington, 1993), 28. He discusses the odes, which, he claims, "show a Milton who is consciously experimenting with form and prosody [and which] evidence a poet concerned with 'standard' religious beliefs, based upon Scripture . . . and with the artifact itself in its form and metric . . . , a believer who accepts mythic substructs while in no way casting that myth out of Truth; and they give further testimony to the preacher/teacher concept and category for the poet. . . . [They] suggest a concern with the writing of poetry as a bid to fame, not observable in works prior to [Milton's] leaving Cambridge in 1632" (23). He points to the possible influence of the *Rime e Prose* of Giovanni della Casa, which Milton purchased late in 1629.

15. Flynn, *John Donne and the Ancient Catholic Nobility* (Bloomington, 1995). The classic study is John Bossy's *The English Catholic Community, 1570–1850* (London, 1975). Also worth perusing is J. Stanley Leatherbarrow's *The Lancashire Elizabethan Recusants* (Manchester, 1947), as well as studies of individual recusant families.

16. Cambridge University Library, MS Add. 22(c) fo. 7. Quoted in Hugh Trevor-Roper. *Catholics, Anglicans and Puritans: Seventeenth Century Essays* (Chicago, 1987), 67.

17. Ibid., 84.

18. Ibid., 109, 115.

19. Shawcross, *John Milton: The Self and the World*, 31.

20. Ibid., 17.

21. Rutland MSS, Historical MSS Commission 12th report, pt. 4 (1888) 1, 490. Schwartz, "'Scarce-well-lighted flame,'" 211–12, proposes a detailed account of the infant's delivery.

22. James Howell, the Marchioness's Spanish tutor, makes this claim in his *Epistolae Hoelianae . . . Familiar Letters domestic and forren; divided into six sections: partly historicall, politicall, philosophicall, upon emergent occasions* (London, 1645), Book Four, letter 49. Her literary prowess is also praised by the Jesuit Pierre Le Moyne in *The Gallery of Heroick Women* (London, 1652).

23. *Ben Jonson,* 11 vols., ed. C. H. Herford, Percy Simpson, and Evelyn Simpson (Oxford, 1947), vol. 8, 268–72 (83 in *The Underwood*). *The Works of Sr William Davenant Kt Consisting of those which were formerly Printed, and those which he design'd for the Press* (London, 1673), 236; Walter Colman, *La Dance Machabre or Death's Duell* (London, 1632?). Schwartz, "'Scarce-well-lighted flame,'" 201, points as well to an elegy by the obscure John Eliot, an anonymous epitaph in Camden's *Remaines,* and a possible manuscript elegy by William Strode.

24. *The Court and Times of Charles I,* 2 vols., ed. R. F. Williams (London, 1848), vol. 2, 106.

25. William Riley Parker, *Milton: A Biography,* 2 vols. (Oxford, 1968), vol. 2, 767.

26. Ibid., vol. 1, 96.

27. *Calendar of State Papers, Domestic series of the reign of Charles I (1629–1631)* Series 3 (Great Britain, Public Record office), vol. 181, 463.

28. Sir Leslie Stephen and Sir Sidney Lee, eds. *The Dictionary of National Biography* 66 vols. (Oxford, 1917), vol. 21, 998.

29. Clarendon, Edward Hyde, Earl of, *A History of the Rebellion and Civil Wars in England begun in the year 1641,* 6 vols., ed. W. Dunn Macray (Oxford, 1888) vol. 4, 508.

30. J. Pironon, "The Images of Woman in the Sonnets and Some Minor Poems of John Milton," *Cahiers Elizabethains* 18 (1980): 47.

31. Ibid.

32. Wilson, "Decorum and Milton's 'Epitaph on the Marchioness of Winchester,'" 14.

33. John Shawcross, personal communication to Emma Roth-Schwartz, 27 April 1994. I am much indebted to these two scholars for allowing me to draw on their learned discussion.

34. Ibid.

35. British Museum, MS Sloane 1446, ff. 37v–38r. See also *The Complete Poetry of John Milton,* ed. John T. Shawcross (New York, 1963), 552.

36. Ibid.

37. William Riley Parker, "Milton and the Marchioness of Winchester," *MLR* 44 (1949): 549.

38. Shawcross, personal communication.

39. Parker, "Milton and the Marchioness of Winchester," 547–50.

40. Mindele Treip, *Milton's Punctuation and Changing English Usage, 1582–1676* (London, 1970), 10.

41. 13 April 1994; 2 May 1994: personal communication.

42. *Oxford English Dictionary* (Oxford, 1884–1928), hereafter cited in the text as *OED*.

43. The carnation (*Dianthus species*) was usually propagated by the insertion during the autumn of pipings or cuttings (as opposed to the modern practice of layering) into rich gritty soil in cold frames until signs of apical growth indicated rooting, with the more choice slips kept in the cold frame all winter.

44. John Donne, *Sermons,* 10 vols., ed. G. F. Potter and Evelyn Simpson (Berkeley, 1953–1962) vol. 6, 175. Another example of the wordplay occurs in lines 37–38 of Donne's *Elegie on the Death of Mrs. Boulstrod:* "Shee was more stories high, hopeless to come / To her soule thou hast offered at her lower roome."

45. Trevor-Roper, *Catholics, Anglicans and Puritans*, 110.

46. Stephen and Lee, eds., *The Dictionary of National Biography*, vol. 21, 998.

47. Sidney had set the precedent for this wordplay in Sonnets 24, 35, and 37 and in the eighth song of *Astrophil and Stella*. The practice was picked up by other poets, for example, Constable and Barnfield.

48. Preeminent among arithmetical studies of *Paradise Lost* are Gunnar Qvarnstrøm's *The Enchanted Palace: Some Structural Aspects of Paradise Lost* (Stockholm, 1967) and Maren-Sofie Røstvig's study of the first edition, *Configurations*, chapter 9, where she acknowledges but does not analyze arithmetical structure in the *Epitaph* (540). Røstvig has also laid out the structure of the Nativity ode (which shares patterns of language and perhaps structure with the *Epitaph*) in "Elaborate Song: Conceptual Structure in Milton's 'On the Morning of Christ's Nativity,'" 54–84 in *Fair Forms: Essays in English Literature from Spenser to Jane Austen*, ed. Maren-Sofie Røstvig (Cambridge, 1975). In this collection H. Neville Davies identifies patterns of structural bifurcation in the Nativity ode, *Lycidas*, and *Elegia Tertia. In Obitum Praesulis Wintoniensis (On the Death of the Bishop of Winchester)*, 85–117. Arithmetical studies of *Lycidas* have been published by John T. Shawcross, "Some Literary Uses of Numerology," *HSL* 1 (1969): 50–62, and Alastair Fowler, "'To Shepherd's Ear': The Form of *Lycidas*," 170–84, in *Silent Poetry: Essays in Numerological Analysis*, ed. Alastair Fowler (London, 1970).

49. "Exegesis before Exegesis," *JDJ* 13 (1994): 191.

50. Røstvig, *Configurations*, 3–74.

51. Wilson, "Decorum and Milton's 'Epitaph on the Marchioness of Winchester,'" 11–12.

52. Shawcross, *John Milton: The Self and the World*, 22, points out that in *Paradise Lost* the number appears related to the hexaemeral seven of Creation.

53. Pietro Bongo, *Numerorum mysteria* (Bergamo, 1591), 464 ff.

54. Fowler, *Triumphal Forms*, 188.

55. Cicero, *De Partitione Oratoria* [23, 82], trans. H. Rackham, (Cambridge, 1942), 371.

56. Cox, *The Arte or Crafte of Rhethoryke* (Robert Redman, 1524), B6v–C1r.

57. *A Fuller Institution of the Art of Logic, Arranged after the Method of Peter Ramus*, in *The Works of John Milton*, ed. F. A. Patterson et al. (New York, 1935), vol. 11, 98–99.

58. Cox, *The Arte or Crafte of Rhethoryke*, C5v.

59. Schwartz, "'Scarce-well-lighted flame,'" 204–6, has discussed in some detail the generic conflict between elegy and epithalamion. For extended discourse on the conflation of epithalamic and elegiac conventions and tropes, see Celeste Marguerite Schenck, *Mourning and Panegyrick: The Poetics of Pastoral Ceremony* (University Park, 1988), 10–16, 77–90.

60. *A Critical Edition of Alexander Ross's 1647 Mystagogus Poeticus, or the Muses Interpreter*, ed. John R. Glen (New York, 1987), 474–75.

61. *John Milton: Poems; the 1645 edition, with essays in analysis by Cleanth Brooks and John Edward Hardy* (New York, 1951), 121.

62. Personal communication with John Rumrich.

63. West, "The *Consolatio* in Milton's Funeral Elegies," 242n, opines that the use of "seize" is appropriate in line 50 since it reflects the inversion of the birth-death trope.

64. *The Poems of John Milton*, ed. James Holly Hanford (New York, 1953), 79n. Schwartz, "'Scarce-well-lighted flame,'" 210–11, 214–15, also notes the connections between Rachel and Jane Paulet, which he ascribes to their sharing the curse of Eve and to their positions as maternal progenitors of noble lineages.

65. Parker, *Milton: A Biography*, 97.

66. I have for rhetorical purposes passed over the order of duchess. The exact royal hierarchical order is: king, duke, marquess, earl, viscount, baron, knight.

DOUBLENESS IN MILTON'S LATE SONNETS

Joseph G. Mayer

O F MILTON'S SONNETS, the five commonly numbered 18–22 hold a special fascination: in each the speaker takes two opposing and mutually exclusive points of view on the issue at hand. One viewpoint overlays the other, so that the sonnet at certain points is like a hologram: turned slightly, it presents a different, even opposite, point of view. As there are contrary points of view expressed in each sonnet, there should be two speakers, because a single statement that makes two contrary assertions unsays itself. The sonnets violate conventions of reasonableness; it is their nonrationality that fascinates.

The main object of this study is to demonstrate the doubleness of sonnets 18–22 by a close study of each. In this process, the sonnets will gain in interest, and several cruxes will cease to puzzle. This study will glance only briefly at the implications of doubleness for our reading of the longer works, and it will leave to later research questions about literary antecedents. This study will not propose that the five sonnets constitute a sequence to be read in a particular order.

The following list gives the titles of the sonnets to be studied, along with the numbers commonly assigned to them. Also indicated is the doubleness of viewpoint that emerges in each:

Sonnet 18 ("On the Late Massacre in Piemont").[1] The speaker is incensed by the massacre and unmoved by it.

Sonnet 19 ("When I consider"). The speaker resigns himself to inactivity while anticipating active service.

Sonnet 20 ("Lawrence of virtuous Father"). Lawrence should allow and deny himself the pleasures that the speaker proposes.

Sonnet 21 ("Cyriack, whose Grandsire"). It is Cyriack's moral duty to stop thinking about duty.

Sonnet 22 ("To Mr. Cyriack Skinner upon his Blindness"). The speaker thinks with pride on his part in affairs of state while dismissing them as empty masquerade.

An argument could be made for adding to this list Sonnet 8 ("When the Assault Was Intended to the City"). However, because the doubleness

of that sonnet's ending is debatable, this study makes only a few references
to Sonnet 8.

Sonnets 18–22 each end on an emphatic note of doubleness, in which
opposed views are expressed concurrently and with equal force. Their doubleness is generated in several ways. A word or phrase in its context may have
double and opposed meanings. In the last line of Sonnet 20, for example,
"spare to" is heard both as "afford to" and "forbear to." The *"Babylonian
woe"* in the last line of Sonnet 18 is a woe both inflicted and suffered by
Babylon. Or, syntax and meter may emphasize a word that resists the very
argument that the same word helps to advance. In the last sentence of Sonnet
22, which urges Cyriack to seize a cheerful hour, the word most emphasized
is "refrain."

Preceding lines introduce the opposing points of view in various ways.
In lines 1–13 of Sonnet 19, two voices are heard in succession: first zeal, then
patience. In the first 12 lines of Sonnet 18 and Sonnet 20, a single voice
expresses the contrary viewpoints, which in Sonnet 18 are zealousness and
detachment; in Sonnet 20, hedonism and austerity. There are two strains to
the same voice, one dominating and providing the poem an ostensible argument; the other, a subversive undertone. Only at the poem's end do both
viewpoints assert themselves concurrently and equally; the effect (reserved
for the end) is arresting.

Several commentators have already noted doubleness in a few of the
sonnets. The full number of "double" sonnets, however, has not been recognized, and the extent of doubleness within specific sonnets has been under-
stated. The most complete treatment of doubleness is found in James Mengert's article "The Resistant Finish of Milton's Sonnets."[2] By "resistant
finish," Mengert means a word or phrase at the end (finish) of the poem that,
even while concluding a line of argument made by the rest of the poem,
counters (resists) that argument.

The crux posed by the word "spare" in the penultimate line of Sonnet 20
serves to illustrate both Mengert's thesis and the nature of doubleness: "He
who of those delights can judge and spare / To interpose them oft, is not
unwise." In a longstanding debate, "spare" is read by some as "afford," by
others as "forbear." As the arguments marshalled for both readings are
equally plausible, Stanley Fish reasonably proposes that both meanings be
admitted.[3] Mengert agrees. He argues that, on the one hand, the context of
the poem, being an invitation, inclines us to understand "spare" as "spare
time for." On the other hand, "forbear" was the more common meaning for

Milton's reader. "What we are dealing with, then, is a context that directs us to one meaning and supports a more or less bold use of a word, and the more common meaning of the word that works against the context. At some level we are reminded of restraint just as we are being conclusively urged to enjoyment" (Mengert, 87).

Mengert's analyses of a sonnet's last lines describe their doubleness with remarkable precision. This study and his differ in two respects. First, Mengert stops short of granting equal weight to the opposing views at the sonnet's end, and so stops short of declaring the end to be nonrational. The qualification in the passage just quoted, "*At some level* we are reminded of restraint. . . .," is characteristic (emphasis mine). Second, Mengert's close analysis is limited to a sonnet's end. He treats the rest of the poem by citing a generally accepted reading of it. In accepted interpretations of the sonnets, they move in a single direction "as a continuous process, a working through some experience or emotion toward . . . a satisfying equilibrium" (83). Usually the direction of movement is from difficulty to resolution; the sonnets exhibit a "positive thrust," a "rising structure of hope" (86, 91). Starting with this general view of the sonnets, Mengert understands the resistant finish as a qualification of the poem's positive thrust. "Its presence qualifies to some extent the positive thrust and logical development of the poem" (86).

The present study takes a different view of those sonnets whose finishes are resistant. A close reading of the whole poem reveals a double direction from the start. Take the first quatrain of Sonnet 8:

> Captain or Colonel, or Knight in Arms
>   Whose chance on these defenseless doors may seize,
>   If ever deed of honor did thee please,
>   Guard them, and him within protect from harms.

These lines pose a oddly dichotomous point of view. One part of the speaker sees clearly his danger and faces up to it in line 2. Another part of him lives in a world of literature: in line 1, his audience changes suddenly from a Royalist officer—a captain or colonel—to an Arthurian "Knight in Arms." In line 4, he preposterously asks the enemy not merely to spare his house but to chivalrously guard it and its occupant from harm by others.

A careful reading of each sonnet with a resistant finish will reveal that a polarized viewpoint is present from the start of each. The whole sonnet, not just the end, is an interplay of opposites. The relation between the earlier polarity and the final doubleness is not always obvious. This study will try to understand how one plays out into the other.

To start with the clearest instance of doubleness and to pair poems with certain similarities, this study will take up the sonnets in the order 20, 19, 21, 22, and 18. At several places, the study will pause to consider a theoretical issue before proceeding to analyze the next poem.

SONNET 20 ("LAWRENCE OF VIRTUOUS FATHER")

Sonnet 20's first sentence introduces the project of seeking refuge from winter, now at hand, in civilized amenities:

> Lawrence of virtuous Father virtuous Son,
>> Now that the Fields are dank and ways are mire,
>> Where shall we sometimes meet and by the fire
>> Help waste a sullen day, what may be won
> From the hard Season gaining?

This invitation is curious. It pursues the usual end of invitations, which is to secure someone's presence, by mentioning a cheerful fire. At the same time, the speaker implicitly suggests that the proffered pleasure is not really attainable or, if attainable, not legitimate. The sentence is both an invitation and a disinvitation, and introduces the mode of doubleness to become explicit at the sonnet's finish.

Mention of the dank fields and miry ways is fitting enough as a foil to a cheerful fire. To extend an attractive invitation, the speaker could stop there. But with mention of the "sullen day" and "hard Season gaining," the forces opposing comfort become menacing and potentially victorious over the rather primitive expedient of sitting by a fire.

The repellent force of the invitation is concentrated in the word "waste." The word, in the present context, has several possible senses. Probably the dominant sense is "to spend, pass, occupy (time)" (*OED* 8).[4] This sense carries the positive tenor of the invitation. A less pleasant sense—"to lay waste, devastate, ravage, ruin" (*OED* 1)—is suggested by an implied state of hostility between the speaker and seasons: pleasures must be "won," or wrested, from "the hard Season gaining" and from the "sullen" day, which is obstinately opposed to human happiness.

A third sense, obvious both to us and to the seventeenth century reader, is "To spend, consume, employ uselessly or without adequate result" (*OED* 9). This sense of "waste" would readily occur to Milton's reader because in the 1650s Puritan "rigorists" often wrote against recreations.[5] With this meaning, the proposal becomes highly problematic: not only is contesting the hard season possibly futile; the effort is reprehensible as well.

The next sentence is more inviting:

> Time will run
> On smoother till *Favonius* re-inspire
> The frozen earth, and clothe in fresh attire
> The Lily and the Rose, that neither sow'd nor spun.

The mythological reference to "*Favonius*" is also a Horatian echo (*Odes* 1.4); together, the allusions transfer us from the reality of dank fields to a neo-classical idyll. Somehow, magically, the proposed series of visits will while away the entire winter. (We are reminded of the speaker's flight to fantasy in Sonnet 8.) But the idyll is troubled by a persistent sense of winter's unfriendly power, which the detail of "frozen earth" epitomizes. The speaker's moral scruples persist too in his allusion to the parable of the lilies (line 8). That allusion, to be sure, is seductively beautiful; in line 8, as at its end, the poem in one moment moves in opposite directions.

The parable of the lilies is part of a tightly knit discourse that extends from Matthew 6:24 to 6:34:

(24) No man can serve two masters. . . . Ye cannot serve God and mammon. (25) Therefore I say unto you, Take no thought for your life, what ye shall eat, or what ye shall drink. . . . (26) Behold the fowls of the air; they sow not, neither do they reap. . . . (28) And why take ye thought for raiment? *Consider the lilies of the field, how they grow; they toil not, neither do they spin.* . . . (30) Wherefore, if God so clothe the grass of the field . . . , shall he not much more clothe you, O ye of little faith? (31) Therefore take no thought. . . . (33) But seek ye first the kingdom of God, and his righteousness; and all these things shall be added unto you. (Authorized Version; emphasis mine)

Jesus here commands an approach to the problem of adversity that is entirely different from the speaker's: do not try to protect yourself by taking thought of the morrow; anxiety over food, drink, and raiment is a distraction from the Kingdom. Instead, seek righteousness in the hope that God will provide.

"O ye of little faith"—the sonnet's speaker falls squarely under the rebuke. He views himself and Lawrence as pitted against the harsh forces of an indifferent cosmos, not as the creatures of a gracious God who protects His servants. The speaker lives not by faith but by common sense, which tells him to provide against natural forces that are much stronger than he. The allusion to Matthew 6:28, when heard in context, exposes the whole project as essentially pagan.

In the third sentence, the speaker shifts ground from fantasy to art:

> What neat repast shall feast us, light and choice,
> Of Attic taste, with Wine, whence we may rise
> To hear the Lute well toucht, or artful voice
> Warble immortal Notes and *Tuscan* air?   (9–12)

The invitation is, for the first time, unchecked by reservations. The reality of the "neat repast" counters the reality of dank fields and miry ways. The speaker has arrived at a shelter from fate that is at once realistic (i.e., effective) and virtuous, in the pagan sense. The notion of virtue, merely mentioned in the first line, is now realized. The meal and the music are the fruits of virtue in the classical sense of skill and discipline. The feast will be moderate—neat, light, and choice. As much as satisfying appetite, it exercises skill and discrimination.

True, the picture verges on a fantasy. "Attic taste" hearkens to a golden age, but it also specifies an aesthetic that can still be emulated. "Warble" smacks of the pastoral, but it can also denote a particular style of singing (*OED* 2a). "Immortal notes" invokes the poetical commonplace of art's immortality; yet echoes of Horace in the sonnet lend weight to the claim. All this ambiguity prepares for the final doubleness.

At this point, we can understand the double ending of the poem as making more pronounced the duality already encountered. Hearing "spare" as "afford," we understand the last sentence to mean: he who has the taste and training to appreciate ("judge") the finer things and can afford them should enjoy them. Such enjoyment is "not unwise" in that it is folly not to employ our advantages against the forces of nature. This is more of the common wisdom voiced earlier in lines 5–8, which counsel Lawrence to let time run on until spring arrives.

On the other hand, hearing "spare" as "refrain from," we understand the last sentence to mean: he who can judge the proffered delights rightly, as a poor, fantastical substitute for the Kingdom, will resort to them as infrequently as possible. According to this interpretation, the speaker regards the proposed entertainment to be a refined delusion. It gives an illusion of immortality, of mastering time and space (by appreciative fellowship with ancient Greece and seventeenth-century Tuscany). Its delicacy, however, is a fragile barrier against the sullen day and hard, frozen earth. The solid good of the Kingdom, alluded to in the second sentence, is won by watchfulness, not wasteful self-indulgence. What from one angle seemed wisdom now appears in the light of Matthew 6:24–34 as pagan folly.

Our examination of Sonnet 20 shows that the doubleness of "spare" has little, if anything, to do with the paradoxes of Metaphysical poetry, which are better called conceits than paradoxes, since they do not truly go beyond (*para*) reason (*doxia*). Of course, in Milton's poetry there are conceits as well as paradoxes. "O dark, dark, dark, amid the blaze of noon" (*SA* 80); "and day brought back my night" (Sonnet 23.14). Unlike a paradox, a conceit can be reduced to reasonable terms through paraphrase; "night" refers to the speaker's blindness. In Sonnet 20, however, a more radical breach of reason is committed. Lines 13–14 give the same "delights" contrary predicates: they are to be both shunned and enjoyed. The curious pleasure that we find in this affront to reason confirms Kierkegaard's observation that "the supreme passion of the Reason is to seek a collision, though this collision must in one way or another prove its undoing."[6]

SONNET 19 ("WHEN I CONSIDER")

In Sonnet 19, opposites play against each other within a monodrama. In imagining this drama, we do well to heed Joseph Pequigney's warning against an autobiographical approach that would narrowly identify the lost talent with that of authorship.[7] Milton avoids naming the speaker's balked talent so that we attend to the dialectical opposition of zeal and blindness.

> And that one Talent which is death to hide,
> Lodg'd with me useless, though my Soul more bent
> To serve therewith my Maker, . . .

This irresolvable dilemma issues at the sonnet's end in a paradoxical solution: the speaker accepts the impossibility of action and, at the same time, expects some commission for action. For, to him, inaction is equally impossible; it is "death" to hide his talent; to live, he *must* employ it.

The speaker, like Samson, is consumed with frustration. By nature, he must act in God's behalf, but cannot. His energy, blocked from action by blindness, seeks outlet in a complaint whose wittiness simmers with compressed emotion: " 'Doth God exact day-labor, light denied,' / I fondly ask." He realizes that his is a foolish accusation while he says it—if, indeed, he does not counter the thought even before saying it. A more telling complaint would fault God for blinding him in this first place, but the reverence that is manifest in his zeal shrinks from accusing God of injustice. So he has to vent his frustration in a way that mocks himself as much as God.

He can escape frustration by resigning himself to inactivity, which he tries to do by giving patience the stage:

> But patience to prevent
> That murmur, soon replies, "God doth not need
> Either man's work or his own gifts; . . ."

His zeal, however, will not yield; and patience, which is really his own voice, becomes ambiguous enough to allow room for activity: "who best / Bear his mild yoke, they serve him best." Although these words point most obviously at those who are consigned to inactivity, they can also be read to include those who serve God actively: since God does not need man's works, it is not the results of action that count but the willingness with which the action is carried out. (This is not doubleness but ambiguity. By doubleness I mean two distinct ideas that oppose each other. The speech of patience, which is very general, allows for multiple possibilities without delineating any.)

Indeed, active service carried out willingly, without stint, is illustrated in the next sentence: "Thousands at his bidding speed / And post o'er Land and Ocean without rest." But how can the speaker count himself among the active, given the uselessness of his talent? In the last line of the poem, he seems to bow to this reality: "They also serve who only stand and wait." But his undeflectable will to serve is no less a reality; so, although the last line starts out contrasting the speaker with active servants, it ends by including him among them. The line asserts two, opposite meanings at once.

The doubleness of the line hinges on "wait." The word has a range of passive and active meanings. At the passive end of the range, it means "to remain in a place, defer one's departure, until something happens" (*OED* 7a). More exactly, it means to remain in a place in expectation of something happening. Nothing may ever happen. Given the speaker's helplessness, nothing *will* happen. His mode of service must be to bear inactivity willingly, without murmuring.[8]

The logic of the dramatic situation requires this passive sense of "wait." Furthermore, this sense of "wait" is activated by the construction "who only stand and wait." Within the construction *only [verb a] and [verb b]*, both verbs bear out the same assertion. For example, in the statement "He only weeps and sighs," both verbs bear out the rejected lover's grief; or, in "Fido only eats and sleeps," both verbs bear out the pet's lethargic lifestyle. Similarly, "stand" and "wait" cooperate to define a passive mode of service that contrasts with the ceaseless posting of the previous lines.

At the other, active end of the spectrum, "wait" means "to be in readiness to receive orders" (*OED* 9a). In this sense, action is imminent, not indefinitely deferred. This sense of wait is logically required by the persistence of the speaker's zeal. It is activated by the metaphor, built in lines 11–13, of God's kingly court. Some of the king's servants have been sent on errands, others wait to be sent.[9] So, with the very argument for resignation, the speaker's zeal reasserts itself in a vision of some imminent commission. The effect of the line is like looking at a reversible figure and ground—a trick picture that commonly illustrates textbook accounts of gestalt psychology. A reversible print by Escher shows red devils or white angels—one cannot decide which. As soon as we read the last line as referring to inactive waiting, we are aware of the meaning being excluded; so we jump to excluded meaning, only to become mindful of the meaning that we have just relinquished.

The mind races back and forth between the two, trying to comprehend both at once.

This double reading of the sonnet's finish agrees with that of Pequigney, who convincingly argues for a "plurisignation of 'waite'" ("Milton's Sonnet XIX Reconsidered," 493). Having done so, however, he is required to smooth over the absurdity of the last line by his view of the whole poem as a drama of spiritual growth. Between octet and sestet, he claims, there is a shift in the speaker "from egocentric concern to theocentric awareness" (490). The speaker, now enlightened, "is fully aware of the mutually exclusive alternatives of awaiting an active mission or of submitting to permanent inactivity. . . . The maturity he attains consists of a toleration of uncertainty and of the emotional flexibility with which he confronts the range of possibilities in an unknown but providentially directed future. He finishes in the spirit, 'Thy will be done'" (494).

To accommodate the scheme of regeneration, Pequigney tones down the doubleness of the sonnet's ending to the contemplation of alternate possibilities. Alternatives, like the antitheses bound in doubleness, are indeed "mutually exclusive" in that both cannot be chosen at once. They can, however, be placed beside each other in a "range of possibilities," whereas doubleness is like a reversible figure and ground: now an angel, now a devil—but not one beside the other. Faced with alternatives, one chooses between them. Faced with doubleness, one tries (futilely) to embrace both possibilities in a single perception.

Sonnet 21 ("Cyriack whose Grandsire")

It is hard not to regard Sonnet 21 as a clever joke. Beginning with weighty praise of Edward Coke's judicial pronouncements and ending emphatically on the word "refrain," it offers an absurd invitation to a moral vacation. Simultaneously, it tells poor Cyriack to indulge in and refrain from a gaudy day. Not that the speaker, like the speaker of Sonnet 20, expresses misgivings over a holiday by using a loaded word like "waste" or by alluding to scripture; rather, his argument's very premise (as distinct from its details), that mirth is a serious moral matter, tilts the poem against mirth.

Lines 5–6 introduce the double project: "Today deep thoughts resolve with me to drench / In mirth, that after no repenting draws." To "resolve" is to come to a decision after some deliberation (as in *PL* 9.97). If the speaker of the sonnet had said, "Drench deep thoughts in mirth with me," the sonnet would be a simple, straightforward invitation to innocent dissipation. By inviting the speaker to *resolve* on dissipation, he leaves open two divergent paths: thinking about a course of action and acting. The rest of the sonnet takes both paths at once.

In lines 7–8, the speaker embarks on a day off (an action): "Let *Euclid* rest and *Archimedes* pause, / And what the *Swede* intend, and what the *French.*" Possibly spoken with a reckless sweep of the arm, these lines banish study and care. But at the same time, they usher in another kind of study, as we learn in lines 9–10: "To measure life learn thou betimes, and know / Toward solid good what leads the nearest way." Cyriack is to put aside geometry and current events—not for lighter matters, but to examine the worth of his familiar studies, their consistency with "solid good." While doing so, of course, he is as far from heedless mirth as before.

Cyriack's deliberations presumably lead him to the speaker's own conclusion (lines 11–14), that he spends too much time thinking:

> For other things mild Heav'n a time ordains,
> And disapproves that care, though wise in show,
> That with superfluous burden loads the day,
> And when God sends a cheerful hour, refrains.

This admonition is far less reasonable than it first seems. The "other things" for which heaven ordains a time certainly include the mirth proposed in lines 6–7. The metaphor of drinking in those lines—"drench / In mirth"—reminds us that mirth, like alcohol, liberates one from the perceived weight of obligations. So, when heaven "ordains" mirth in line 11, an absurdity arises: in ordaining mirth, heaven appeals to the very sense of duty that mirth puts aside.

As the thought of ordaining clashes with that of mirth, so does the thought of refraining. Mirth means letting go, refraining means holding back. "[R]efrains" (line 14) must be accented because it follows a heavy caesura. We pause heavily between "hour" and "refrains" to pronounce the two successive "r"s. Thus, the poem's conclusion on a very emphatic "refrains" undermines its advocacy of mirth. Mengert also observes this countercurrent: "The end of the poem does not so much condemn refraining as it makes refraining a decisive presence."[10]

By the time "refrains" arrives to close a tortuous periodic sentence, we have lost a clear sense of its distant subject—of who or what is doing the refraining. The word has become detached from its function in the ostensible argument that heaven frowns on people who refrain too much. Heard in this isolation, "refrains" denotes an act that is commendable; for in common discourse, people refrain from doing something wrong. Rarely is someone said to refrain from doing good. So, even though "refrains" (unlike "spare" and "wait") has a single meaning, the word still carries us in contrary directions. To the extent that we hear it in the context of the argument that heaven disapproves needless cares, "refrains" comes under condemnation. To the extent that "refrains" is isolated from this argument by syntax and meter, we hear the word with approbation. In short, the last sentence works against itself, and the sonnet ends in doubleness.

SONNET 22 ("TO MR. CYRIACK SKINNER UPON HIS BLINDNESS")

In Sonnet 22 Milton carries doubleness almost to the point of indecorous contradiction. In lines 9–14, the speaker gives two, contrary answers to Cyriack's imagined question: What supports the speaker in his blindness? Lines 9–12 give one answer:

> What supports me dost thou ask?
> The conscience, Friend, to have lost them overplied
> In liberty's defense, my noble task,
> Of which all Europe talks from side to side.

The speaker is supported by the satisfaction of having served liberty and by the praise that his service has received. In the discussion to follow, this answer will sometimes be referred to as "reason 1 (conscience)." Lines 13–14 give a second, conflicting answer:

> This thought might lead me through the world's vain mask
> Content though blind, had I no better guide.

He is supported by a better guide than satisfaction in works. This guide—some form of Christian faith—accounts the world, including public affairs and repute, a vain masquerade. This answer will be referred to as "reason 2 (better guide)."

The second answer seems to take back the first. Mengert states the problem precisely: "The reader wonders why the conditional verb [i.e., 'might'] when the speaker has already affirmed that this thought *does* lead him. . . . The affirmation, a ringing, even proud one, of the previous four lines is not only qualified . . . ; it is displaced in favor of a stronger support that had not really been present in the poem until now" (88).

These lines contain a cruder kind of doubleness than we have seen before. In the other sonnets examined, the speaker concurrently expresses opposite views, undercutting one view even while expressing it. That is a satisfying kind of irony. In this poem, the opposing views are more serial than concurrent. Milton seems to contradict himself—not inadvertently but deliberately, as an affront to the reader. It is indeed surprising how few commentators have noted Milton's disconcerting maneuver.[11]

Concurrent doubleness is found along with the serial type. Even while taking back reason 1 (conscience) with reason 2 (better guide), he reasserts reason 1. Mengert continues: "But Milton gets still more effect from his conclusion, for the negative conditional structure allows him to qualify the displacement itself: 'no better guide.' He has the better guide, so all other supports are secondary or superfluous. But the possession is conditional in the first place, and, in addition, 'no better guide' invites the reader to recall that superfluous support, which has just been displaced" (88).

Within line 13 alone there are simultaneous, conflicting statements: "This thought might lead me through the world's vain mask." On the one hand, the speaker allows the possibility of reason 1 (conscience), which "might" lead him through the world. But by calling the world a "vain mask," the speaker disallows the possibility of reason 1; for the speaker cannot be consoled by his part in the world when that world is an empty show. The sentence undoes itself.

Actually, the poem's doubleness begins earlier, in line 12. That line completes the initial assertion of that reason 1 (conscience) with "Of which all Europe talks from side to side." In view of line 12, it is not quite accurate to say, with Mengert, that the initial assertion of reason 1 is "a ringing, even proud one" (88). The word "talks" in Miltonic usage is usually tinged with contempt. The contempt heard in "talks" anticipates the explicit disparagement of public affairs heard in "the world's vain mask" (line 13). As the great events of the day are ephemeral and meaningless, so is the talk that these events excite.

John Bradshaw's concordance finds thirteen instances in Milton's poetry of "talk" used as a noun or verb.[12] Of these, ten connote some sort of disapproval. For example, in *Paradise Regained* Jesus tells Satan: "I never lik'd thy talk, thy offers less" (4.171). Disparaging the Stoic's "Philosophic pride" (4.300), Jesus says, "For all his tedious talk is but vain boast"(4.307). Underlying Milton's scorn of talk is a high valuation of action. In *Samson Agonistes,* after the chorus makes Samson an offer of consolation, he proudly replies, "Your coming, Friends, revives me, for I learn / Now of my own experience, not by talk, / How . . ." (187–88). In other words, although blind, he is still a man who deals in action, not (like the chorus) in talk. Finally, in *Paradise Lost* Satan scornfully contrasts talk with action when he confronts Gabriel in Eden: "Then when I am thy captive talk of chains, / Proud limitary Cherub" (4.970–71).

The satire introduced into Sonnet 22 by "talks" is amplified by the phrase "from side to side" (line 12). The phrase can mean "from one limit to another" or "back and forth." The second sense calls up the ludicrous picture of gigantic mouths gossiping back and forth across Europe.

As in the other sonnets under discussion, the opposition that becomes prominent in the final lines is prepared for from the beginning. In the octet we find opposing personae who correspond, respectively, to the opposing thoughts expressed in the sestet. Of course, there is only one person speaking, but that person sounds different in the first and second sentences of the sonnet. Here is the first sentence:

> Cyriack, this three years' day these eyes, though clear
>   To outward view of blemish or of spot,
>   Bereft of light thir seeing have forgot;
>   Nor to thir idle orbs doth sight appear
> Of Sun or Moon or Star throughout the year,
>   Or man or woman.

The speaker is reflective and sensitive to the spiritual implications of things. He sees more than one level: phenomena have an "outward" and an inward aspect, a literal and metaphorical significance. The diction and idiom are free from the conventional. In the Metaphysical manner, intellectual vitality generates emotional intensity: the sad irony of clear eyes that don't see, idle orbs that have forgotten the sight of the heavenly orbs. This is the private persona.

The speaker of the second sentence uses language and ideas that are much more commonplace; his tone is hearty.

> Yet I argue not
> Against heav'n's hand or will, nor bate a jot
> Of heart or hope; but still bear up and steer
> Right onward.

The expressions "bate a jot," "bear up," seem to roll off the tongue without thought.[13] "[H]eav'n's hand and will" initially may seem to evidence a religious turn of thought; the phrase turns out, however, to be the first of three coordinate constructions ("heav'n's hand and will," "heart and hope," "bear up and steer") that give the sentence a singsong, rather superficial quality. By the end of the sentence, it seems likely that the speaker says "heav'n's hand and will" quite mindlessly, as a person today might say "God willing" or "Heaven forbid" without any real reverence.

Because of his outgoing tone and common expression, the speaker of the sentence may be called the public persona. His distinctive qualities continue into the next three lines, which tell the first reason for his cheerfulness in adversity:

> What supports me, does thou ask?
> The conscience, Friend, to have lost them overplied
> In liberty's defense, my noble task . . .

His address of Cyriack as "Friend" emphasizes the public nature of this disclosure, and (accompanied perhaps by a clap on the shoulder) reinforces the general heartiness of his tone. "Liberty," then as now, was a political catchword invoked by several sides, including the Levellers, who opposed the same government that Milton defended.

As reason 1 (conscience) is expressed by the public persona, reason 2 (better guide) amounts to a reemergence of the private persona. The whole poem is the portrait of someone with two contrary natures; its doubleness occurs when the two natures overlay each other. In his prose work, Milton made the same claim found here that his defenses of the regicide greatly affected European opinion.[14] Douglas Bush and Mark Pattison correctly regard Milton's claim to be exaggerated. But these biographers assume too readily that Milton wholly believed his fantasy of grandeur. Sonnet 22 raises the distinct possibility that only one part of him (or persona) believed the fantasy.[15]

The link between the private persona (lines 1–6) and reason 2 (lines 13–14) is not obvious, for, by definition, the private persona is more reserved than his counterpart; his thoughts are more obscure. Yet a link does exist. Reason 2 (better guide) can be called unworldly; it invokes a better, spiritual guide that is aloof from human affairs. There is an unworldly quality also in the first sentence of the poem, spoken by the private persona.

In the first sentence, implied spiritual meanings lie behind more obvious, "outward" ones. "[C]lear / To outward view of blemish or of spot," most obviously, is a report on his physical appearance. "[B]lemish" does not have to connote a defect of character; and "spot" is a technical term for a disfigurement of the eye (*OED* I.3.a). At the same time, the speaker's choice of words strongly suggests that he has formed a spiritual interpretation of this physical catastrophe. The books of Exodus and Leviticus in innumerable places prescribe temple offerings that are without "blemish." Priests, too, are to be without blemish; that is, neither lame nor blind (Lev. 22:18). "Spot" can be a cultic term like "blemish"; it is so used in Sonnet 23: "Mine as whom washt from spot of child-bed taint, / Purification in the old Law did save" (5–6). Finally, change of "light" to "sight" by the sonnet's seventeenth-century editor, Edward Phillips, suggests that "sight" was a more conventional way of referring to eyesight, and that "light" recommended itself to Milton by its spiritual overtones.

Cooperating with the speaker's spiritual orientation is his removal from sensible reality. The speaker has not only lost his sight but also is forgetting what things look like—to us. "[T]hir seeing have forgot" can mean both that he has lost the capacity to see and has forgotten what things look like. The latter sense is borne out by the extreme abstractness of his world: "Of Sun or Moon or Star throughout the year, / Or man or woman." There is no detail in his recollection of creation. Nor, strung together by "or," are these abstract phenomena in any specific relationship to each other. He lives in a strange world of his own, from which, with the words "Yet I argue not" he emerges in a public guise. The private persona's spiritual orientation, his loneliness, and his removal from the familiar world can be heard again in the statement of reason 2, which talks of an empty world and a mysterious guide—obscurely, as words spoken to oneself.

To summarize the pattern of the poem: In lines 1 6, the speaker talks to us of his own, peculiar world. In lines 6–10, he rouses himself to speak as someone who has a public role, and gives a public reason for his contentment (which repeats Milton's published account of himself in *The Second Defense* [YP 4.587–91]). In line 12, the initial persona, who follows a better guide, intimates another reason by satirizing the first one. Lines 13–14 develop the assertion of reason 2 (better guide) while concurrently (and doubly) reaffirming reason 1 (conscience). The A–B–AB form roughly resembles that of Sonnet 19, which presents zeal and patience separately and then paradoxically combines them.

The rarity of comment on the doubleness of this and other sonnets may well provoke some skepticism: if doubleness is indeed a prominent feature of the late sonnets, how could centuries of criticism have missed it? The answer lies in the nature of doubleness: as a form of absurdity, it seems out of place, un-Miltonic. And as seemingly un-Miltonic, doubleness is ignored by criticism.

Doubleness is "un-Miltonic" on several counts. The sonnets have a strongly rhetorical character, and can be classed under different types of rhetorical address: panegyric, diatribe, exhortation, etc. Considering their rhetorical cast, we expect the poems to observe the axioms of common discourse: for example, a precept is true or false. In the discourse of doubleness, however, a precept is both true *and* false. Doubleness jars with the poet's apparent intent of persuading the listener; it is a troublesome inconsistency.

As a form of absurdity, doubleness borders on humor, and one sometimes suspects that Milton is playing a joke on us. This is especially true of

Sonnet 21, the invitation to a gaudy day. At the same time, the sonnets are lofty and authoritative. As observed by John H. Finley, Milton "constantly addresses persons with a kind of social authority springing from his conception of the poet's office."[16] How can such an address be humorous? So, again, when one encounters doubleness, it seems a kind of mistake, like a naked emperor, and it is usually ignored.

In Sonnet 22 doubleness jeopardizes both the poem's argument and its loftiness. The trouble begins with line 12, which concludes the speaker's ringing affirmation of his noble task and at the same time, with the word "talks," brings the nobleness of his task into question. The textual history of the sonnet, and especially of line 12, illustrates the tendency of Milton criticism to evade the complications posed by doubleness.

Written in the mid-1650s, the poem existed only in manuscript until its first publication in 1694 by Milton's nephew Edward Phillips. Phillips altered the manuscript reading of Sonnet 22 in six places. In the last three lines, he changed "talks" to "rings," "the world's" to "this world's," and "better" to "other." All of these changes—most notably the first—work to soften the reversal of meaning that takes place in these lines.

The manuscript has been accessible since 1736, in the Trinity College library. By the late nineteenth century, most editors adopted its version of Sonnet 22 over Phillips's. Phillips's invention of "rings" persisted, however, even in editions that otherwise adhered to the manuscript. Editions by Masson (1874), Chalmers (1881), Bradshaw (1892), Moody (1899), and Rouse (1909) all retain "rings" while discarding Phillips's other changes. The sentiment behind this anomaly must be that since Milton's task was "noble," the irreverent "talks" is a mistake and must be elevated to "rings." A note by J. S. Smart, in his 1921 edition of the sonnets, reports such a sentiment. "Bishop Newton [an 18th century editor of Milton] suggests that '*rings* may be thought better than *talks from side to side,*' because—'There is something very pleasing as well as noble in this conscious virtue and magnanimity of a great poet.' But *talks* is the only reading which has Milton's own authority."[17] After Smart's edition of the sonnets, "talks" became the standard reading.

Sonnet 18 ("On the Late Massacre in Piemont")

The doubleness in Sonnet 18, as in Sonnet 22, centers on the speaker's attitude towards history. Sonnet 18 is occasioned by the persecution of protestants in Northern Italy by their Roman Catholic ruler, the Duke of Savoy, in 1655. The speaker is both incensed by the recent massacre and detached from it; the intertwining of these attitudes produces a tone of lofty passion for which the poem is much admired.

To consider the impassioned, partisan side of the speaker: his appeal for vengeance assumes that God, as in the Hebrew scriptures, assists His people against their enemies; and that His people and their enemies can be identified with particular nations, parties, or sects. The speaker is zealous to champion the people of God. In Sonnet 22, he is proud of having sacrificed his sight for the defense of English republicans against their detractors; in Sonnet 18, taking the role of prophet, he calls upon God to avenge the Waldensians and prophesies the form of God's response.

Another, less partisan (and less vocal) side to the speaker holds that, while wickedness should be punished, the wicked and the good do not belong exclusively to different parties, and the triumph of one party over another rarely can be celebrated as the triumph of good over evil. (We recall the friendships that Milton formed in Italy, and his admiration of the court composer and Royalist, Henry Lawes.) As for a particular party's cause, if it prevails, it usually does so by the means of violence, no matter how worthy its goal and adherents. This dilemma faces Jesus in *Paradise Regained* when he ponders, at the outset of his career, how "to subdue and quell o'er all the earth / Brute violence and proud Tyrannic pow'r" without augmenting the evil (1.218–19). These considerations restrain the speaker from allying himself completely with a particular cause. His "better guide" is hope for the new creation that is promised at the end of time. In the meantime, however, he must use his talents, and the controversies of the day allow him to do so. The speaker's two attitudes correspond roughly to the public and private personae of Sonnet 22; this discussion of Sonnet 18 will retain those labels.

The poem's first lines exhibit the double viewpoint just defined: "Avenge, O Lord, thy slaughter'd Saints, whose bones / Lie scatter'd on the Alpine mountains cold." Although the slaughter that excites the speaker's wrath in the first line is recent, the image in the second line is not of slaughtered corpses but of bones, scattered (as if by the passage of time) on the Alpine mountains cold. The passionate call for vengeance paradoxically carries us to a realm that is remote, clear, and cold. It is remote from the present and from passion. This is the realm inhabited by the private speaker.

The remoteness persists into the next line: "Ev'n them who kept thy truth so pure of old." The purity and remoteness of the Alpine peaks metamorphose into the doctrinal purity of an ancient and ideal church.[18] To be sure, this distancing also advances the case for vengeance: "the Alpine mountains cold" alludes to the suffering of the Waldensian refuges; their purity aggravates the atrociousness of their slaughter. Such is the paradoxical nature of doubleness.

In the fourth line, the public persona stokes his indignation with thoughts of idolatry: "When all our Fathers worship't Stocks and Stones." "Fathers" refers first to the audience's Papist ancestors in England, then to the more ancient heritage of idolatry that is denounced by the Hebrew prophets: "Saying to a stock, Thou art my father; and to a stone, Thou has brought me forth" (Jer. 2:27). The timelessness of idolatry transcends distinctions between Protestant and Catholic. Furthermore, the very mention of stocks (blocks of wood) and stone, while embedded in an expression of angry scorn, reinforces the initial imagery of hard, cold, unfeeling objects. Finally, the implication of *all* our fathers in idolatry can only temper our condemnation of it. For all these reasons, the line blows both hot and cold.

This paradox of dispassionate passion in the first quatrain has been noticed independently by John S. Lawry: "A series of immediate affective protests against the massacre is closely linked with, but also effectively opposed by, a series of reflections upon that act. . . . The sickening . . . sight of slaughter yields . . . to an elegiac vision of now-cleansed bones, strewn as if in lonely space."[19]

In the sonnet's next sentence, the tension between opposites continues:

> Forget not: in thy book record their groans
>   Who were thy Sheep and in their ancient Fold
>   Slain by the bloody *Piemontese* that roll'd
>   Mother with Infant down the Rocks.

Before, the speaker called on God to avenge; here, to write in a book. This is not action but a deferral of action. But while stepping back from retributive action, the speaker brings closer to us the massacre that demands such action, by showing us the perpetrators ("the bloody *Piemontese*") and their victims ("Mother with Infant"). Within this double movement away from and towards action, there are finer ones. The bloody action is stylized by the detail of the Mother and Infant being *rolled* down the rocks.[20] How are we to imagine the pair? As a sphere? "Hurled" would be easier to visualize. Unable to picture the scene, our mind may resort to a preexisting, iconographic image of the Holy Mother and Child.

Of course, this association would be a mistake, as it contains implications directly contrary to the speaker's ideological position. The association might be discounted out of hand, were there not several opportunities for similar mistakes. The first occurs with line 4: "When all our Fathers worship't Stocks and Stones." Readers understand "Fathers" to be their Papist ancestors in England, but not, perhaps, after briefly identifying "Fathers" with the pagans in England who, before their conversion, literally did worship stocks and stones. In that case, those who kept the faith pure (in line 3) would be the early Romanists—a proposition which, of course, must be rejected as soon as entertained. Kathryn Brock has noticed two more possible mistakes.[21] The

phrase "slaughter'd Saints" can be misconstrued as a Roman Catholic elevation of believers to sainthood after death by martyrdom; that is, the saints
could be Roman Catholic, not Protestant. Also, says Brock, the mention of
saints' bones may put the reader in mind of sacred relics and their veneration.
As for mother with infant being rolled down the rocks, that detail for Brock
"evokes the casting down of the statues of the Virgin and Child" by militant
Protestants.[22] It may seem unlikely that the reader would embrace any one of
these mistakes, but taken together, they do impart to the poem a subtle aura
of surrealism: as in a dream, labels become unanchored from their proper
objects; good and bad figures appear in each others' places.

To return to the larger and more visible movement between passion and
detachment: The account of the massacre, after angrily denouncing the
"bloody *Piemontese*," comes to a stylized close: "Their moans / The Vales
redoubl'd to the Hills, and they / To Heav'n." Hills, vales, and echoes are all
fixtures of the Pastoral. In keeping with the pathetic fallacy (another fixture),
nature sides with the victims, broadcasting their moans to heaven. Innocent
blood cries out to heaven for revenge; but those cries, because described in a
conventional manner, are not intensely stirring.

So far, the public persona has been making a case for God's intervention
by establishing the purity of the Waldenses and the brutality of their persecu-
tors. In the final sentence, he urges God to a specific act of vengeance. This
brings the poem to a crisis: somehow, the envisioned vengeance must satisfy
the two contrary principles that are active in the poem. From this point, we
can best proceed by keeping in mind the two personae. Their requirements
jointly steer the vision's progress toward "the *Babylonian* woe" (14), where
their attitudes, though opposed, assert themselves concurrently. The course
they steer is zigzag; the direction taken by one is corrected by the other.

The poem's last sentence begins on a note of prophetic passion that
consists with the public persona:

> Their martyr'd blood and ashes sow
> O'er all th' *Italian* fields where still doth sway
> The triple Tyrant: That from these may grow
> A hundredfold ...   (10–13)

With this sentence, responsibility for the massacre settles on the Pope,
who is here depicted as exercising spiritual sway over all of Italy and so as
accountable for religious persecution, even distant from Rome. (Actually, it
was the Duke of Savoy who ordered the massacre.) The phrase "triple Tyrant" refers to the three tiers of the Papal crown, which represent the Pope's
authority over heaven, earth, and hell, respectively. The usurpation of earthly

authority aggravates the Pope's guilt, in the speaker's eyes, and intensifies the speaker's audible anger.

Who or what will grow a hundredfold from the blood and ashes sown in the Italian fields? We think of Cadmus, who sowed a crop of armed men, and also of Tertullian's apothegm: "The blood of the martyrs is the seed of the church."[23] The two images fuse into the vision of militant Protestants scattered over Italy, threatening the Roman Catholic church. The Reformation of Italy would be ample recompense for the massacre; but there would be violence; and, besides, the notion is fantastical, even though powerfully expressed.

The final words of the poem admit the voice of the private persona:

> who having learnt thy way
> Early may fly the *Babylonian* woe.

There is a drop in emotional intensity, and the situation imagined becomes more mundane. With the phrase "who having learnt thy way," the speaker, in effect, recasts his prophecy. The metaphorical crop of Protestants that sprang up earlier in the sentence asked to be imagined fully armed, as it were, like Cadmus's soldiers. That is, they sprang up as Protestants. The phrase "who having learnt thy way" is senselessly redundant if the speaker is understood to be talking still about the metaphoric crop, which by definition is Protestant. The phrase escapes redundancy, however, if there is understood to be a shift in the speaker from the public to private persona, who now translates the earlier, heated metaphor into cooler, literal terms. The speaker now imagines Italians who learn God's way and convert to the Protestant faith.

Still thinking realistically, the private persona naturally imagines conversion to be followed by persecution; once again, the saints must "fly." The conclusion is anticlimactic. It quite fails the expectations roused by the earlier appeals to divine justice. The most the speaker hopes for is that the persecuted Protestants, having learned from the experience of history, will flee in time (i.e. "early"). (As Stanley Fish argues, "thy way" may have a secondary meaning of "the ways of Providence.")[24] The resigned pessimism of the conclusion consists with the private persona's relative detachment from the massacre, and may contribute to that detachment.

But the pessimism of the last sentence is only one facet of a double ending. There is a triumphant aspect too. "*Babylonian* woe" can refer either to the woe *inflicted* by Babylon (such as renewed persecution) or to the woe *suffered* by Babylon that is prophesied in Revelation. The reference in line 5 to a book of judgement ("in thy book record their groans") prepares for this association of "*Babylonian* woe" with the apocalyptic destruction of that city.

Since Rome is the seat of the triple Tyrant, whom the poem now holds responsible for the massacre, the devastation of Rome/Babylon satisfies the call for vengeance that began the poem. Nor does this vengeance violate the dispassionate principle of the poem, for the destruction of Babylon is carried out solely by God, who pours plagues and fire on the city (Rev. 18:8).

Far from being agents of wrath, the Protestant converts are possible victims who must flee for their lives. A gloss on their flight is found in Revelation 18:4: "And I heard another voice from heaven, saying, Come out of her my people, that ye be not partakers of her sins, and that ye receive not of her plagues." The same warning comes from Jeremiah, who prophesies the fall of the literal Babylon at the hand of Cyrus: "Flee out of the midst of Babylon, and deliver every man his soul: be not cut off in her iniquity; for this is the time of the Lord's vengeance" (51:6). Both constructions of *"Babylonian* woe," then, include flight from destruction. Flight is the common term that allows the reader's mind to shuttle between woe suffered by Babylon and woe dealt by Babylon.

However we imagine *"Babylonian* woe," there is flight, wrath, and terror. The poem's last line tolls a knell of woe. It is hard to agree with Lawry that the "speaker ascends into the awareness that both past isolation and present martyrdom are not pathetically terminal but productive and generative."[25] This optimistic reading says less about the poem than about a modern predilection for stories in which a character experiences some sort of enlightenment.

The doubleness of Milton's late sonnets can guide us to a fresh way of approaching his longer poetical works. The fresh approach may called dialectical. In all the sonnets studied here, Milton poses a pair of opposed principles (activity/inactivity, indulgence/refraining, involvement/detachment, etc.). The principles are of equal strength, or validity; one cannot banish the other. At the same time, being antitheses, neither can they tolerate the other. These conditions eventuate in the concurrent assertion of both principles at the end of the poem. The interplay of opposed principles under these conditions is the plot of the poem.

The similarity of Sonnet 19 to *Samson Agonistes* invites a dialectical approach to the drama. The initial opposition of principles is the same in both works: imperative zeal, innate in the sonnet's speaker and in Samson, meets an immovable obstacle in the form of blindness. To review the dialectical interplay in Sonnet 19: frustrated by blindness, zeal turns into complaint; then, zeal embarrassed by its own complaint, tries to desist from itself and take the form of its opposite: patience. But, unable to desist from itself, it finally combines with patience in an act of doubleness that leaves us in wonder.

The dénouement of *Samson Agonistes* too is full of doubleness: An heroic Nazarite, separate to God, plays before the Philistines at a festival in honor of their god, Dagon. Wearing the livery of the Philistian court, he acts of his own free will. He is simultaneously slave and conqueror. Might not criticism of the play undertake to trace the course of Samson's zeal that leads to these paradoxical events?

Most commentary on *Samson Agonistes* takes a far different approach, which has been termed regenerationist. It is applied broadly to the works of Milton: in a poem's speaker or hero, pride and its derivatives give way to piety. The speaker's zeal in Sonnet 19 is initially tainted with willfulness but later tempered by humility. Samson lacks, then learns, repentance.

A regenerationist reading of Sonnet 19 may be plausible, but in *Samson Agonistes* the approach runs afoul of detail. The various accounts of Samson's journey from sin to repentance to salvation are detailed and eloquent—but they simply do not fit the play. Several critics have pointed out this inadequacy, but they have not offered a better alternative, and the regenerationist reading rules by default.[26] A fresh approach to the play is needed, and the late sonnets, as here explicated, point the way.

Belmont, Massachusetts

NOTES

1. Quotations of Milton's poetry are from *John Milton: Complete Poems and Major Prose,* ed. Merritt Y. Hughes, (New York, 1957). Milton's prose is quoted from *Complete Prose Works of John Milton,* 8 vols., ed. Don M. Wolfe et al. (New Haven, 1953–82), hereafter cited as YP, with volume and page number.

2. James G. Mengert, "The Resistance of Milton's Sonnets," *ELR* 11 (1981): 81–95; see also Stanley E. Fish, "Interpreting the *Variorum*," *CritI* 2 (1976): 465–85, and Joseph Pequigney, "Milton's Sonnet XIX Reconsidered," *TSLL* 8 (1967): 485–98.

3. Fish advances this solution to the crux by way of championing "reader-oriented analysis" against "formalist analysis" ("Interpreting the *Variorum*," 468). The present study is not aligned with either methodology.

4. References are to the second edition of the *Oxford English Dictionary.*

5. *Milton's Sonnets,* ed. E. A. J. Honigmann, (New York, 1966), 179–80.

6. Søren Kierkegaard, *Philosophical Fragments,* trans. David Swenson, translation revised by Howard V. Hong (Princeton, N.J., 1962), 46.

7. "The verbal and dramatic qualities of the poem become more demonstrable if intrusive biographical inquiry is initially set aside and the central character is regarded, at least provisionally, as fictional" (Pequigney, "Milton's Sonnet XIX Reconsidered," 487).

8. Whiting and Grossman correctly insist on this logical consequence of blindness in arguing against Fitzroy Pyle's characterization of the speaker as belonging to those "who though inactive are eagerly prepared for action when the call comes" (Pyle, "Milton's First Sonnet on his Blindness," *RES* 9 [1958]: 383). But Grossman and Whiting are themselves mistaken in asserting that the speaker "resolves to heed the voice of Patience counselling resignation" (Grossman and

Whiting, "Milton's First Sonnet on his Blindness," *RES* 12 [1961]: 369). Both sides err in allowing only a single meaning.

9. Pequigney also finds in "wait" a passive and active sense. In his reading, the court metaphor controls both senses. The passive sense of "wait," in his view, is "to attend a superior ceremoniously," that is, to serve by one's mere presence ("Milton's Sonnet XIX Reconsidered," 493). This is certainly a possible reading.

10. Mengert, "The Resistance of Milton's Sonnets," 87.

11. Mengert, as just quoted, and John Carey, in a passing remark: "The sage, shrugging off the world as a 'vain mask', keeps odd company with the excited pamphleteer who imagines himself the talk of Europe" (John Carey, *Milton* [London, 1969], 16).

12. John Bradshaw, *A Concordance to the Poetical Works of John Milton,* (London, 1894), 353.

13. Anna Nardo thinks that the diction of the second sentence betrays insincerity: "The commonplace phrase *bate a jot;* the alliterative cliché, *heart or hope;* the trite nautical metaphor [*sic*] of putting up the helm and steering to the wind . . . suggest that the speaker protests too much" (Anna K. Nardo, *Milton's Sonnets and the Ideal Community* [Lincoln, Neb., 1979], 154–55).

14. "I have in the *First Defense* and shall in the *Second* speak again to the entire assembly and council of all the most influential men, cities, and nations everywhere" (YP 4:554).

15. Bush calls line 12 of the sonnet "a pardonable exaggeration" (Douglas Bush, ed., *The Complete Poetical Works of John Milton* [Boston, 1965], 197). Pattison remarks, "He consoles himself with the fancy that in his pamphlet, the *Defensio,* he had done a great work . . . for his country. This poor delusion helped him doubtless to support his calamity" (Mark Pattison, *Milton* [London, 1887], 110–11).

16. John H. Finley Jr., "Milton and Horace: A Study of Milton's Sonnets," *Harvard Studies in Classical Philology* 68 (1937): 40.

17. J. S. Smart, ed., *The Sonnets of Milton* (Glasgow, 1921), 106.

18. Line 3 of the sonnet invites the common Protestant perception of the Waldenses as directly and uniquely preserving the purity of the Apostolic church. As Milton knew, they were actually another reformed church. In *Considerations Touching the Likeliest Means to Remove Hirelings from the Church* (1659), he accurately refers to the Waldenses as Reformed, while not completely disallowing their idealized genealogy: "Hence those ancientest reformed churches of the *Waldenses,* if they rather continu'd not pure since the apostles, deni'd that tithes were ever to be given" (YP 7:291–92).

19. John S. Lawry, "Milton's Sonnet 18: 'A Holocaust,' " *MQ* 17 (1983): 11–12.

20. In contemporary accounts of the massacre quoted by Honigmann, some victims (of unspecified gender and age) were bound in such a way that they could be rolled down precipices (Honigmann, 164–65). In an account written a few years after the event, and quoted by Mark Pattison, "A mother was hurled down a mighty rock with a little infant in her arms" (*The Sonnets of John Milton,* ed. Mark Pattison [London, 1883], 200–201). It seems that Milton, rather than strictly following reports of the event, recombined their details.

21. Kathryn Gail Brock, "Milton's *Sonnet XVIII* and the Language of Controversy," *MQ* 16 (1982): 3–6. Brock's observations belong to an argument that is very different from the one advanced by this study: "By recreating the ever present threat posed by the perversion of language and reasoning, the sonnet shows that the Catholic attack on the Waldensians is one manifestation of the continual war of falsehood against true belief" (5).

22. Ibid., 5.

23. Tertullian, *Apologeticus* 50; Migne, *Pat. Lat.* 1.535; cited by A. S. P. Woodhouse and

Douglas Bush, ed., *A Variorum Commentary on the Poems of John Milton* (London, 1972), vol. 2, part 2, 440.

24. Fish, "Interpreting the *Variorum*," 470.

25. Lawry, "Milton's Sonnet 18: 'A Holocaust,'" 14.

26. Mason Tung writes, "Until his final hour, he stubbornly holds to his own wisdom, his own will to act or not to act, his own 'vain reasoning'" ("Samson Impatiens: A Reinterpretation of Milton's *Samson Agonistes*," *TSLL* 9 [1968]: 492); G. A. Wilkes writes, "It is an improvement of *Samson Agonistes* that is offered, a play endowed with a singleness and coherence that (as a psychological drama) the original does not possess" ("The Interpretation of *Samson Agonistes*," *HLQ* 26 [1963]: 366); Stanley Fish writes that proponents of the regenerationist theory have "tended to assume a linear progression, more or less visible, from accusation of God to acceptance of responsibility to rejection of temptation to a reaffirmation of faith. But an examination of the text will not support this reading" ("Question and Answer in *Samson Agonistes*," *CritQ* 11 [1969]: 248).

MILTON AND THE REASONING OF ANIMALS: VARIATIONS ON A THEME BY PLUTARCH

Bruce Boehrer

BURIED TOWARD THE END of Plutarch's *Moralia* are two minor dialogues on the intellectual capacities of animals, one titled "Whether Land or Sea Animals Are Cleverer" (Πότερα τῶν ζῴων φρονιμώτερα τὰ χεπσαῖα ἢ τὰ ἔνυδρα) and the other called simply "Beasts Are Rational" (Περὶ τοῦ τὰ ἄλογα λόγῳ χρῆσθαι). Despite their relative obscurity, even within the limited canon of Plutarch's own works, these discourses leave their mark upon carly modern learning theory, and one aim of the present essay is thus to trace their Renaissance *Nachleben*, especially as it extends into seventeenth-century England. In the process, I will also bring sustained attention to bear upon Milton's debt to these two dialogues, a debt whose profundity and ambivalence extend beyond the poet's limited work on the theory of education. For Milton, as well as for at least one author—Bathsua Makin—writing in response to Milton, Plutarch's dialogues on animal intelligence raise broader questions about the nature of human understanding in general: who has it and why, whether closed or open educational communities can best foster and preserve it, and how it helps to structure the relations between men and women that form the basis of the poet's major works.

In what follows, I will argue that Plutarch's dialogues raise questions of knowledge in a way that associates them with gender difference; that in doing so the dialogues figure a tension between competing ways of knowing, ways that are associated with masculine and feminine figures and communities, respectively; and that this tension likewise directly informs Milton's work, both in his earlier and later periods. Since this study concerns mainly the sources and originary formation of a gender tension central to Milton's verse, I will focus upon early Miltonic texts—the prolusions, elegies, and *Comus*. While I will end with some broad and suggestive remarks about the reemergence of themes from Plutarch's dialogues in *Paradise Lost*, sustained discussion of Milton's later work is well beyond the scope of the present study.

I

Plutarch's *Moralia* were printed fairly early and often in the Renaissance. The *editio princeps* (produced with the assistance of Erasmus) issued from the Aldine press in 1509, and by 1570 Wilhelm Holzmann (Xylander) had completed a monumental edition of the work, settling the Greek text in its modern sequence and also supplying a Latin translation and some critical notes.[1] This edition, in turn, superseded a number of other, partial Latin translations of the *Moralia,* including exercises by such figures as Politian, Melanchthon, Willibald Pirckheimer, and Sir John Cheke.[2] Early vernacular translations, on the other hand, were "comparatively few" in number,[3] but even so, Philemon Holland had rendered the *Moralia* into English by 1603, in a version based on Plutarch's Greek but massively influenced by Jacques Amyot's epochal French translation of 1572. (North's famous version of Plutarch's *Lives,* in contrast to Holland's *Moralia,* was a straight translation from Amyot's French.) Thus by the time Milton matriculated at Cambridge he could have had easy access to the *Moralia* in Greek, Latin, English, French, and a number of other languages as well. Surviving evidence suggests that most readers of Greek in early modern Europe "seem to have depended very much on Greco-Latin bilingual editions" of the *Moralia* such as Holzmann's,[4] referring to the Greek largely in order to clarify difficulties in the Latin translation, and one is tempted to suppose that Milton would have proceeded in this manner himself. But this point is uncertain; Plutarch is not cited in Milton's surviving commonplace book, and the Miltonic allusions with which this essay is concerned are sufficiently diffuse in form to have come from almost any contemporary edition or translation of the *Moralia.*

Of the two Plutarchan dialogues in question here, "Animals Are Rational" is in a sense mistitled, for instead of seeking to persuade the reader that animals can reason, it takes their reasoning ability as a given and proceeds instead to demonstrate that they are also supremely virtuous. It is the piece on "Whether Land or Sea Animals Are Cleverer" that makes the more direct case for the reasoning abilities of beasts, in part through arguments like the following:

Logicians assert that a dog, at a point where many paths split off, makes use of a multiple disjunctive argument and reasons with himself: "Either the wild beast has taken this path, or this, or this. But surely it has not taken this, or this. Then it must have gone by the remaining road." Perception here affords nothing but the minor premiss, while the force of reason gives the major premises and adds the conclusion to the premisses.[5]

This passage seems to have been fairly popular among seventeenth-century English readers, whose general esteem for dogs (particularly hunting dogs)

grew rapidly under the early Stuart monarchs.[6] Thus, for instance, King
James I could attend a public debate, held in Cambridge in 1615, on "whether
dogs could make syllogismes,"[7] and the victor of the disputation, John Preston, could carry the day in part by reproducing Plutarch's argument almost
verbatim: "An Ethymeme [sic] (said he), is a lawfull & reall syllogisme, but
dogs can make them; he instanced in a Hound, who has ye major proposition
in his minde, namely, the hare is gone either this way, or that way, smells out
the minor wth his nose, namely, she is not gone that way, & follows the
conclusion, "Ergo," this way, wth open mouth."[8]

     In 1615 Milton was too young to have attended this debate, but he was
most certainly in Cambridge and participating in public debates himself
seventeen years later, when he worked the same passage from Plutarch into
the end of Prolusion 7. In this speech—a standard forensic exercise in defense of learning against the claims of ignorance—the young poet summa-
rizes his arguments in a way that must be quoted at length:

Finally, we may well ask, what is the happiness which Ignorance promises? To enjoy
what one possesses, to have no enemies, to be beyond the reach of all care and
trouble, to pass one's life in peace and quiet so far as may be—this is but the life of a
beast. . . . If such is the argument, we will offer Ignorance Circe's cup, and bid her
throw off her human shape, and walk no longer erect, and betake her to the beasts. To
the beasts, did I say? they will surely refuse to receive so infamous a guest, at any rate
if they are . . . endowed with some kind of inferior reasoning power, as many maintain. . . . For Plutarch tells us that in the pursuit of game, dogs show some knowledge
of dialectic, and if they chance to come to cross-roads, they obviously make use of a
disjunctive syllogism.[9]

     Unlike Preston, who simply appropriates Plutarch's argument for his
own purposes, Milton forces the argument to acquire unexpected resonance
through a series of powerful juxtapositions and reversals. First, Milton's reference to canine logic inverts his preceding association of ignorance with beasts
and makes claims for the preeminence of learning even within the customary
territory of ignorance. At the same time, too, Milton's prose distinguishes
canine reason from an ignorance that loses its personhood through a variety
of Circean transformation; in doing so Milton tropes the feminine principle
into deviations from an implied standard of rational masculinity. Further, the
allusion to Circe constitutes yet another reference to Plutarch, this time to
the dialogue "Beasts Are Rational," which cleverly inverts the themes and
commitments of the Circe-story as related in the tenth book of the *Odyssey*.

     To consider this last point at some length: "Beasts Are Rational" mocks
the ingenuity of Odysseus by subjecting him to the moral instruction of one
of Circe's swine. The occasion for this mockery is Odysseus' own determi-

nation to abandon Circe's company and resume his journey homeward to Ithaca, for, as Circe herself observes, this choice involves an element of unreason that far exceeds the effects of her own magic:

Haven't you already worked a stranger magic than [mine] on yourself? You who refused an ageless, immortal life at my side and would struggle through a thousand new dangers to a woman who is mortal and, I can assure you, no longer so very young—and this for no object other than to make yourself more gaped at and renowned than you already are, pursuing an empty phantom instead of what is truly good. (985F–986A)

To represent her own views to Odysseus, Circe introduces him to a former Greek, the hog Gryllus, who persuades him at length that beasts surpass men in courage, temperance, chastity, and reason, and who thus ingeniously reverses the mental and emotional effects of Circe's enchantments in the *Odyssey*. There, Homer relates that the witch's victims grow inarticulate yet retain their human consciousness, weeping at their unhappy metamorphosis,[10] yet Plutarch's Gryllus not only remains capable of speech but also resists with inexorable logic any opportunities for retransformation.

So in Plutarch's dialogue, the wily Odysseus is apparently not so clever after all; the plight of Circe's victims is no plight after all; Circe herself is not so much an evil enchantress as an instructress in that most Neoplatonic of self-help projects, the pursuit of spiritual metamorphosis;[11] and to emphasize these points Plutarch's dialogue goes out of its way to revise its Homeric pretext by conceiving Circean enchantment as a transformation not only of the body but of the mind as well. Thus Gryllus remarks to Odysseus that "just as children dread the doctor's doses and run from lessons, the very things that, by changing them from invalids and fools, will make them healthier and wiser, just so you have shied away from the change from one shape to another" (986D). For Gryllus, Circean transformation is a learning process. And thus, too, Odysseus can remark in horror that "To me, Gryllus, you seem to have lost not only your shape, but your intelligence also under the influence of that drug" (986E). For both of the major characters in this dialogue, the inner metamorphosis wrought by Circe's magic acquires preeminence over its physical consequences.

This notion proves appealing to Milton, who employs it in his own version of the Circe-tale, *Comus*. There the Attendant Spirit traces Comus's descent from Circe and then describes the effects of his "orient liquor" (65) upon the travellers who partake of it:

> Soon as the potion works, their human count'nance,
> Th'express resemblance of the gods, is chang'd,
> Into some brutish form of Wolf, or Bear,

Or Ounce, or Tiger, Hog, or bearded Goat,
All other parts remaining as they were,
And they, so perfect is their misery,
Not once perceive their foul disfigurement,
But boast themselves more comely than before
And all their friends, and native home forget
To roule with pleasure in a sensual stie.   (68–77)

Critics have spent little time trying to account for this variation upon Homer's Circe-myth, and when they have paid attention to it at all, they have usually traced it to Ariosto.[12] Yet Plutarch is at least an equally viable candidate, and probably a better one, for the source of this material. The *Moralia* predate *Orlando Furioso* and were equally familiar to the young Milton; they have the additional advantage of offering Milton a sustained early treatment of his masque's central fable, while *Orlando Furioso* does not. Moreover, while scholars have usefully identified a parallel between *Comus*'s beasts and the monsters outside of Alcina's bower at *Orlando Furioso* 6.60–66, they have wrongly extended that parallel by claiming that both Ariosto's and Milton's "victims . . . are entirely oblivious to the[ir] transformation."[13] While this is true of *Orlando Furioso*, it is simply false in the case of *Comus*, whose monsters are well aware that they have changed and believe that the change is for the better. The pattern for this latter detail of *Comus* thus cannot be found in Ariosto, but on the other hand it is readily available in Plutarch.

By emphasizing the internal transformation that Comus's victims undergo, Milton would seem to be abandoning Homer for Plutarch in his use of source-material. But he is reworking Plutarch in the same gesture: revising those features of "Beasts Are Rational" that appear to challenge Odyssean wisdom most directly, replacing the rational attainments of Gryllus with an empty fantasy of personal comeliness, and insisting with *The Odyssey* that there really is no place like home. It is as if Milton has gone out of his way to recall Gryllus' feminine riposte to Homer, but with the specific aim of putting it unequivocally and finally in its place. And that place, in turn, is the place of ignorance; the "human count'nance" that Comus's victims lose is an "express [i.e. pressed out, externalized] resemblance" of the more essential interior quality of reason itself. Hence the Attendant Spirit can elsewhere describe the human countenance specifically as "reasons mintage/ Character'd in the face" (528–29); for Milton's *Comus*, as for the Prolusion 7, ignorance thus acquires feminine associations concomitant with the Plutarchan opposition between Odysseus and Circe.

Finally, there is another reference to the Circe-tale in Milton's early works, a reference less clearly derivative of Plutarch but that likewise invokes the opposition between masculine learning/reason (Odysseus) and feminine ignorance/unreason (Circe), once more in a way that seems to promote the former at the expense of the latter. The text in question here is Milton's Elegy 1—the verse epistle to Charles Diodati that Milton wrote to describe his brief removal from Cambridge to London (apparently, although not certainly, due to rustication)[14] in 1626—and the reference in question comes at the poem's end. There, after a lengthy description of the delights of London's theater and women, the poet abruptly resolves that he must return to Cambridge, and he casts this resolution in the Odyssean mold: "Yet, while blind Cupid permits, I am getting ready to leave these city walls quickly, and with the aid of the divine plant moly to run away from the ill-famed halls of deceptive Circe. I am resolved to return to the reedy marshes of the Cam, and again to face the uproar of the noisy University"(85–90).

Once more, for Milton, learning has triumphed over ignorance, Odysseus over Circe, and this triumph, repeated thus in the elegies, the prolusions, and *Comus,* would seem to constitute a definitive motif of the poet's early work. But in each of the foregoing cases, the very terms of reason's triumph render the triumph itself equivocal. In Prolusion 7, for instance, reason may discover itself unexpectedly amongst the beasts, but ignorance is likewise banished from human company and relegated to bestial form. In *Comus,* the sorcerer's blandishments are ultimately rejected, but that rejection is couched as a *refusal* to engage in rational discussion ("Fain would I somthing say, yet to what end?" [783]). And the opposition between school and city in Elegy 1 is disabled from the start by the poet's insistence that the former is less hospitable to true learning than the latter:

Now I am in no rush to see the reedy Cam again, nor am I pining for love of my hearth gods there, this long time denied me. I find no pleasure in barren fields that offer no gentle shade; how ill-adapted is such a place to the worshippers of Phoebus! I am not of a mind to bear the constant threats of an unbending tutor, and all the other trials that are to be met by a nature such as mine. (11–16)

In sum, scholars have described the Circe-myth as being of "central importance . . . within the Milton corpus,"[15] and I believe this is so because, for Milton, the myth embodies a tension not between learning and ignorance or reason and unreason, but between competing models of learning and reason. I believe this tension finds its *locus classicus,* in turn, in the conflict between the Circe-myth as presented in Book Ten of *The Odyssey* and as revised in Plutarch's *Moralia.* Hence Milton's Elegy 1 is structured by the opposition between Cambridge and London, university and city, tutors and women, classroom and theater, and one of the most curious features of this poem is its ultimate rejection of the urban mode of life that it initially presents as a model of true literary education: "If only the poet had never had to

put up with more [than life in London]—that famous bard who was a weeping
exile in Tomis: he had then been a match for Ionia's son Homer, and you,
Vergil, outdone, and the first prize of praise would not now be yours!" (21–
24). At a moment like this, London can be associated with a poetic inspiration capable of overcoming Homer, just as Homeric myth is overcome by
Circe and Gryllus in Plutarch's *Moralia;* yet even so, by the poem's end
Milton has abandoned this inspiration in favor of the "raucae murmur . . .
Scholae." Conversely, just as Elegy 1 watches the differential terms of learning and ignorance switch places between London and Cambridge, Prolusion
7 expands upon this paradox by discovering that ignorance exists nowhere
in nature:

Rocks, too, show a certain aptitude for learning in that they reply to the sacred words
of poets; will not these also reject Ignorance? Therefore, driven lower than any kind of
beast, lower than stocks and stones, lower than any natural species, will Ignorance be
permitted to find repose in the famous "non-existent" of the Epicureans? No, not
even there. (872)

And if Prolusion 7 thus finds itself in the peculiar position of arguing against a
nonentity, *Comus* presents its viewers with a debate in which the advocate of
unreason famously gets all the best lines,[16] while the defender of reason takes
refuge in a vision of unrestrained violence:

> Yet should I try, the uncontrouled worth
> Of this pure cause would kindle my rap't spirits
> To such a flame of sacred vehemence,
> That dumb things should be mov'd to sympathize,
> And the brute Earth should lend her nerves and shake
> Till all thy magick structures rear'd so high,
> Were shatter'd into heaps o're thy false head.   (793–99)

If Milton finds the Circe-myth useful for representing the tension between competing bodies of knowledge, that is arguably because Plutarch's
Moralia revise the myth to much the same end. In the process, Plutarch also
represents intellectual conflict as coextensive with gender conflict, and here
again he points the way for Milton; much recent criticism, for instance, has
tended to read *Comus* as a document essential to the formation of early
modern domestic political economies,[17] and the opposition figured in Elegy 1
between Cambridge, with its schoolboys and harsh tutors, and London, with
its crowds of beautiful girls, speaks for itself in this regard. Beyond the
limited body of Milton's early work, moreover, the Circe-myth maintains a
broad currency in early modern European discussions of feminine liberty
and learning theory, where it repeatedly figures difference on the levels of

social rank, gender, and ethnicity. Indeed, in its references to the Circe-myth as presented in Homer and Plutarch, Milton's early writing activates a popular set of literary associations whose ultimate focus includes the educability of women and the feasibility of coeducational study. Early Miltonic works like *Comus,* Prolusion 7, and Elegy 1 thus beg to be read in light of these issues and the contemporary literature that addresses them, and it is to that literature that I therefore now turn.

II

Of course, it is not strictly necessary to use the Circe-myth as a vehicle for questions about education and gender-difference, nor is it necessary to use Plutarch's *Moralia* in such a way. This essay does not wish to suggest anything of the sort, nor does it seek to supersede earlier critical appraisals of the function of the Circe-myth in Renaissance discourse. On the contrary, in these pages I would simply like to expand previous scholarship on the resonance of the Circe-motif in Milton's work by noting that it *could* be—and was—sometimes associated with feminine liberty, license, and education. Moreover, Plutarch's adaptation of the Circe-myth has obvious relevance to this pattern of association, insofar as it presents Odysseus, the darling of Athena, as worsted in formal debate by a hog who claims to represent Circe's views on the nature of reason. One of the interesting features of early modern responses to Circe and Gryllus is the length to which such responses can go in order to ignore the unacceptable but apparent conclusion that a major classical author could present a hog and a witch as cleverer than the "King of Brains."[18]

In some cases, the preferred mode of dealing with this problem was apparently to ignore it. Thus none of the great Renaissance mythographers mention Gryllus in their dictionaries of mythology, and one—Cartari—mentions Circe herself only in passing, in connection with the metamorphosis of Scylla.[19] (Natale Conti includes a broad selection of pieces from Plutarch's *Moralia* in his "Catalogus Nominum variorum Scriptorum, & operum," yet ignores Gryllus anyway.)[20] But Boccaccio and Conti both devote a fair amount of space to Circe, and for both she figures as an embodiment of feminine license: a "malefica mulier . . . formossissima . . . & meretrix famosa"[21] who "utebatur . . . carne in veneficiis, sed in amatoriis praecipue."[22] As John Mulryan has recently noted, Circe's use of "veneficia"—potions and poisons— leads Renaissance mythographers to view her as an avatar of the original disobedient woman, Eve herself.[23] Further, Conti lends a moral reading to Circe's "veneficia" and the bestial transformation they induce, noting that such transformation offers a visible emblem of Circe's own depravity:

Circe Solis & Perseidis filiae Oceani filia fuisse dicitur, quia libido ex humore & calore
fit in animalibus. Haec cum naturalis sit titillatio ad voluptates excitans, si nobis
dominetur, beluarum vitia in animis nostris imprimit, facitque cum siderum aspectu,
& cum illis conspirat, quorum alia ad Venerem, & ad commesationes, alia ad iram,
crudelitatem, improbitatemque omne[m] nos alliciunt: idcirco si his cupiditatibus
aliquis paruerit, eum fabulantur in aliquam formam belue a Circe fuisse conversum
per veneficia.

Circe is said to be the daughter of the Sun and of Perseis the daughter of Oceanus,
because desire is born in bodies through moisture and heat. When this natural tickling
is exciting us to pleasures, if it masters us, it imprints the vices of beasts in our souls,
and it makes itself felt with the appearance of the stars, and it interacts with them,
some of which entice us to Venus and to couplings, others to anger, cruelty, and all
impropriety; for that reason, if anyone has yielded to these desires, they say that he has
been changed into some beastly form by Circe through her potions.[24]

Here is the traditional association of Circe with feminine "libido," cou-
pled to the equally traditional association of libido with bestial degeneration.
Milton reproduces these associations in *Comus,* and they also reappear—
together with the figure of Gryllus himself—in an acknowledged source of
Comus, Book Two of *The Faerie Queene.* There Spenser's Guyon revises
Plutarch in what can only be called an excess of Odyssean wishful thinking.
First, Gryllus appears to Guyon as one of the rout of monsters accompanying
Acrasia, and in this case the bestial transformation is specifically connected to
sexual intercourse. As the Palmer explains matters,

> These seeming beasts are men indeed,
> Whom this enchauntress hath transformed thus,
> Whylome her lovers, which her lustes did feed,
> Now turned into figures hideous.[25]

Moreover, having thus emended Plutarch to stipulate a prior sexual relationship between woman and beast, *The Faerie Queene* then transforms the
Plutarchan story further by having the Palmer do what Gryllus exhorts Odysseus not to do: return the beastly men to their original, natural form. Nor
does Spenser allow Gryllus to retain his bestial articulacy, or any of his abilities in formal debate. Instead, after resuming human shape, he simply calls
the Palmer bad names, thus confirming a lowliness of mind to parallel his
lowliness of spirit:

> One above the rest in speciall,
> That had an hog been late, hight Grylle by name,
> Repined greatly, and did him [the Palmer] miscall,
> That had from hoggish form him brought to naturall.[26]

In a sense, this is the crowning irony to Spenser's adaptation of Plutarch, for in Plutarch it is *Odysseus,* not Gryllus, who resorts to name-calling; thus Gryllus exhorts him early on, "If it is your pleasure to discuss the matter instead of hurling abuse [λοιδορεῖσθαι], I shall quickly make you see that we [beasts] are right to prefer our present life in place of the former one" (986E).

In keeping with this wholesale revision of Plutarchan materials, another antecedent of Milton's *Comus,* William Browne's *Inner Temple Masque* (1614), manages to ignore the philosophical and social ramifications of its source material almost entirely. Browne reduces Plutarch's porcine philosopher Gryllus to the status of an antimasque grotesque; introduced out of "Plutarche . . . in his moralles,"[27] Gryllus performs an antic dance in the company of horned beasts and baboons, then disappears with the rest at the following lines:

> Grillus is gone, belyke he hath hearde
> The dayry-maid knocke at yᵉ trough in yᵉ yearde
> Through thicke & thinne he wallowes
> And weighes nor depths nor shallowes.[28]

Addicted to his trough and divested of his articulacy (he is a non-speaking character in Browne's masque, and the Greek word for "irrational"—ἄλογοσ —literally means "wordless"), this Gryllus embodies the qualities to which he stands in the *Moralia* as an ironic antithesis. In a sense, he is a comforting figure to incorporate into a masque whose concluding vision is of Odysseus' companions liberated from the enchantments of Circe; stripped of the attributes that make him troublesome to Odysseus in the *Moralia,* Gryllus appears in Browne's masque without challenging the rational capacities of the masque's hero. Unlike his counterparts in *Comus* (or his own alter ego in "Beasts Are Rational"), Browne's Gryllus is unable to "boast [himself] more comely than before," and thus he fails to raise troubling questions about the relative validity of competing claims to comeliness, reason, and virtue.

Thus, on one hand, Boccaccio, Cartari, and Conti overlook the figure of Gryllus entirely while casting Circe in her traditional form as an emblem of feminine impiety and libido.[29] On the other hand, Spenser and Browne silently revise Plutarch, in massive and startling ways, so as to produce a Gryllus who is consistent with the mythographers' traditional view of Circe, and in the *Pegma* of Pierre Coustau (Costalius; 1555) one encounters another, subtler example of this same tendency to revise the wisdom out of Plutarch's Gryllus. Coustau offers his readers an emblem, consisting of a woodcut that depicts Odysseus in disputation with the porcine Gryllus, an accompanying brief poem, and an additional brief prose commentary, all

under the heading "Le vice plait au mechant."[30] The eight-line poem opens
with Coustau's only direct reference to Gryllus, a rhetorical question that
reiterates the Plutarchan Odysseus' horror at Gryllus' refusal to resume human shape:

> *Qui t'a si fort molesté en ce monde*
> *Paouure Grillus, & quel motif te meine*
> *De demourer à iamais truye immunde,*
> *Et ne uouloir reprendre face humaine?*

Who in the world has harmed you so badly, poor Gryllus, and what reason persuades
you to remain forever a dirty sow, and never again to recover your human face?[31]

The accompanying prose commentary supplies the obvious answer to this
question, that Gryllus has in fact harmed and degraded himself through his
bestial lowness of mind and spirit:

Ceux qui sont do–nés aux voluptés & perturbations d'esprit, encores qu'ilz le veulent,
ne se peuuent remettre en la liberté de vertu: & comme ie croy si le pouuoient faire,
ne le voudroient.

Those who are given to pleasures and perturbations of the spirit could not return
themselves to the liberty of virtue even if they wished; and I believe that even if they
could do so, they would not.[32]

In sum, Spenser and Browne rewrite the details of Plutarch's "Beasts
Are Rational" so as to render Gryllus morally and culturally untroubling; they
make him inarticulate, they stipulate a prior sexual relationship between him
and Circe, they force him to return to human form, and when he has (in *The
Faerie Queene*) reassumed human shape, they divest him of his formidable
eloquence. Coustau, on the other hand, simply takes Odysseus' side of the
debate with Gryllus and assumes by fiat that Odysseus' arguments have carried the day. Such revisions of "Beasts Are Rational" serve an obvious purpose: to enlist Plutarch in the long tradition of mythological and mythographic discourse that identifies Circe with feminine disruptions of the order
of culture. Indeed, this is the dominant tradition in early modern English
treatments of the Circe-myth, and it has undeniable relevance for Milton's
verse. Roger Ascham, for instance, regards the figure of Circe as "a paradigm
of the southern cultural threat to English morality," and William Miller has
seen a source for Milton's association of Comus with "the perversions of art"
in Ascham's work:[33] "I am afraid, that over-many of our travellers into Italy do
not eschew the way to Circe's court, but go, and ride, and run, and fly
thither . . . ; yea, I could point out some with my finger, that never had gone
out of England, but only to serve Circes in Italy."[34] Further, the myth of Circe

is unquestionably prominent in early English diatribes aginst such related abuses as theatrical entertainment and general sensuality.[35]

But when it comes to Plutarch's "Beasts Are Rational," the dominant tradition in Renaissance responses to the Circe-myth is built upon a solid foundation of collective denial. Boccaccio and Cartari and Conti ignore Gryllus; Coustau and Spenser and Browne all revise his story to one degree or another; and these authors treat the character this way because, when traced to his *locus classicus*, Gryllus simply refuses to do what they want him to do. For one thing, Gryllus gets the last word in "Beasts Are Rational," and even given the incomplete form in which Plutarch's dialogue has been preserved, there is no doubt as to who is the star of the piece. "Beasts Are Rational" takes the form of a Socratic dialogue, with all the relevant textual markers—the length of the speeches, their informational content, the fact that Gryllus' remarks go unrebutted and that the text itself draws attention to this fact (see, e.g., 988F), the gradual diminution of Odysseus' objections, etc.—clearly designating the pig as Plutarch's substitute for Socrates himself. It is true that at one point Odysseus calls Gryllus a sophist (988E–F), and that Gryllus accepts the tag in passing (989B), and these two remarks might be used to read "Beasts Are Rational" as an indictment of the sophist predilection for empty debate. But by rendering Gryllus inarticulate, Spenser's and Browne's revisions of Plutarch minimize the issue of sophistry, while even Coustau depicts Gryllus not as a corrupt manipulator of words but rather as an obdurate voluptuary.

On the whole, Renaissance readers of Plutarch seem to have viewed Gryllus not as an ironic caricature of sophism but as an emblem of unregenerate vice, and thus they tend to downplay his forensic skills while concentrating instead upon his pig-headed appearance. This tendency, in turn, conveniently undercuts the central conceit of Plutarch's dialogue: the contrast between Gryllus' swinish physicality and his startling articulacy. Likewise, just as Plutarch draws attention to Gryllus' skills in debate, he also relegates Odysseus to the role of a semi-articulate dupe. These two features of his work pose an inevitable challenge to the politically correct, dominant line in Renaissance interpretations of the Circe-myth, and in consequence Renaissance authors tend to ignore them as much as possible.

One writer who faces these matters more squarely than most is Philemon Holland, the first translator of Plutarch's *Moralia* into English. Since, unlike Spenser, Browne, et al., Holland closely engaged with Plutarch's text in the process of translating it accurately, he cannot so easily ignore or revise the inconvenient features of "Beasts Are Rational." Yet Holland is clearly just as uncomfortable with the dialogue as is anyone else, and his response to this discomfort is novel. In the translator's headnote with which he prefaces the piece, Holland concedes that Plutarch's Odysseus is intellectually inferior to Circe and Gryllus, but he reads this inferiority through the medium of Christian allegory: "This disputation, conteineth a forme of processe against all Pagans and Atheists, to prove that brute beasts excell them, and be in more happie estate than they."[36] Thus Odysseus' inferiority is testimony not to Circe's strength but to the weakness of classical polytheism. This ingenious reading manages both to preserve traditional mythographic interpretations of the Circe-myth and to do so without massively violating Plutarch's text: "[Plutarch] sheweth sufficiently, that if men have no other approach to rest upon, than a naturall habitude of an earthly vertue, and can assure the repose of their consciences upon nothing but upon humane valliance, temperance, and wisedome, they doe but goe in the companie of beasts, or rather come behind them."[37] To be sure, there are problems with this argument. For one thing, Plutarch's Gryllus is no mere "brute beast," any more than is Milton's serpent. For another, to credit Plutarch with the writing of antipagan invective is to contradict the evidence of his contemporary reputation as well as the rest of the works attributed to him. Yet for an author in Holland's position, these are inevitably minor inconsistencies: an acceptable price to pay for an ingenious trick of hermeneutics.

Although no Renaissance author makes the point directly, Plutarch's treatment of Circe and Gryllus is consistent with his tendency in other works to champion the character and capacities of women. Renaissance writers use the *Moralia* not only, as we have seen, to argue that dogs and other animals can reason, but also to argue that women should receive schooling. When Richard Mulcaster makes his case for cross-gendered education in 1581, he adduces Plutarch as his most commanding authority on the subject: "I will not medle with any moe writers to whom wymen are most bound, for best speaking of them, and most spreading of their vertues, then with one onely man a single witnes in person, but above all singularitie in profe: the learned and honest *Plutarch,* whose name emporteth a princis treasure, whose writings witnes an unwearied travel, whose plaine truth was never tainted."[38] This aspect of Plutarch's reputation perhaps inspired Queen Elizabeth herself to translate part of the *Moralia* in 1598.[39] At any rate, Plutarch's name was clearly associated in the sixteenth and seventeenth centuries both with a liberal view of the rational capacities of beasts and with an equally liberal view of the educability of women. Moreover, whether early modern authors acknowledge the fact or not, "Beasts Are Rational" tends to coordinate and conflate these two issues in a variety of ways. For one thing, Circe was—as we have already seen—a standard emblem of feminine license and promiscuity in the Renaissance mythographic tradition, while the dialogue's interest in the reasoning ability of animals is manifest from its title onward. For another thing, Plutarch's dialogue associates animals with women so that Gryllus and Circe form a united front of argument against Odysseus. This association speaks to—and reverses—traditional views of the intellectual inferiority of both women and beasts. Furthermore, Plutarch's reversal of Homeric myth provides an ironic mode that can be usefully exploited by later satirists to debunk various kinds of social injustice, not least of all masculine educational privilege.

That is how Erasmus uses Plutarch in his colloquy on women's education, "The Abbot and the Learned Lady" ("Abbatis et Eruditae," 1524). In this dialogue the ignorant abbot Antronius takes to task the learned woman Magdalia (apparently "drawn with Margaret Roper, the eldest . . . daughter of Thomas More, in mind")[40] for reading and collecting Greek and Latin books. Magdalia responds with a dry irony that culminates when, echoing Gryllus' comments about the parallelism of physical and mental transformation, she asks Antronius why he himself neglects learning:

ANT.   [Because of] long prayers, housekeeping, hunts, horses, court functions.

MAGD.   So these are more important to you than wisdom?

ANT.   It's what we're used to.

MAGD.   Now tell me this: if some heavenly power enabled you to turn yourself and your monks too into any animal whatever, would you change them into hogs and yourself into a horse?

ANT.   Not at all.

MAGD.   But by doing so you'd prevent anybody's being wiser than you.

ANT.   I shouldn't much care what sort of animal the monks were, provided I myself were a human being.

MAGD.   Do you think one is human if he's neither wise nor wants to be wise?

ANT.   I'm wise enough—so far as I'm concerned.

MAGD.   And swine are wise enough so far as *they're* concerned.[41]

As one of the editors of the 1509 Aldine *Moralia,* Erasmus knew his Plutarch well, and it shows at moments like this. Where Plutarch's "Beasts Are Rational" arrays a woman and a hog in debate against a man and ironically engineers the man's defeat, Erasmus's colloquy pits woman against man in such a way as to identify the latter metaphorically with swine. Plutarch reverses Homer by casting the Circean transformation from man to pig as an ontological advancement; Erasmus, on the other hand, reverses Plutarch by locating a kind of ontological degradation—from person to pig—in the man who refuses to educate himself. Yet while inverting Plutarch's pattern, Erasmus nonetheless preserves his commitment to the ironic deflation of masculine authority; whether Gryllus emerges as a superior being or Antronius as an inferior one, the end result of Plutarch's and Erasmus's satire is to this extent the same.

Bathsua Makin, writing during Milton's last years, effects yet another reversal of the Circe-myth, again in support of women's education.[42] In her *Essay to Revive the Antient Education of Gentlewomen* (1673), Makin argues that

> Meerly to teach Gentlewomen to Frisk and Dance, to paint their Faces, to curl their Hair, to put on a whisk, to wear gay Clothes, is not truly to adorn, but to adulterate their Bodies; yea (what is worse) to defile their Souls. This (like *Circes* cup) turns them to Beasts; whilst their Belly is their Godd, they become Swine; whilst Lust, they become Goats; and whilst Pride is their God, they become very Devils.[43]

Here Makin upends the traditional association of Circe with feminine deceit in a way that anticipates the twentieth-century feminist claim that woman is made, not born. The degradation of dances and cosmetics and gay clothing, rather than bespeaking women's essential inferiority, attests instead to the injustice of a patriarchal social order that imposes preconceived limitations upon its women as a strategy of masculine self-aggrandizement. Ironically, the model of the witless and inferior woman emerges as a fundamentally masculine construct, representative of male insecurity and protective of male privilege.

As for the essential nature and capacities of women, Makin emphatically places reason among them, and in doing so she returns us to the triad of man, woman, and beast invoked so suggestively by Plutarch: "Had God intended Women onely as a finer sort of Cattle, he would not have made them reasonable. Bruits, a few degrees higher than Drils or Monkies, (which the *Indians* use to do many Offices) might have better fitted some mens Lust, Pride, and Pleasure; especially those that desire to keep them ignorant to be tyrannized over."[44] By locating within feminine nature the capacity for reason, Makin implies that women should deserve educational opportunity, denial of which would be a tyrannical violation of the claims of nature itself. Thus it may be one mild irony of Makin's argument that it leads her to reinscribe a nonnegotiable opposition between rational humanity and "bruit" creation—an opposition that Plutarch's *Moralia*, as we have seen, undercuts concomitantly with that between men and women.

In addition, Makin's words call into question the relative status of and distinctions between man and woman, man and beast, and woman and beast. These distinctions, together with their nature and validity and purpose, provide the raw material for Plutarch's humor in "Beasts Are Rational," and they likewise provide the basis for some of Milton's more enduring literary preoccupations. Moreover, these distinctions constitute a vital point of disagreement between the educational writings of Milton and Makin. This disagreement may not be coincidental; although scholars have generally argued that Milton's and Makin's works "need not be causally related,"[45] Frances Teague has recently suggested that Bathsua Makin's *Essay to Revive the Antient Education of Gentlewomen* may in fact have been composed as a deliberate riposte to Milton's *Of Education* (which was reissued in 1673, the year of Makin's work) and his treatise on *Accedence* (published in 1669).[46]

My argument may offer some additional evidence in support of Teague's findings. At the very least, the present essay demonstrates that Milton and Makin both allude to the Circe-myth in educational contexts; that both are interested—albeit for different reasons—in determining the intellectual status of men and women relative to that of beasts; and that this common interest may be traced to Plutarch, whose admission of beasts into the society of rational creatures creates inevitable problems for any effort to conceive of gender difference in terms of a difference in intellectual equipment. For Makin, no such difference exists, and thus she enthusiastically espouses the coeducational initiatives of writers like Erasmus, Anna Marie van Schurman, and John Amos Comenius.[47] As for Milton, his tractate *Of Education* famously snubs Comenius[48] while espousing a pedagogical model that "shows no interest in . . . the participation . . . of girls of any class,"[49] and that reserves for its headmaster the authority to administer corporal punishment of the sort that Milton himself apparently suffered under at Cambridge. To this extent *Of Education* repeats the patterns of discrimination enacted in Prolusion 7, *Comus,* and most obviously in Elegy 1, where the poet abandons the Circean blandishments of London's women in order to return to Cambridge's severe world of schoolboys and tutors. Here once again we may be tempted to see Milton casting himself in an Odyssean mold of rational masculinity that receives short shrift in Plutarch's *Moralia.*

III

Despite the obvious differences between John Milton and Bathsua Makin, both as to their relative interest in coeducational pedagogy and as to the authors from whom they draw, their thought converges in at least one particular. The issue in question, oddly enough, is bestiality: what is wrong with it and why, and what differentiates it from normative heterosexual intercourse. For Makin, bestial intercourse becomes the logical consequence of masculine efforts to deny the rational capacities of women; by repudiating women's native ability to reason, men subject their spouses to a degrading bestial transformation of the Circean variety, with the result that there is no longer any meaningful difference between sex with women and sex with animals. Hence, as Makin pithily observes, "Bruits, a few degrees higher than Drils or Monkies, (which the *Indians* use to do many Offices) might have better fitted some mens Lust, Pride, and Pleasure; especially those that desire to keep [women] ignorant to be tyrannized over." For Makin, feminine reason is not simply intrinsic to feminine nature; it is also constitutive of licit sexuality and healthy domestic relations. It becomes a moral and social discriminator of the first importance.

Here we have one particular version of a model of family relations famously documented by Lawrence Stone, a model "inspired by the principle of Affective Individualism" and committed to notions of personal free will, legal and educational equality, and spiritual and emotional nurturance.[50] A similar domestic model emerges, interestingly enough, in *Paradise Lost,* where Raphael counsels Adam on the nature of attraction between husband and wife:

> Love refines
> The thoughts, and heart enlarges, hath his seat
> In Reason, and is judicious, is the scale
> By which to heav'nly Love thou maist ascend,
> Not sunk in carnal pleasure, for which cause
> Among the Beasts no mate for thee was found.   (7.589–94)

For Milton, as for Makin, "Reason" is central to legitimate conjugal relations, serving as a primary marker of difference between such relations and the various sexual perversities for which bestiality stands as a synecdochic emblem. On one hand, the exercise of reason enables one to "ascend" to "heav'nly Love," and possibly to engage in various sorts of dramatic personal transformation in the process, as Raphael hints elsewhere (5.493–503); on the other hand, abandonment of one's reason leads to a far less happy transformation, of a sort for which the Circe-myth may once more provide an appropriate paradigm.

But Milton complicates the picture here in a way that Makin does not. Makin exerts no effort to examine the rational capacities of beasts; on the contrary, she assumes a traditional Aristotelian distinction between human and bestial nature, in which the ability to engage in abstract reasoning differentiates the former from the latter.[51] Hence the force of her accusation that men who seek to deny women their rightful education do violence to nature: reason is something that men and women both possess, whereas animals apparently have to do without it. Milton allows no such clear distinction. On the contrary, in *Paradise Lost* he returns to the youthful themes of Prolusion 7, this time attributing Plutarch's views on the reasoning ability of beasts to no less an authority than God the Son, who remonstrates thus with Adam:

> Is not the Earth
> With various living creatures, and the Aire
> Replenisht, and all these at thy command
> To come and play before thee, know'st thou not
> Thir language and thir wayes, they also know,
> And reason not contemptibly; with these
> Find pastime, and beare rule; thy Realm is large.   (8.369–75)

In effect, where Makin presents us with a binary distinction between human and bestial nature, reason and unreason, Milton offers us a continuum, in which reason finds its place even among the brute orders of creation, and in which gender difference expresses itself in part through the *relative* intellectual superiority of the male. Thus Adam can observe of Eve that

> Well I understand in the prime end
> Of Nature her th'inferiour, in the mind
> And inward Faculties, which most excell.   (8.540–42)

And Raphael can thus warn Adam against "attributing overmuch to things/ Less excellent" (8.566–67) than "Wisdom" (8. 563)—among which things Eve's "fair" "outside" receives particular attention (5.568).

Here once more one encounters a Miltonic pattern, already documented at length in this essay, whereby the poet associates femininity with bestial transformation and differentiates it from a masculine principle identified with the (relative) exercise of reason. But this pattern, which as I have argued repudiates certain tendencies in Plutarch's *Moralia*, is complicated because Milton also borrows from Plutarch the idea that other genders and even species can be endowed with reason. The effort to resolve this complication by invoking a continuum of rationality ultimately cannot work if reason is also to serve as the cornerstone of successful domestic relations. Adam himself is clever enough to recognize the difficulty here, and he states it succinctly when insisting to the Son that he deserves companionship other than that of the beasts:

> Among unequals what societie
> Can sort, what harmonie or true delight?
> Which must be mutual, in proportion due
> Giv'n and receiv'd;
>
> .   .   .   .
>
>   Of fellowship I speak
> Such as I seek, fit to participate
> All rational delight, wherein the brute
> Cannot be human consort.   (8.383–92)

The key phrases here—"among unequals what societie," "must be mutual," "all rational delight"—leave little room for nuance or equivocation; Adam clearly believes (and the Son agrees) that a conjugal relationship founded in reason will suffer if there is any intellectual inequality between the principals involved. This belief, in turn, coexists uncomfortably with the Son's insistence elsewhere that Eve is in fact Adam's inferior, and that her inferiority manifests itself largely through the exercise of reason and choice ("Reason also is choice" [3.108]):

> Was shee thy God, that her thou didst obey
> Before his voice, or was shee made thy guide,
> Superior, or but equal, that to her
> Thou did'st resigne thy Manhood, and the Place
> Wherein God set thee above her made of thee.   (10.145–49)

In fact, Milton's poem seems to promote two separate and incompatible notions of Eve's rational capacity: one in which she is Adam's "likeness" and "other self" (8.450), perfectly fitted to participate with him in a society of peers based upon the exercise of reason; and one in which she is gently but firmly situated as his mental and therefore political inferior. The result is a domestic utopia of near-Orwellian proportions, in which both animals are equal, but one is more equal than the other.

IV

I hope the foregoing discussion will prove useful to scholars in a variety of interrelated ways. First, it tracks the recurrence of references to and motifs from Plutarch's *Moralia* in early modern European literary texts dealing with gender difference, the nature of human understanding, and the education of women. Second, it provides a particular account of how those references and motifs inform the work of Milton and invest that work with certain of its signature characteristics and unifying concerns. It also argues that Plutarch's "Beasts Are Rational" has been undervalued as a source for one of *Comus*'s principal variations upon its Homeric pre-text: the belief of Comus's victims that they have in fact been improved by their bestial transformation. And finally, this essay argues that Plutarch's *Moralia* may anticipate and inform a particularly fruitful tension in Milton's work: what James Grantham Turner has called the "irresolvable doubleness at the heart of Milton's apprehension of wedded love."[52]

Milton's conflicted sense of matrimony parallels his ambivalent use of Plutarch; one is almost tempted to view tensions in the former as an outgrowth of uncertainties in the latter. Thus, on one hand, Milton's repeated use of the Circe-myth—in Prolusion 7, in Elegy 1, in *Comus,* and less directly in *Paradise Lost*—functions almost as a calculated rejection of Gryllus' views in Plutarch: a sustained and heroic effort to hold the line against feminine unreason and brute ignorance, to prevent these qualities from regaining the ascendancy they wield in "Beasts Are Rational." Yet on the other hand, Milton subscribes both in the prolusions and in *Paradise Lost* to Plutarch's opinion that beasts are capable of reason, and this opinion renders the relation of man to woman particularly unstable. Insofar as beasts are rational yet insufficient companions for Adam, there is no justification for creating a less-than-perfectly-equal Eve; however, if Eve is indeed Adam's absolute equal, then there is no ground for discriminating between husband and wife on the basis of their relative capacity for reason. Thus, an inconsistency in Milton's response to Plutarch's *Moralia* anticipates and informs one of the most fascinating inconsistencies in the poet's larger social vision.

In both cases, the inconsistencies could easily be resolved: Milton could have employed any number of venerable arguments to insist upon the absolute rational inferiority of women to men, and of animals to people. But he refuses to do so, and by this refusal he opts for a view of human nature and gender difference that is a good deal messier and more conflicted than strictly necessary. If this is so, in turn, I believe that it is because Milton finds the resulting messiness to be a condition of possibility, and because he refuses to sacrifice such possibility in the name of greater doctrinal consistency. Again, Plutarch yields a good case in point: the *Moralia* unquestionably create problems for any view of domestic relations that presents man as intrinsically more rational and therefore superior to woman, and in certain moods Milton clearly likes this view of matters too much to relinquish it entirely. Yet at the same time, Plutarch's dialogues on animal-intelligence also offer one a sense of the perdurable connectedness of creation—the commonality and wondrousness of all things under the sun—and this feeling of connectedness is indispensable to Milton's vision of conjugal love. Rather than choosing a consistent view of marriage that undercuts either the comforts of equal intimacy or those of masculine hegemony, Milton opts instead for a condition of fruitful conflict. In doing so, he repeats on a grand scale the ambiguities through which he responds to two minor dialogues by Plutarch.

The Florida State University

NOTES

For their help in developing this essay, I am grateful to Paula Barbour, Albert Labriola, John Mulryan, Jeffrey Tatum, and Frances Teague. A short version of this work was presented to the

Hudson Strode Renaissance Studies Program of the University of Alabama on October 31, 1998; I would like to thank my host on that occasion, Gary Taylor, and my audience for comments, questions, and suggestions which have substantially affected the essay's final form.

1. For a detailed study of Plutarch's influence see Rudolf Hirzel, *Plutarchos* (Leipzig, 1912), 74–206; D. A. Russell (*Plutarch* [London, 1973], 143–58) supplies a much briefer but more up-to-date synopsis of the subject. Robert Aulotte provides a complete list of early Latin and vernacular translations of the *Moralia* in his study of Plutarch and Amyot (*Amyot et Plutarque: La tradition des Moralia au XVIe siecle* [Geneva, 1965], 325–62).

2. Aulotte, *Amyot et Plutarque*, 325.

3. Russell, *Plutarch*, 148.

4. Russell, *Plutarch*, 149.

5. Plutarch, "Whether Land or Sea Animals Are Cleverer," 969A–B, in *Plutarch's Moralia*, 15 vols., trans. Harold Cherniss and William Helmbold (Cambridge, 1957), vol. 12, 377–79. All further references to Plutarch will be to this edition and cited parenthetically in the text.

6. For the growth in popularity of dogs during the Jacobean and Caroline periods, see Keith Thomas, *Man and the Natural World: Changing Attitudes in England 1500–1800* (London, 1983), 101–9.

7. Thomas Ball, *The Life of the Renowned Doctor Preston* (London, 1885), 23.

8. Ball, *The Life of the Renowned Doctor Preston*, 23.

9. John Milton, Prolusion 7, in *The Riverside Milton*, ed. Roy Flannagan (Boston, 1998), 872. All further references to Milton's works will be to this edition and cited parenthetically in the text.

10. The relevant passage occurs in *The Odyssey* 10.239–43: "Now when [Circe] had given them the potion, and they had drunk it off, then she immediately struck them with her wand, and penned them in the pigsties. And they had the heads, and voice, and bristles, and shape of swine, but their minds remained unaltered, just as they were before. So they were penned there weeping, and before them Circe flung mast, and acorns, and the fruit of the cornel tree to eat" (*The Odyssey*, 2 vols., trans. A. T. Murray and George E. Dimock [Cambridge, 1995], vol. 2, 375).

11. See Paul Barolsky, "As in Ovid, So in Renaissance Art" (*Renaissance Quarterly* 51 [1998]: 451–74) passim for a recent discussion of metamorphosis as an artistic and philosophical principle in the Renaissance. Barolsky regards metamorphosis first and foremost as an Ovidian trope that extends from the literary to the visual arts and also speaks to the concerns of Renaissance Neoplatonism, so that—for one instance—Michelangelo's poetic emphasis upon mutability, transformation, and incompleteness, "in the language of Pico, . . . speaks of his own incompleteness, forever aspiring to an unattained spiritual perfection" (461). Likewise, Michelangelo's *Prisoners* "have been justly interpreted in terms of [his] Neoplatonic or Neo-Aristotelian philosophy, expressed in his poetry, where he speaks of liberating the figure from the stone . . . The struggle to free the figure from the marble is implicitly tied to the aspiration of the soul to escape from the 'earthly prison' of the body" (462).

12. See Douglas Bush, *Mythology and the Renaissance Tradition in English Poetry* (Minneapolis, 1932), 260 n.30; Edward Ainsworth, "Reminiscences of the *Orlando Furioso* in *Comus*," *Modern Language Notes* 46 (1931): 91 (whom Bush also cites); and William Miller, *The Mythology of Milton's "Comus"* (New York, 1988), 24 (who cites Bush citing Ainsworth). Leonora Brodwin also discusses Ariosto as a source for Milton ("Milton and the Renaissance Circe," in *Milton Studies* 6, ed. James Simmonds [Pittsburgh, 1974], 26–28), without mentioning Plutarch. John Carey's edition of *Comus* does draw attention to Plutarch as a possible source for the material traced by Ainsworth et al. to Ariosto (*Milton: Complete Shorter Poems* [London, 1968], 180n.75–76)—although Carey does not specifically claim Plutarch as a source for the self-satisfaction of

Comus's victims—and Carey usefully notes the reappearance of Plutarch's Gryllus in Spenser's *Faerie Queene* 2.12.86–87 and William Browne's *Inner Temple Masque* (for which see below). While Merritt Hughes's edition of *Comus* mentions Spenser and Browne, it makes no direct reference to Plutarch (*John Milton: Complete Poems and Major Prose* [Indianapolis, 1957], 91 n.72). Roy Flannagan's notes to the *Riverside Milton* (Boston, 1998) likewise do not mention Plutarch, focusing instead upon resonances of Sandys's *Metamorphoses* (126 n.63). In a list of sources for *Comus* that includes seven plays by Shakespeare and works by "Marlowe, Spenser, Sylvester, Drayton, Jonson, Peele, John Fletcher, and William Browne . . . ; Tasso and Guarini . . . ; possibly . . . Erycius Puteanus; and among the ancients . . . Homer, Virgil, Ovid, Horace, Aeschylus, and Euripides," Angus Fletcher omits Plutarch (*The Transcendental Masque: An Essay on Milton's "Comus"* [Ithaca, 1971], 202).

13. Ainsworth, "Reminiscences of the *Orlando Furioso*," 91.

14. For the surviving biographical records, see John Milton French, *The Life Records of John Milton,* 3 vols. (New Brunswick, 1949), vol. 1, 106. For critical commentary that takes Milton's rustication for granted, see E. K. Rand, "Milton in Rustication," *Studies in Philology* 19 (1922): 109–35 passim, esp. 109–14; John Shawcross, "Form and Content in Milton's Latin Elegies," *Huntington Library Quarterly* 33 (1970): 332–33; and Stella Revard, *Milton and the Tangles of Neaera's Hair: The Making of the 1645 "Poems"* (Columbia, 1997), 14. John Carey, on the contrary, argues that the exile mentioned in Elegy 1 "is probably merely the university vacation" (Carey, ed., *Milton: Complete Shorter Poems,* 18).

15. Brodwin, "Milton and the Renaissance Circe," 22.

16. For one classic formulation of this view, see G. Wilson Knight, *The Burning Oracle: Studies in the Poetry of Action* (London, 1939), 66–67: "Comus urges the fecundity of nature in poignant phrases, the ones so praised by Dr. F. R. Leavis . . . for what he considers an un-Miltonic sincerity . . . Indeed, Milton never in all his work shows so convincing a cosmic apprehension . . . We have all cosmic and natural excellence such as Shakespeare incorporates into *Antony and Cleopatra* ranged with the evil force, whereas the brothers and the Lady are, in their earlier moralizing, dull."

17. See, for instance, Maureen Quilligan, *Milton's Spenser: The Politics of Reading* (Ithaca, 1983), 209–18; William Kerrigan, *The Sacred Complex: On the Psychogenesis of "Paradise Lost"* (Cambridge, 1983), 22–72; Richard Halpern, "Puritanism and Maenadism in *A Mask,*" in *Rewriting the Renaissance: The Discourses of Sexual Difference in Early Modern England,* ed. Margaret Ferguson, Maureen Quilligan, and Nancy Vickers (Chicago, 1986), 88–105; and Katharine Maus, *Inwardness and Theater in the English Renaissance* (Chicago, 1995), 198–209, all of whom tend to read *Comus* in ways that foreground the masque's construction of gender economies. For Quilligan, the masque exemplifies the feminine qualities of chastity, obedience, and silence; for Halpern, it constructs a model of wedded chastity to function as a domesticated alternative to the threatening virginity of classical maenadism; for Kerrigan, the masque serves as "a ritual for the unification of a family" (22) through "the sacrifice of [oedipal] desire" (24); for Maus, *Comus* neutralizes anxieties concerning the vulnerability and penetrability of the feminine body.

18. Plutarch's Loeb editors offer this phrase as an alternative translation of the punning "βασιλεύ[σ] Κεφαλλήνων" ("King of the Cephallenians" [986E]; vol. 12, 499, note b).

19. Vincenzo Cartari, *Le Imagini degli Dei* (Venice, 1571; facs. New York, 1976), 248.

20. Natale Conti, *Mythologiae* (Padua, 1616; facs. New York, 1979), sig. a3v.

21. Giovanni Boccaccio, *Genealogiae* (Venice, 1494; facs. New York, 1976), fol. 32.

22. Conti, *Mythologiae,* 306.

23. John Mulryan, *"Through a Glass Darkly": Milton's Reinvention of the Mythological Tradition* (Pittsburgh, 1996), 167.

24. Conti, *Mythologiae,* 308.

25. Edmund Spenser, *The Faerie Queene* 2.12.85, 1–4, in *The Complete Poetical Works of Edmund Spenser,* ed. R. E. Neil Dodge (Cambridge, 1908).

26. *The Faerie Queene* 2.12.86, 6–9.

27. William Browne, *The Inner Temple Masque,* in *The Whole Workes,* ed. W. C. Hazlitt (rpt. New York, 1970), 251.

28. Browne, *The Inner Temple Masque,* 252.

29. For another instance of this traditional reading, John Mulryan cites Johannes Spondanus' 1583 commentary upon Homer, which reads the myth of Circe as signalling "Satan's presence in the world," insofar as Circe, like Eve, has the power to turn a man [Adam] into a beast (*"Through a Glass Darkly,"* 15). See Brodwin, "Milton and the Renaissance Circe" passim, for a sustained discussion of this mythographical tradition.

30. Pierre Coustau, *Le Pegme de Pierre Coustau* (Lyon, 1555; facs. New York, 1979), 214. This text (the Garland facsimile) is a copy of the French translation of Coustau's 1554 *editio princeps.*

31. Coustau, *Le Pegme,* 214.

32. Coustau, *Le Pegme,* 215.

33. Miller, *The Mythology of Milton's "Comus",* 158.

34. Roger Ascham, *The Scholemaster,* ed. R. J. Schoeck (Don Mills, 1966), 64–65.

35. See, for instance, Stephen Gosson, *The School of Abuse,* ed. Edward Arber (London, 1906), 20: "These [i.e., the words of poets] are the Cuppes of *Circes,* that turne reasonable Creatures into brute Beastes." Also see William Prynne's claim that actors offer their audiences "*Circes* cuppe to drink of, and so of men to make them beasts" (*Histrio-mastix* [London, 1633], 170).

36. Philemon Holland, trans., *The Philosophie, commonlie called, The Morals . . . of Plutarch* (London, 1603), 561.

37. Holland, *The Philosophie,* 562.

38. Richard Mulcaster, *Positions concerning the Training Up of Children,* ed. William Barker (Toronto, 1994), 174.

39. Russell, *Plutarch,* 150.

40. Craig Thompson, trans., *The Colloquies of Erasmus* (Chicago, 1965), 218.

41. Desiderius Erasmus, "The Abbot and the Learned Lady," in *The Colloquies of Erasmus,* trans. Craig Thompson (Chicago, 1965), 220–21.

42. For the definitive biographical account of the genesis of Makin's essay, together with an edited text of the essay itself, see Frances Teague, *Bathsua Makin, Woman of Learning* (Lewisburg, 1998), 91–150.

43. Bathsua Makin, *An Essay to Revive the Antient Education of Gentlewomen* (Los Angeles, 1980), 22.

44. Makin, *An Essay,* 23.

45. See, for instance, James Helms, "Bathsua Makin's *An Essay to Revive the Antient Education of Gentlewomen* in the Canon of Seventeenth-Century Educational Reform Tracts," *Cahiers elisabethains* 44 (1993): 45, and Jean Brink, "Bathsua Makin: Educator and Linguist," in *Female Scholars: A Tradition of Learned Women before 1800,* ed. Jean Brink (Montreal, 1980), 94–97.

46. For the full argument, see Frances Teague, "A Voice for Hermaphrodotical Education," in *The Double Voice,* ed. Elizabeth Clark (London, forthcoming), ms pp. 4–11.

47. For instance, see Makin, *An Essay,* 23 for a favorable reference to Erasmus. In its general structure and argument, Makin's tract is modeled upon van Schurman's *De Ingenii*

Muliebris (1659), and Makin concludes her work with a five-page endorsement of Comenius' system of Latin-learning, the *Janua Linguarum,* which she extols as an improvement upon Lily's classic *Grammar* (Makin, *An Essay,* 37–41).

48. See *Of Education,* 980: "To tell you . . . what I have benefited herein among old renowned Authors, I shall spare; and to search what many modern *Janua's* and *Didactics* more than ever I shall read, have projected, my inclination leads me not." The present argument accords with Karen Edwards's recent claim that Milton recoils from the Comenian "impulse to epitomize" ("Comenius, Milton, and the Temptation to Ease," in *Milton Studies* 32, ed. Albert Labriola [1995], 26), an impulse that Milton visualizes as a "broad, easy path which leads only to superstition and delusion" (36). In contrast to the easy and delusory epitomization of knowledge —an epitomization readily associated with such slothfully effeminate Miltonic villains as Comus —Milton himself emphasizes a "dynamic" and "arduous" model of education whose aim is "the nurturing and strengthening in students of 'that act of reason which in *Ethics* is call'd *Proairesis:* that they may with some judgement contemplat upon morall good and evill' " (35).

49. Ernest Sirluck, ed., in *Complete Prose Works of John Milton,* 8 vol.s, gen. ed. Don M. Wolfe (New Haven, 1953–1982), vol. 2, 193–94.

50. Lawrence Stone, *The Family, Sex and Marrige in England 1500–1800* (New York, 1979), 411–12.

51. Aristotle (*De Anima,* trans. Hugh Lawson-Tancred [Harmondsworth, 1986]) subdivides the soul into a series of faculties: "the nutritive, perceptive, desiderative, locomotive, and intellective" (162). Of these, the nutritive is common to all living things, while the perceptive, desiderative, and locomotive are distributed to a variable degree throughout the animal kingdom. Finally "and most rarely, some [animals] have reasoning and thinking"—the animals in question being "man and any other creature there may be like him or superior to him" (163). For a clear Renaissance statement of this formulation, see Cervantes' *Dialogue of the Dogs* (in *Exemplary Novels,* 4 vols., trans. John Jones and John Macklin [Warminster, 1992], vol. 4, 85): "The difference between man and animal is that man is a rational being and the animal an irrational creature" (also see vol. 4, 95). Michel de Montaigne argues directly against this traditional view in the *Apology for Raymond Sebond:* "We must infer from like results like faculties, and consequently confess that this same reason, this same method that we have for working, is also that of the animals" (*The Complete Essays of Montaigne,* trans. Donald Frame [Stanford, 1957, rpt. 1998], 336–37).

52. James Grantham Turner, *One Flesh: Paradisal Marriage and Sexual Relations in the Age of Milton* (Oxford, 1987), 145.

THE *TELOI* OF GENRES: *PARADISE LOST* AND *DE DOCTRINA CHRISTIANA*

Phillip J. Donnelly

ALTHOUGH A CONSENSUS has not yet developed out of the re-cent debate over whether Milton authored *De Doctrina Christiana,* the controversy is helpful in sharpening some specific questions about how we read even those works upon which Milton's authorship is agreed. The results of this debate will be far-reaching and could lead to a reassessment of over a century of scholarship that has assumed Miltonic authorship of the theologi-cal text. Over the last several years (publicly since 1991), William Hunter has been advancing and defending the view that Milton did not author the trea-tise. In his recently published monograph, *Visitation Unimplor'd,* Hunter presents the most complete defense of his position to date. His basic strategy is twofold: first, he demonstrates how weak is the assumption that Milton did indeed write the tract—this makes the central issue one of offering compet-ing hypotheses to see which best explains the facts (historical and textual); then he examines the character of the differences between *De Doctrina* and the Miltonic canon (prose and poetry) to demonstrate that his hypothesis offers a better explanation of those differences. The nature of the question, as constituted by Hunter's argument, has made it far more difficult for either side to base conclusions on definitive proof—leaving both dependent pri-marily upon circumstantial evidence. Attempts "to develop external biblio-graphical or stylistic criteria" for establishing the provenance of *De Doctrina* "have not yet reached fruition," but as Paul Sellin points out, we can still test the compatibility of the treatise with *Paradise Lost* (especially on central issues that they share in common) to see whether their relation supports the skeptical position advanced by Hunter or leaves the question open.[1] Such an approach is, in itself, common enough (among both skeptics and those af-firming the attribution), but this debate reveals some of the pivotal interpre-tive practices shared by both sides. In particular, when the interlocutors attempt to compare *Paradise Lost* with the treatise, as Sellin does, too little allowance is made for the crucial generic differences between a biblical epic theodicy and a Ramist theological treatise.

In one sense, *De Doctrina's* Ramist organization of dogma generally involves the same task of persuasion as the epic's attempt to "justify the ways of God to men." However, the differences between the two works' respective means of persuasion entail a qualitative difference in the belief to which they attempt to persuade their readers. A fair consideration of them must keep in view the fact that Milton was aware of the respective generic constraints *and* possibilities of the two works. This invites two considerations: the apparent differences between the two works could be a result of Milton's attempt to exploit their generic differences in support of a larger theological project that encompasses both—a view Hunter finds doubtful in the extreme; or Milton could have begun revising *De Doctrina* for publication, in a manner similar to his recension of Downame's text in the *Artis Logicae*—a possibility suggested by Campbell and others and not precluded by Hunter's argument.[2]

　　I shall here argue a further specification of the second hypothesis: if Milton had begun revising *De Doctrina* for publication under his own name, he would have abandoned the theological project specifically because he understood the doctrinal implications of re-ordering biblical content according to Ramist method. The problem is that the present practices of the debate over *De Doctrina* tend to obscure the basic differences in genre between the two works. Because I am sufficiently persuaded by Hunter's argument and expect it ultimately to become a widely accepted account of *De Doctrina* (though its acceptance may require the passing of an entire generation of Milton scholars), my analysis here will focus on how even such a skeptical position is overly optimistic concerning the ways in which statements from one generic context can be immediately compared with those from another.[3] We shall first consider how Sellin's argument in support of Hunter's position offers a sharply focused instance of this central interpretive problem. We can then see how the same difficulty inhabits Hunter's treatment of Miltonic monism and Christology. In doing so, we can begin to understand how keeping in view the different ends of the respective textual genres illumines the debate over *De Doctrina* and also alerts us to the perils involved in a quest for any kind of demonstrative gloss on the epic. In this way, the investigation will ultimately lead us to consider Milton's handling of the relation between theological intelligibility and biblical narrative form.

I

Sellin's argument focuses specifically on how *Paradise Lost* and *De Doctrina* handle the central issue of predestination. He concludes that the deep differences between them "indicate that Hunter has put his finger on a problem that is real" (Sellin, 58). Ultimately Sellin proposes four alternative explanations for the "sharp variance" (52) between the two treatments of predestination: "(1) Milton authored neither work—an alternative absurd to everyone, presumably; (2) Milton authored both the treatise and *Paradise Lost,* but did not put down what he really thought in one or the other of them; (3) Milton changed his mind between the times he wrote the two texts; (4) the author of *Paradise Lost* is not the author of the treatise, as William Hunter maintains" (Sellin, 58). Of course, there are other possible explanations, including some partial combination of the various alternatives Sellin proposes (whether partial authorship, partial changes in thinking, or incomplete textual revision, etc.). However, these propositions (*as* alternatives) logically depend upon the accuracy of Sellin's argument regarding the character of the "variance" between the two works. Are the two treatments of predestination indeed irreconcilable (Sellin, 52)? Certainly the two works are not theologically identical, but that does not constitute their being irreconcilable on this point.

In order to contrast effectively the treatment of predestination in the two works, Sellin, using a paradigm established by Dutch scholar Klaas Dijk, examines each work in the following terms: "(1) end or purpose of the decree; (2) the position of predestination among the other divine decrees preceding or following it; (3) the object of, or creature subject to the decree; and (4) the nature of the acts of election and reprobation that the decree entails" (Sellin, 48). In discussing the ends of predestination, Sellin points out that while the purpose of the decree in *De Doctrina* is explicitly to manifest "the glory of [God's] mercy, grace and wisdom," the purpose of the decree in *Paradise Lost* is limited to mercy and justice.[4] Although different, none of these terms necessarily excludes the other. The deeper problem in Sellin's analysis is that it demands that the terms of the doctrinal treatise be directly and explicitly transposed onto the epic, effectively ignoring the very generic differences that Milton understood and could exploit. Sellin focuses upon the dialogue between the Father and Son in Book Three of *Paradise Lost* as the primary proof-text for his discussion of predestination in the poem. In that passage he finds the explicit references to "mercy" and "justice" but ignores the fact that the Father calls the Son "my wisdom" (3.170). Wisdom is not explicitly named as an "end" of predestination because wisdom is presently manifest as a character in the drama of the poem in which that predestination is acted out. If the theodicy is finally effective, both the wisdom and the grace of God (as well as the explicitly named justice and mercy) will be manifest in the reader's experience of the poem's drama. Furthermore, although the epic's emphasis upon mercy (which "first and last shall brightest shine" [3.134]) does not directly correlate with the emphasis of the treatise, the difference in emphasis is not irreconcilable. In this one respect at least, there is no necessary contradiction between the two works.

The second and more important point of comparison between the two works is the relative location of the decree of predestination. These differences, Sellin maintains, are "both essential and undeniable" (52) because the order of decrees will determine the logic upon which a theologian bases the concept of human liberty (55). According to the treatise, election (being general and contingent) is *"ante iacta mundi fundamenta"* (CM 14:90)—decreed "before the foundations of the world were laid" (YP 6:168). Sellin calls this a "supralapsarian" view of predestination, because the decree is made *before* Creation and before the Fall (50–51). Because the decree of predestination in *Paradise Lost* appears to come *after* Creation but before the Fall, Sellin calls it a "prelapsarian" view of election and argues that it "runs exactly counter" to that of the doctrinal treatise (52). The "sharp variance" between the two accounts of predestination results, therefore, from the fact that the treatise places the divine decree before Creation, while the poem places the divine decree after Creation. As noted, he bases his account of predestination in *Paradise Lost* upon the dialogue between the Father and Son in Book Three. The problem is that the entire speech that Sellin takes to be *"the* divine decree" regarding human and angelic predestination is actually nothing of the kind. Sellin maintains that in Book Three (lines 56–134) God is "issuing the decree of predestination itself right before our nose" (Sellin, 46). His comparative argument depends on this assertion, because if this particular passage in the epic is not the actual decree of predestination, then the entire poetic side of his comparison fails.

Before God the Father ever speaks, Milton describes him in terms indicating that his speech will be one of providential prescience, not predestination:

> God beholding from his prospect high,
> Wherein past, present, future he beholds,
> Thus to his only Son foreseeing spake.   (3.77–79)

Throughout the passage, God is declaring not his determination of what shall be (such decrees, conditional or otherwise, are already in place) but his *knowledge* of what shall be. The problem that Milton faces here is one of how to represent in narrative form the actions of a God who beholds "past, present, future" as a continuous present. How could Milton represent within the form of an epic the unspeakably originary character of the predestination decree described in *De Doctrina*? He could do so by using precisely the kind of narrative structure we find in *Paradise Lost*, where God recounts as knowledge, within the narrative temporal sequence, those decrees he made before the creation of the universe. Thus, although the treatise and the poem differ in form, their treatments of predestination do not necessarily conflict, because God's speech is one of prescience and not predetermination. Ultimately, Sellin's entire comparison of divine decrees within the two works depends upon this mistake of treating the Father's statements in Book Three of the poem as the decree of predestination itself rather than an articulation of foreknowledge.

The third main point of comparison on which, Sellin argues, "the epic and the treatise clash irreconcilably" regards the creature(s) subject to the predestination decree (Sellin, 52). The two texts are "utterly different" because where the treatise takes the usual view that humans are the object of the decree, the poem seems to treat both angels and humans as the objects of predestination. Sellin rightly points out that lines 111–19 in Book Three of *Paradise Lost* are concerned with the angelic rather than human fall in relation to free will (Sellin, 46); however, because he again mistakes this speech for a dramatic representation of the decree of predestination itself, he interprets the lines to be a "predestination" of past events (i.e., retroactive, and hence, a constitutionally incoherent decree):

> They [Ethereal Powers] therefore as to right belong'd,
> So were created, nor can justly accuse
> Thir maker, or thir making, or thir Fate;
> As if Predestination over-rul'd
> Thir will, dispos'd by absolute Decree
> Or high foreknowledge; they themselves decreed
> Thir own revolt not I.   (3.111–17)

Sellin takes this passage as a decree that the angels "have already undergone creation but also effected their own fall" (52), but such a decree (in the past tense) could not itself be the decree of *pre*destination. Moreover, the point of this passage is completely independent of whether or not angelic predestination is actually being proposed. The implication is that no matter how angels or humans conceive of divine efficacy within the universe, whether they call it "fate" or "predestination" or "absolute decree," they cannot rightly deny their own responsibility or blame God for their fall. The qualifier "as if" is pivotal: it allows a recognition of predestination as an aspect of divine efficacy without making any necessary connection between that efficacy and the angelic fall. The passage actually emphasizes that there is *no* sufficient causal relation between the divine capacity for predestination and the fall of "Ethereal Powers." Ultimately, the poem does not state explicitly whether or not angels are an object of predestination, but it clearly does not dictate an affirmative view. Thus the poem does not necessarily conflict with *De Doctrina*'s view that humans are the object of the predestination decree, because, although the epic does not rule out the possibility of angelic predestination, this remains only a possibility.

The fourth area in which Sellin contrasts the epic and the treatise is in the actual character of the election and reprobation that the predestination decree involves in each account. He is right to point out that the poem's notion of "peculiar grace" (*PL* 3.183) does not have a direct parallel in *De Doctrina*. To argue, however, that the "mind behind the treatise could not possibly" endorse the Calvinist view of election implicit in the poem is to find mutual exclusion where none exists (Sellin, 53). Sellin overlooks the fact that such "peculiar grace" (pertaining to vocation to service) does not bear on the pivotal question of salvation or damnation, because the latter is a function of the general and conditional election on which (as he points out) the treatise and the poem agree. Sellin's main point is that the order of these decrees in *Paradise Lost* is precisely the reverse of what it should be if Milton had a genuinely intelligible account of human liberty: "Mere endorsement of 'free will' does not in and of itself mean much. What counts is the way one reasons towards it, and the order of decrees has probably more to do with determining a theologian's stand on human 'liberty' than the other way around" (55). Within the usual terms of Arminian theology there is a specific sequence to the divine decrees: the first decree is the appointment of the Son as mediator; the second is the general decision to receive in grace those who repent, leaving the unrepentant under wrath; the third is to give "the means necessary for repentance and belief sufficiently and powerfully"; finally, "and only then," ensues the decree regarding the eternal destiny of specific persons (54–55). Thus the ingenuity of Arminius' reasoning is that he places these three intermediary decisions between the Fall and the decree of election and reprobation (54). All this theological subtlety, however, according to Sellin, was apparently lost on Milton, because in *Paradise Lost* the order of these decisions is in "virtually reverse order to that posed by Arminius" (55). At this point Sellin's argument returns to the mistaken premise that the Father's speech in Book Three is the actual divine decree of predestination.

Thus Sellin's analysis proceeds through each step of the speeches in Book Three to show that the decision of predestination to salvation precedes the decree of the means of salvation, which precedes, in turn, the appointment of the Son as mediator. One example is sufficient to demonstrate that this last stage of his analysis shares the same root interpretive error. The following passage (continuing to line 202 of the poem) Sellin takes to be the "secondary decrees determining the means of carrying out the primary edict" (Sellin, 55):

> My word, my wisdom, and effectual might,
> All thou hast spoken as my thoughts are, all
> As my Eternal purpose hath decreed:
> Man shall not quite be lost, but saved who will,

> Yet not of will in him yet grace in me
> Freely voutsaf't.   (*PL* 3.170–75)

Because the Son has earlier spoken what were already the Father's thoughts, these speeches are plainly not themselves the primordial decrees that they describe. The explicit mention of God's "Eternal purpose" reminds us that these decisions to offer grace (human volition is necessary but not sufficient in itself) were actually made "before the foundations of the earth were laid": that is, constitutionally outside the reach of any humanly conceivable narrative. The thirty lines following the colon in line 172 are then simply a recounting of the means of grace that have already been decreed. The attempt to treat the speeches of the Father in Book Three as though they were divine decrees, rather than articulations of prescience, leads the argument to mistake the order of discussion in the dialogue for the order of decrees. Therefore, the attempt to assess how *Paradise Lost* treats the order of divine decrees by following the sequence of the Father–Son dialogue narrative in Book Three is deeply mistaken and can only lead to confusion.

All of this should not be taken to imply that there are no points of disagreement between the poem and the doctrinal treatise. Rather, if we make allowance for the generic differences between an epic theodicy and a Ramist theological treatise, we will find that the poem does not necessarily exclude an interpretation that agrees with the doctrinal work. The poem and the treatise are, therefore, not as irreconcilable on the issue of predestination as Sellin argues. But what then is the character of the relation between the two works? We can begin to get a more detailed answer to that question by considering Hunter's arguments and then focusing specifically on his analysis of materialism and Christology, which are often ascribed to Milton and often used to link the poem with the treatise.

II

The strongest part of Hunter's argument in *Visitation Unimplor'd* is that which draws upon a combination of historical data to show that the circumstantial evidence linking Milton with the specific manuscript treatise is virtually nonexistent. At the most basic material level, the history of the manuscript demonstrates that the text originally had no authorial inscription and that Milton's name was a late addition, possibly as late as 1823 (*Visitation*, 42–48). Hunter's analysis of the early biographers is also compelling. He demonstrates that, aside from the anonymous biographer (Cyriac Skinner) who seems familiar solely with Chapter 10 of Book One, only Edward Phillips had any basis other than rumor upon which to base the claim that Milton was composing a "body of divinity" at all (*Visitation,* 19–25). But even if the existence of such a text is granted, there is no concrete basis for identifying it with the *De Doctrina* manuscript. More importantly, Hunter makes a strong case for attributing *De Doctrina* to one of Milton's students. He does so by putting the biographical details in the preface together with Phillips' account of Milton's practice of pedagogical dictation and with the dates of publication for the known source texts of *De Doctrina* (*Visitation,* 25–33). In short, if we accept the biographical details of the preface writer as true and applicable to the author of the whole text, then Milton could not have been the author, but one of his students might have been (given the publication dates of the theological compendia upon which the treatise draws and which its author claims to have read as a boy [*adolescens*] [CM 14:4]). Also valuable to Hunter's argument is his discussion of the authorities that the treatise engages, whether in disagreement or agreement. The tract employs almost exclusively Continental authorities, and even more notable is the omission of any mention of major English writers whom Milton engages on the same topics elsewhere in his prose (*Visitation,* 71–86). Most importantly, Hunter also discusses a series of doctrinal points on which the content of the treatise disagrees with explicit statements that Milton makes in other prose works (56–70). All of which leads me to agree generally with Hunter that Milton was likely not the original author of the *De Doctrina Christiana* manuscript.

The story is complicated by two factors. On the one hand, Milton could still have undertaken (as we noted earlier) to revise the manuscript, as he did George Downame's logic text, and publish it under his own name. Even if we admit such a hypothesis, it is simply not possible to know what stage of the revision process the extant manuscript represents. On the other hand, to deny that Milton is the original author of *De Doctrina* does not preclude any of the heterodoxy of the treatise from appearing in *Paradise Lost.* Moreover, when Hunter undertakes to compare the treatise with the epic (rather than just the canonic prose), he meets the same difficulty as Sellin, in not making sufficient allowance for the differences in generic context. Once again, this is not to claim that two works agree completely. Many of Hunter's distinctions are sound, but his specific treatment of monism and Christology in *Paradise Lost* raises questions about the whole attempt to compare the two works.

In contrast to the "near-creedal acceptance" of the view that *Paradise Lost* is consistent with the monism of *De Doctrina,* Hunter contends that the poem clearly contradicts the tract's assertion that the originary *ex Deo* matter of the universe was inherently good (*Visitation,* 121–25; q.v. YP 6:307–10). Hunter points out that the figure of Chaos (as depicted in Books Two and Seven of the poem) is evil (or, at best, neutral), but that critics, assuming Milton wrote the treatise, have tried various ways of reconciling the two accounts of matter (*Visitation*, 122–24). Clearly such divergent views of matter would be a problem, and the two works have typically been taken to be in tension on this point. The apparent contradiction disappears, however, if we recall the narrative context in which the figure of Chaos appears and if we allow that Milton's usage in *Paradise Lost* is intentionally precise and accurate. First, we need to remember that the introduction of "Chaos" as a character is consistent with the epic's deployment of allegoresis elsewhere (e.g., the allegory of Satan, Sin, and Death) specifically to portray evil—that is, to depict the privation of being.[5] Chaos is the personification of a *principle*, the opposite of which is the goodness of dynamic order. The key point here is that "Chaos" per se is simply not "matter." Insofar as the originary matter "exists" at all, it is, in a minimal sense, good. Although matter is made subject to the rule of Chaos, in so far as it still *is* matter, it is good, does not participate in the ontic privation of Chaos, and cannot be identified with the evil of Chaos (much like the way the subjects of a corrupt monarch can remain virtuous themselves). Thus the appearance of a contradiction between the two treatments of matter is based on the mistaken premise that the allegorically depicted principle of Chaos represents in itself the *ex Deo* substance of the universe, rather than the condition to which that substance (*materia prima*) was initially subjected.

In considering Milton's materialism, one of the central points to keep in mind is that neither *Paradise Lost* nor *De Doctrina* equates "matter" (*materia*) with "body" (*corpus*). The distinction is important because, although the epic presents a vision of the universe in which all existents are differentiated by God out of the "one first matter" (*PL* 5.472), it still assumes a distinction between those things which are corporeal (body) and those which are spiritual. Despite Milton's precision on this point (at least in *Paradise Lost*), the tendency of some readers to equate matter with body has led them to render Milton's position incoherent, by implying that although Milton believes everything to be corporeal, he still employs the distinction between corporeal and spiritual substances. Once the incoherence is introduced, critics can work around it by formulating new terms, as, for example, Stephen Fallon does by suggesting that Milton shares with Thomas Hobbes a belief in the corporality of spirit.[6] However, when the distinction between matter and body is maintained, not only is there precise agreement between the theological treatise and the poem, but the materialism in the epic is articulated by means of a close proximity to biblical idiom.[7]

In discussing the treatise's handling of materialism there are at least two main passages to which we should attend: the description of the human spirit (YP 6:319), and the account of first matter's procession from God before its differentiation into existents (YP 6:305–11). Regarding the first issue, the treatise states: "the idea that the spirit of man is separate from his body, so that it may exist somewhere in isolation, complete and intelligent, is nowhere to be found in scripture, and is plainly at odds with nature and reason" (YP 6:319). By denying the separability of the body and spirit in the constitution of a given human being, this passage clearly rejects what could be described as traditional "anthropological dualism." But the statement does not imply that the soul is "corporeal"; moreover, to insist that two things are inseparable does not entail their being the same thing but implies rather the opposite. Even if the above passage is taken as an outright denial of the existence of a human "spirit" per se, the anthropological corporealism is not applied to the entire universe; the treatise goes on later to defend a precise understanding of the human soul as well as "spiritual" substance. According to the treatise, "all form—and the human soul is a kind of form—is produced [*ex potentia materiae*]" (YP 6:322, 325). But given that matter is, in itself, "only a passive principle" (YP 6:307), such forms result only from the *potentia* specifically "implanted in matter" by God (YP 6:325). In this sense, all forms are "material" (though not all corporeal) because each creature (whether a corporeal or spiritual being) is constituted as an indivisible union of matter and form (YP 6:308).[8] Thus, the claim that body and soul are not separable follows logically from the premise that the soul is the form of a whole embodied human being produced *ex potentia materiae* (YP 6:317–18, 322; never *ex potentia corporis*). But this entire account is rendered incoherent if "matter" is taken to be synonymous with "body."

Because the treatise articulates a kind of materialist monism that nevertheless maintains the distinction between spiritual and corporeal substances, it also offers a unique intellectual foundation for the possibility of theodicy that is consistent with *Paradise Lost*. We see this most clearly in Book One, Chapter 7, where the author initially argues that the creative first matter is *ex Deo* and then argues that a corporeal substance could be derived from a spiritual substance (YP 6:305–11). In short, by maintaining that "it is not the matter nor the form [of a given being] that sins" (YP 6:309), the treatise keeps evil's origin (in the free choices of individual rational creatures) distinct from matter (which is incorruptible). In effect, corruptibility is only possible after a creature is individuated and thus enters a "mutable state" (YP 6:309). Because of the way this passage in the treatise progresses from using the paired terms "God" and "matter" to using "spiritual substance" and "corporeal substance" (YP 6:305–11) some readers have been led to treat "matter" as a substitute for "corporeal substance."[9] But in fact, the precise development of the argument implies that the terms "spiritual substance" and "God's own substance" (not "essence")[10] are used as synonyms for the incorruptible originary matter, specifically removed from the corruptibility of any individuated creature (corporeal or spiritual). That this monist *ex Deo* account of Creation maintains the matter–body distinction is therefore pivotal to the argument that God is not the sufficient cause of evil—a basic precondition for theodicy.

The monism of *Paradise Lost* turns on the distinction between "sensible" (corporeal) and "extended," and implies that spiritual beings are the latter but not necessarily the former. To suppose that everything made of first matter is corporeal implies that indeed everything is corporeal and renders the poem's use of the distinction between corporeal and non-corporeal substances incoherent (e.g. *PL* 5.413 or 4.584–85). The key passage here is Raphael's account of created order in Book Five, a passage commonly cited on this issue but which Hunter dismisses as only "superficially" similar to the materialism of the treatise (*Visitation*, 131):

> O Adam, one Almighty is, from whom
> All things proceed, and up to him return,
> If not deprav'd from good, created all
> Such to perfection, one first matter all,
> Indu'd with various forms, various degrees
> Of substance, and in things that live, of life;
> But the more refin'd, more spiritous, and pure,
> As nearer to him plac't or nearer tending
> Each in thir several Spheres assign'd,
> Till body up to spirit work, in bounds
> Proportion'd to each kind.   (*PL* 5.469–79)

The main problem that Hunter sees in this account of matter is that it does not fit with the two-stage account given in the Creation narrative (7.210–42), where chaos is first circumscribed and stilled by the Son before being indued with forms. In effect, the problem for Hunter is that Raphael "does not mention [matter's] earlier existence as undivided chaos—indeed, he does not mention chaos at all" (*Visitation*, 128). Once again, there is no problem if we recall that chaos is not matter. Raphael's silence regarding chaos is no longer puzzling: the angel is describing the operation of matter in the order of Creation, not in the state of absolute chaos; the plenitude of being, not the principle of its privation. Moreover, Raphael's account is consistent with *De Doctrina*, in that "corporeal" and "incorporeal" (*PL* 5.407–14) both designate "degrees / Of substance" (5.473–74), which result from the "one first matter" being "indu'd" with form. At the same time, the claim that humans could one day "ascend" in status from corporeal to spiritual substances (5.491–500) only makes sense if those terms are understood to indicate both a clear distinction between forms and a common "material" substrate.

In a later statement by Raphael, regarding the way in which Adam should undertake to think about the celestial spheres, the poem's handling of monism is characterized by a precise interpretive openness:

> The swiftness of those Circles attribute,
> Though numberless, to his Omnipotence,
> That to corporeal substances could add
> Speed almost Spiritual.   (*PL* 8.107–10)

The assumed distinction between corporeal and spiritual substances fits precisely with the above account of Milton's monism. Although both substances are implicitly extended in space (both being differentiated out of matter), they have a different relation to human sensation and understanding. However, at the same time, the passage could also be understood within its immediate context to be assuming a more orthodox dualism. Hunter objects precisely to those who would ascribe to Milton such a subtle duplicity that the materialism of the epic could only be discerned after the publication of *De Doctrina* (*Visitation,* 114). But duplicity is not the only alternative explanation to Hunter's treatment of the interpretive issues at stake. Regarding, for example, Raphael's comment about taking the lesser part of a day to travel from heaven to earth (*PL* 8.110–14), the problem is that to speak at all regarding angelic travel, whether in a biblical story or the epic, implies (if taken literally) a spatially located, though not corporeal, heaven. In effect, Raphael's comment could be taken to presume a kind of materialist monism, but it entails such a position only to the same extent dictated by biblical narratives that speak of angels coming to earth.

Where Hunter sees a specious ascription of duplicity, I find that Milton's subtlety is the ultimate vindication of his materialist monism. What could appear as duplicity in describing the relation between corporeal and spiritual substances is only a result of Milton's precise biblicism. In this respect, it could be argued that the poem's consistency with Scripture implicitly faults those readers who do not find the same monism in the biblical text. Nevertheless, the interpretive issues at the root of Hunter's central objection on this point still require further elucidation. But we can speak to those issues more fully only after we consider further the epic's biblicism in its treatment of Christology.

III

Milton's treatment of God as a character—specifically in the Father–Son dialogue of Book Three—presents theological issues in a way that allows but does not necessitate interpretive agreement with *De Doctrina*. There is obviously a certain amount of flexibility in depicting the actions of created beings such as angels, but a theodic narrative involves itself in a complex set of potential problems when it attempts to treat the immutable God as a character. Completely aside from the artistic challenge, how does Milton avoid contravening the advice that Raphael gives to Adam?

> Solicit not thy thoughts with matters hid,
> Leave them to God above, him serve and fear;
>
> . . . .
>
> Heav'n is for thee too high
> To know what passes there; be lowly wise:
> Think only what concerns thee and thy being;
> Dream not of other Worlds.   (*PL* 8.167–68, 172–75)

Milton himself raises the issue of the propriety of his treatment of God (whether as the "light" of pre-incarnate logos or otherwise) in the invocation to Book Three, when he asks, "May I express thee unblamed?" (3.3); however, he still continues to ask that he would be able to "see" "things invisible to mortal sight" (3.55). The attempt to communicate this vision, Wendell Berry argues, is the central problem of the poem, because it forces Milton to "bring God on stage in person, not as inscrutable mystery and power, visible blindingly, but as a heroic king conversing in Homeric dialogue with the Son."[11] In effect, by "aspiring to 'see' the one God of Abraham, Isaac, and Jacob, Milton Falls onto Olympus" (105). Thus the poem's primary weakness, according to Berry, is that by using the epic voice to treat God as a character, the narrative violates its own principle of created hierarchical order, as pronounced by Raphael. However, if we look more closely at Raphael's comments and the scene in heaven in Book Three, we can see whether Milton actually does violate Raphael's advice.

By bringing together biblical narrative with the form of classical epic, Milton places within the fabric of his work a tension, as Erich Auerbach argues, that had animated much of western literature up to his time:

The world of Scripture stories is not satisfied with claiming to be historically true reality—it insists that it is the only real world, is destined for autocracy. All other scenes, issues, and ordinances have no right to appear independently of it, and it is promised that all of them, the history of all mankind, will be given their due place within its frame, will be subordinated to it. The Scripture stories do not, like Homer's, court our favor, they do not flatter us that they may please us and enchant us—they seek to subject us, and if we refuse to be subjected we are rebels.

Let no one object that this goes too far, that not the stories, but the religious doctrine, raises the claim of absolute authority; because the stories are not, like Homer's, narrated "reality." Doctrine and promise are incarnate in them and inseparable from them; for that very reason they are fraught with "background" and myste-rious, containing a second, concealed meaning.[12]

By contrasting the way in which the obscurities of biblical narrative intimate the character of "a hidden God" (15) with the Homeric need to "externalize" thought (11), Auerbach emphasizes not only the differences in form between biblical and classical narrative but also the unavoidably theological implica-tions that follow from those differences in form. This makes the character of Milton's undertaking all the more daunting: how can he maintain his commit-ment to the theological integrity of the biblical narrative if he is using the epic form and the omniscient Homeric voice to shape that story?

Milton overcomes this problem primarily through typological inter-pretation of the Bible. Figural interpretation depends upon the view that both a type (e.g., Isaac) and its fulfillment (e.g., Christ) have the status of concrete historical persons, but that their essential unity inheres in the eter-nal "divine plan" (Auerbach, 555). In this way, typology affords an oppor-tunity to make the story of revealed faith intelligible while still maintaining the historical status of the events recounted in the biblical narrative. Al-though such "figural realism" has its roots in patristic writers like Augustine, Jerome, and Tertullian (Auerbach, 196), that tradition of interpretation was mediated through Renaissance humanist biblical scholarship. In contrast to its deployment of allegoresis to portray ontic privation, *Paradise Lost* draws upon a figural, or typological, reading of Scripture to present biblical narra-tive in a way that is consistent with the externalized elaboration of epic style. Milton is not simply reshaping a biblical narrative into a classical form and ethos; he is, in a crucial sense, converting the epic genre itself by relocating it within the biblical metanarrative and shaping it according to a Christian heroism defined by that narrative.

The other major characteristic of *Paradise Lost* that both allows and instigates this combination of forms is its central concern with theodicy. The theodic parameters of the work are limited precisely to humans, to "thee and thy being," and, as Dennis Danielson points out, the goal of the poem is to justify the ways of God specifically "*to men.*"[13] Milton could justifiably main-tain that the conversation we overhear in heaven between the Father and the Son tells us nothing that we could not already find in Scripture. The purpose of the dialogue is to initiate the debate concerning human freedom that con-tinues throughout the poem (Danielson, 108). The theological difficulty that this passage creates results not so much from any explicit theological content but from the dramatic form itself. The difficulty is not the Father's defence of free will but the fact that he feels compelled to tell the pre-incarnate Son his plans at all, as though the Son does not already know (*PL* 3.173–216).

If a reader begins with the orthodox assumption that any extra-incarnational relation between the Father and the Son would be hidden and internal to the Godhead, then the dialogue clearly presents some difficulty. At the same time, the Father does address the Son explicitly as "My word, my wisdom, and effectual might" (3.170) and states that the Son has spoken the Father's own thoughts even in asking the questions that he does (3.171). Here we find a clear interpretive opportunity, despite the dramatic structure, to understand that the dialogue is already, in a sense, internal to God. This implies, not that the dialogue is a sham conversation like Satan's mock parliament in Book Two, but that the conversation is intended primarily for the benefit of those listening. It is entirely consistent with the character of the orthodox Godhead that the Father would reveal himself to his creatures (in this case angels) precisely through his Son *in relationship* to himself. Milton affirms the standard orthodox view that the Son is not simply "wise" but *is* indeed *the* "wisdom of God" himself. Thus, the apparent difficulties created by the dramatic form of the dialogue, regarding the Son's knowledge, can be interpreted as consistent with orthodoxy or with a more heterodox subordinationism.

We can see a more precise instance of the same kind of subtle monist consistency when the poem mentions the Father–Son relationship directly. When the narrative voice says that, in the Son, the "Father shone / Substantially expressed" (*PL* 3.139–40), the poem is consistent with the materialism of *De Doctrina* in exactly those terms that still leave the text susceptible to a Trinitarian (as well as dualist) reading. Because, according to *De Doctrina*, the Son is created (YP 6:205–12), he is also a substantial differentiation within matter. Although the Son is the supreme spiritual created being, the fact that he is created means that he is only the "Son" of God in the sense that he is the most perfect substantial expression (among many) of God's image (out of the potential of matter). At the same time, the usual theological equation of "essence" with "substance" allows orthodox readers to interpret these lines to imply that the Son shares the Father's essence (which *De Doctrina* denies because it identifies "essence" as a biconditional equivalent of "individual"). The pivotal distinction in the poem depends upon whether we understand the adverbial modifier "substantially" as synonymous with or distinct from "essentially." If we believe that Milton's position is similar to the one offered in *De Doctrina*, then we can see how the poem accords with a subordinationist view of the Son; however, the poem itself is also open to an orthodox reading.

Hunter takes up this same set of issues in discussing one of the most common points of connection scholars make between the theological treatise and the Miltonic prose canon, where *Artis Logicae* directly echoes *De Doc-*

trina and seems to make the same point. The author of the theological treatise ultimately bases his argument against the Trinity upon the insistence that both "person" and "essence" are numerically distinct—that is, equatable with individuated being (YP 6:216). In the *Artis Logicae* Milton makes a similar point that "things which differ in number also differ in essence, and never do things differ in number without also differing in essence" (YP 8:233). It thus seems that Milton, in this passage of the logic text, lays the foundation for *De Doctrina's* anti-Trinitarianism and then emphasizes the connection between the two works by adding and italicizing a phrase not found in the source logic texts: "*Here let the Theologians take notice.*" Hunter cites the essay by Thomas Scott-Craig as one of the better analyses making this apparent connection between the two works.[14] Following the lead of Bishop Burgess, however, Hunter maintains that the passage in the logic text actually implies the opposite of what it is customarily taken to imply, because Milton (unlike the author of *De Doctrina*) goes on to distinguish between two different senses of the term "essence." Thus Milton's warning is that theologians should not confuse the two senses of the term or reduce them to one. Hunter quotes and emends the passage from *Artis Logicae* as follows: "the essence of anything is partly common [that is, what constitutes in this case the members of the Godhead] and partly proper [that is, what individuates them]; matter [or better, substance] constitutes the common essence [of the Trinity] and form the proper [essence of each of its three members]."[15] Hunter rightly points out that the anti-Trinitarian arguments of *De Doctrina* depend upon limiting "essence" to indicate individuation exclusively.[16] However, the reason why Hunter can take this passage from *Artis Logicae* as an argument *supporting* the Trinity is because he has already rejected the ascription of materialism to Milton. The passage quoted above could just as easily be rephrased to demonstrate that Milton makes the distinction between "proper essence" and "common essence," not in order to support Trinitarian definitions, but to support the *De Doctrina's* distinction between God's individual essence (identified as the Father) and the "substance" or *ex Deo* matter out of which all things (including the Son) are created. Such a reading follows because: 1) even the logic treatise specifically refers to common essence as "matter" (*De Doctrina's* term of choice); 2) proper essence is referred to as "form" and corresponds directly to those forms with which first matter is "indu'd" in the epic (*PL* 5.473).

As we now consider the form of the Father–Son dialogue in heaven in more detail, two important points are worth noting. First, the Bible does not provide much explicit information about the pre-incarnational existence of the Son of God. Second, given the characterization of the Son in the gospels, the orthodox insistence upon the differences in "person" between Father and Son, and the logical necessities of narrative presentation, Milton's portrayal does not exceed the biblical limits of artistic license. The subtlety of Milton's presentation of the Son in *Paradise Lost* is that although it is literally consistent with the subordinationism presented in *De Doctrina*, the poetic portrayal does not necessitate such a reading. More importantly, the poem does not presume to depict events in heaven without some biblical precedent. Aside from the numerous "throne room" scenes transcribed from various visions of heaven (e.g., Isaiah 6 or Ezekiel 1), the three biblical passages that bear most directly upon the question of Milton's artistic license are: Revelation 5, Zechariah 3:1–10 and Job 1–2.

Although none of these biblical scenes is identical to that presented in Book Three of *Paradise Lost,* each of them contains formal elements that Milton clearly incorporated into his own account of the heavenly dialogue. In his edition of *Paradise Lost,* Merritt Hughes provides (as does Alastair Fowler in his edition)[17] a gloss on the words, "And silence was in Heav'n" (3.218), by citing Revelation 8:1, which mentions the half-hour silence that followed the opening of the "seventh seal." The correspondence between the two occurrences of silence seems obvious enough; but in Revelation 5 we find the biblical precedent for the specific dramatic dynamics that precede the silence in Milton's poem. In the biblical passage, before even the first seal of the prophecy is ever opened the question is asked in heaven, "Who is worthy to open the book [beside the throne], and loose the seals thereof?" (Rev. 5:2):

And no man in heaven, nor in earth, neither under the earth, was able to open the book, neither to look thereon. And I wept much because no man was found worthy to open and to read this book, neither to look thereon. And one of the elders saith unto me, Weep not: behold the Lion of the tribe of Judah, the Root of David, hath prevailed to open the book, and to loose the seven seals thereof. (Rev. 5:3–5)[18]

Although it is an angel in this scene, rather than God the Father, who asks the pivotal question, the dynamics of the drama are similar to those in *Paradise Lost* (3.217–26). The challenge is pronounced and only the Son is able to answer the challenge because he is willing to sacrifice himself for humanity. Of course, there are a number of important differences between this scene in Revelation and Milton's presentation in *Paradise Lost*. First, the throne of God the Father is also that of the Lamb in Revelation—differences between Father and Son are minimized by the dramatic structure. The same one on the throne who is clearly God, "Alpha and Omega," "the Almighty" (1:8), "the first and the last" (1:17), is also Christ who says, "I am he that liveth and was dead; and, behold, I am alive for evermore" (1:18). Second, as implied by this unity, God the Father never appears as a character separate from the Son through whom he has chosen exclusively to reveal himself. Third, the narrative voice in Revelation is in the first person so that the vision of God's throne is not treated from the perspective of an epic voice. However, if we look at the passages from Job and Zechariah, we can see that each of these points of difference also has a biblical precedent.

In the passages from Job and Zechariah, the central human characters (Job and the high priest Joshua) are normally understood as types of Christ. In both cases Satan appears as a dramatic character who comes before the throne of God to accuse the central figure. Zechariah's account is important because typologically it emphasizes the role of "Joshua" ("Jesus" in Greek) as a supernatural high priest who represents the sinful chosen nation (by wearing rags) before God the Father. For later interpreters, the direct association of the high priest with Christ is unavoidable (q.v. Hebrews), so that what may be a "vision" for Zechariah becomes a reality for Christians. In Zechariah's story, the rags are replaced so that Joshua can stand before God in pure white clothes (3:3–5); however, the important point for Milton's purposes is that here we find two of the persons of the (orthodox) Godhead effectively presented as dramatic characters face to face, an encounter that Christians claim to be made actual (in some sense) by Christ. Still, Zechariah's vision is just that: a vision recounted in a first person narrative voice that would not for a moment presume to treat God as simply "one character among many" within its story. The biblical precedent for that kind of treatment of God is the initial framing story (rather than the conclusion) of the Book of Job.

The Book of Job, like Zechariah, presents a Satan figure in dramatic action before the throne of God in heaven. The main difference between them is that, in Job, God the Father interacts with the Satan character (initially at least) as if the plot were not of his design. More importantly, God is treated by a third-person omniscient narrator. The pivotal question is how Milton would have interpreted the Book of Job. As Barbara Lewalski demonstrates in her study of *Paradise Regained,* Milton was familiar not only with the patristic tradition of treating Job as an epic but also with the humanist practice of treating Job typologically.[19] Because typological interpretation maintains the historical status of the "type" (in this case Job) as well as its fulfillment (Christ), Milton remains well within the limits of standard Protestant hermeneutics in holding that the framing narrative in Job consists of historical events. On this basis, Milton had a firm biblical precedent for presenting the dialogue and dramatic events at the very throne of God using the externalized verisimilitude of epic (in contrast to the metaphysical realism of allegoresis) and thus for treating God as a character within an epic narrative. Ultimately, we find in *Paradise Lost* a poem that admits both a materialist and a subordinationist interpretation consistent with *De Doctrina,* specifically through retaining a rigorous consistency with biblical models for representing divine action.

In discussing how different critics have tried to find the subordinationism of *De Doctrina* in *Paradise Lost,* Hunter points out that the passages in the epic that seem to support such a reading are actually based on biblical passages that orthodox readers always had to interpret in ways that might seem forced to theologically naive readers today.[20] The obvious implication is that Milton would not have expected his readers to discern heterodoxy in the poem unless they were already liable to interpret the Bible in such a way. Thus, against the arguments of Lewalski, who maintains the importance of *De Doctrina* in helping scholars to discern the peculiar and, as it were, secret meaning that Milton gives to the relevant scriptural texts, Hunter insists that "it is incredible that [Milton] could disguise such heterodoxy so well that generations of readers were duped until the treatise was recovered" (*Visitation,* 114). As Hunter rightly points out, if we begin with the assumption of Miltonic authorship of the treatise and suspend the usual orthodox ways of reading the relevant passages of the epic (or the Bible), we can get a rather doubtful picture of Milton's ingenuity: "one can make [Milton] out to be an extraordinarily subtle or devious author who had such double meanings in mind, though his 'fit audience,' who could understand his hidden messages [in the epic], would indeed be very few until the recovered [*De Doctrina*] manuscript set them straight" (*Visitation,* 114). Because many of Milton's "fit," anti-Trinitarian readers in the Restoration would not have thought it wise, safe, or even possible to publish their views, the existing textual record (or at least the well-known one) may be misleading.[21] There is, however, an alternative to seeing Milton in the way described above, if we consider more closely how the epic handles the relation between the Father and the Son. Even if we do not ascribe to Milton the outright anti-Trinitarianism of the theological treatise, Milton explicitly stated elsewhere that differences over such a point of doctrine do not constitute heresy (e.g., YP 8:423–25)—demonstrating that he could choose to present his epic in such a way that the dispute is effectively rendered moot. Even if Milton did believe in the doctrine of the Trinity (as Hunter quite justifiably maintains), he insisted on the right of others to disagree with him on that point. Regardless of the authorship of the treatise, based on Milton's possession of the manuscript and his known heterodox associations, Milton clearly had friends who were anti-Trinitarians. For that reason, we need not ascribe to him some strategy of extraordinary duplicity or devious subtlety in his writing of the epic. Milton knew both the Bible and Trinitarian hermeneutics well enough to know that all he needed was to remain rigorously consistent with biblical literary form, as well as content, in order for the resulting poem to preserve an interpretive openness that neither precluded a Trinitarian reading nor provided such a reading the certitude to make it a defining article of faith. Thus, even if we grant that we cannot know how much of *De Doctrina* is Milton's or was influenced directly by him, we can still maintain that *Paradise Lost* is written in such a way that neither precludes nor dictates a Trinitarian reading.

IV

We are now in a position to return to the question of the epic's success as a theodicy (in view of its generic *telos*), in order to see how these various elements shape our perception of Milton's lowly wise undertaking to "justify the ways of God to men." Central to the success of the poem's stated intentions is the issue of human freedom. In order to maintain both the justice of the human Fall and the blameless position of God in relation to the Fall, Milton must maintain that the human will (at least in the unfallen state) is free. Dennis Danielson outlines *Paradise Lost*'s relation to various other positions in the debate over free will and determinism. Besides the libertarians and the determinists, there were the "compatibilists" who maintained that "free will does not preclude determinism and vice versa."[22] Danielson points out that, although Milton is an anticompatibilist (libertarian), many critics mistakenly impose a compatibilist view onto *Paradise Lost*, resulting in a "serious misjudgement of his theodicy" (142). If we consider just briefly some aspects of the compatibilist and anticompatibilist positions, we can begin to see how an accurate apprehension of the materialism in the epic bears upon the poem's theodic objectives.

The central points of difference between the compatibilism that characterized many Calvinist accounts of postlapsarian existence and the libertarian view hinged upon the issues of necessary versus sufficient causation and internal versus external freedom:

The compatibilist will hold Jones responsible for a given action because Jones could have *acted otherwise*, had he chosen to do so; the incompatibilist (or libertarian) holds Jones responsible because he could have *chosen otherwise*. The compatibilist believes that one can ask, and in principle answer, the question why Jones chose as he did— believes, in other words, that there is a sufficient cause for Jones's choice. The libertarian sees that belief as begging the question, for given a sufficient cause of Jones's choice, it follows that Jones could not have acted otherwise. (Danielson, 133)

The libertarian will certainly recognize the role of causes that are necessary but not sufficient to produce a given decision, but those causes could never constitute a complete explanation for a truly free decision. At the same time, in order to maintain that "things *could* be other than they are," compatibilism must distinguish between "acting" and "choosing"; thus "freedom" is defined in terms of physical constraint while still maintaining psychological determinism (Danielson, 133–35). However, the central problem for compatibilist theodicy is that if it admits determinism to be true, the causal matrix cannot avoid making God the author of evil (Danielson, 135–37).

In order for the distinction between "acting" and "choosing" to be effective as a defense of free will, the compatibilist argument must imply some kind of anthropological dualism that allows for the operation of two independent causal matrices. A dualist account is the only way to maintain that a given psychological choice is determined while the action itself remains unconstrained. By contrast, in *Paradise Lost* the "one first matter" is the basis for prelapsarian liberty:

> one Almighty is, from whom
> All things proceed, and up to him return,
> If not deprav'd from good, created all
> Such to perfection, one first matter all,
> Indu'd with various forms.   (5.469–73)

In opposition to the mechanist corporeal monism of writers like Hobbes, the intrinsically moral and conditional character of first matter (note the explicit, "if not") results ultimately from its status as a gratuitous (substantial but nonessential) *ex Deo* creation. (Although initially subject to Chaos, as a state of completely disordered *potentia,* matter itself still derives ultimately from God rather than from Chaos.) At the same time, that freedom is part of what constitutes the rational order of Creation. In maintaining the mutual dependence of "Will and Reason (Reason also is choice)" (3.108), Milton attempts to avoid the extremes of both irrational voluntarism and deterministic rationalism. Prelapsarian Creation therefore consists not of a tension between freedom and rational order but of a complementary fulfillment of rational causation and free choice in one another (bifurcation of human will and reason being a consequence of the Fall). This account fits precisely with the libertarianism of *De Doctrina,* where each event "is the result of particular causes which, by [God's] decree, work quite freely" (YP 6:164). But the connection between the monism and the anticompatibilism of *Paradise Lost* will be missed if the reader attempts a dualist reading of the poem. If the phrase "one first matter" is taken to imply simply a neoplatonic ontology, the ensuing dualism will then allow for a compatibilist reading of the main argument. The reader can then maintain the central objection against compatibilist theodicy and dismiss the poem as a failure because it seems that God is still the ultimate cause of evil. Thus the poem's success in justifying the ways of God to men is inextricably connected not only to the libertarian account of human freedom but also to the conditional monism upon which the latter depends.

If we now recall Paul Sellin's criticism of *Paradise Lost* (discussed in Part I, above), we can see that, in effect, he ascribes to the poem (and the treatise) a compatibilist position. He does this by first minimizing the distinction between "predestination" and "determinism" (even though Milton's view of salvific election is both conditional and general), and then implying that, although Milton claims to believe in freedom of the will, his account of predestination is deterministic. This interpretation (as noted earlier) is substantiated by his problematic analysis of Book Three of the poem, yet the simple fact that such a compatibilist account renders the very idea of theodicy incoherent is apparently no cause for concern. If the poem's self-declared objectives are preemptively dismissed by the theological assumptions ascribed to the work, is it not fair to ask whether that ascription is accurate?

In arguing as strongly as I have that monism and subordinationism are implicit in *Paradise Lost,* my intention has not been to discount the many other points of disagreement between the epic and *De Doctrina* regarding, for example, Christology. Nor is my intention to dismiss Hunter's broader claim that Milton is not the original author of the treatise. At the outset of this investigation, I pointed out two possible ways in which the differences between the two works could be explained, suggesting that Milton may have either attempted to exploit the generic differences to support a larger theological project, or that he could have abandoned his revision of *De Doctrina* because he understood the broader theological implications of substituting the form of Ramist dialectic for the form of biblical narrative. The latter possibility fits well with the few commonly established facts regarding the *De Doctrina* manuscript upon which Hunter and the report by Campbell and others concur.[23] However, the two possibilities are not, in fact, mutually exclusive. Milton could have begun intending to accomplish the former but finally resigned himself to the latter. This hypothesis would explain both the points of unique congruence and the important differences between *Paradise Lost* and *De Doctrina.*

Hunter is certainly correct to point out that much of the evidence to support common authorship of the two works is simply evidence that both drew upon the Bible and the commonplaces of Reformation theology (50). This is why those arguing for Miltonic authorship of the treatise need to focus their arguments on specific points of unique heterodoxy upon which the treatise and the canon agree, and why Hunter bases his argument on those points of explicit disagreement that cannot be explained away. However, the initial fact of such generally similar theological sources for the particular two works raises an even deeper question that inhabits much of Reformation writing. Regardless of what we believe about their author(s), if both *Paradise Lost* and *De Doctrina* issue from within a theological ethos of *sola scriptura* (or even *sola conscientia*), why was either work written? What could either text claim to be offering that was not already present in the Bible (or conscience)? Even as the author of *De Doctrina* claims to be submitting entirely and solely to the authority of Scripture, his very writing of such a text simultaneously judges the logical arrangement of Scripture to be in need of some correction. Clearly, few people would have been more sensitive than Milton to the theological implications that follow from a Ramist ordering of biblical content that effectively deletes narrative. But how does Milton in *Paradise Lost* avoid involving himself in a similar presumption to improve upon Scripture? In brief, Milton shares in common with the author of the treatise a conscious antecedent submission to the authority of the scriptural text and a desire, not to improve upon Scripture, but rather to understand it in relation to their present situation. There is one crucial difference between them, however. Milton's sense of the truth of the biblical text includes submission to its literary form.

Although the epic involves numerous crucial elaborations and generic re-orderings of the biblical text, it reflects a clear understanding of the inextricable relation between biblical narrative form and doctrinal content. As a matter of course, Milton's elaboration of biblical narrative does potentially result in some important doctrinal implications, but the challenge for a writer like Milton, having such a rigorously biblicist orientation, is to make those embellishments so deeply scriptural in form and content that they are consistent with the "spirit," or *telos*, of the biblical metanarrative even in their substructure. This kind of teleonomic consistency with scriptural form is not even possible within the genre of a Ramist theological treatise, regardless of who the author may be, and I think Milton came to understand this limitation. It is therefore especially revealing that readers on both sides of the debate over the authorship of *De Doctrina* share in common a tendency to treat statements from the epic as if they were Ramist logical axioms. One possible objection to the account that I have just given is that Milton clearly had no qualms about attaching his name to the explicitly Ramist *Artis Logicae*. If so, why would he come to think so differently about employing Ramist method in theology, which simply amounts to an application of the kind of logic that he advocated? In fact, the idea that Milton would have *tried* to apply the principles of his own logic text fits perfectly with the account that I am proposing. Only after he had undertaken to revise *De Doctrina* (almost certainly the initial work of another writer) as an application of Ramist logic did he come to see the severity of the limitations imposed upon the biblical texts by stripping them from their narrative embedding.

University of Ottawa

NOTES

Financial support from the Social Sciences and Humanities Research Council of Canada enabled me to take the time required to complete this paper. I am very grateful to David L. Jeffrey and Nicholas von Maltzahn for their responses to earlier versions of the essay.

1. Paul R. Sellin, "John Milton's *Paradise Lost* and *De Doctrina Christiana* on Predestination," in *Milton Studies* 34, ed. Albert C. Labriola (Pittsburgh, 1996), 45. For a detailed account of the results of the stylistic analyses, see Gordon Campbell et al., "Final Report on the Provenance of *De Doctrina Christiana*," *Milton Quarterly* 31 (1997): 67–121. William Hunter, *Visitation Unimplor'd: Milton and the Authorship of De Doctrina Christiana* (Pittsburgh, 1998).

2. Hunter, *Visitation,* 148, 154–55. Cf. Cambell et al., 104–10. Arguments against Hunter's claim can be found in the essays by Christopher Hill, "Professor William B. Hunter, Bishop Burgess, and John Milton," *SEL* 34 (1994): 165–93, and Maurice Kelley, "The Provenance of John Milton's *Christian Doctrine:* A Reply to William B. Hunter," *SEL* 34 (1994): 153–63. Compare Barbara K. Lewalski, "Milton and *De Doctrina Christiana:* Evidences of Authorship," in *Milton Studies* 36, ed. Albert C. Labriola (Pittsburgh, 1998), 203–28. Lewalski's argument also attends specifically to Sellin's other related essay, "The Reference to John Milton's *Tetrachordon* in *De Doctrina Christiana*," *SEL* 37 (1997): 137–49. Most recently, Hunter and Sellin have published "Responses" and "Further Responses," respectively, in *Milton Quarterly* 33 (1999): 31–37, 38–51.

3. My analysis here focuses upon the arguments of Sellin and Hunter (cited parenthetically in what follows) because I find the ultimate direction of their position more credible. However, let me emphasize that both sides of this debate share in common the root interpretive problem that I am addressing. In fact, the opposing arguments are typically no less prone to the same difficulties that I point out here, but they suffer from even more basic logical errors and weaknesses. Unlike those of Sellin or Hunter, the arguments of their opponents cannot be remedied by qualification or nuance. For instance, to prove that both *De Doctrina* and *Paradise Lost* advocate an Arminian view of predestination does not, in itself, demonstrate that Milton wrote the treatise. It only shows a correlation that would exist between any two consistently Arminian works. At best, such proof can only (as Sellin points out) leave the question open. See, for example, Stephen M. Fallon's essay, "Milton's Arminianism and the Authorship of *De doctrina Christiana*," *Texas Studies in Literature and Language* 41 (1999): 103–27. Despite its exceptionally lucid exposition of the Arminianism in both works, and of Reformation theology more broadly, the essay never addresses the real crux of the debate over the authorship of the treatise —that is, the points of disagreement between the treatise and Milton's prose (q.v. Hunter, *Visitation,* 60–70, 90–98). Claims like Fallon's could be successful only as part of a much larger project based on what would amount to an argument from overwhelming circumstantial evidence. But even that kind of undertaking (as we find in Christopher Hill's essay cited above)

cannot succeed unless it first addresses the points of substantial inconsistency raised by Hunter. Otherwise, no amount of circumstantial correlation would ever prove conclusive.

Also important to emphasize at this point is that there is no logically necessary connection between a skeptical view regarding Miltonic authorship of the treatise and the attempt by some to normalize Milton's heterodox theology. Unfortunately, Hunter generally frames his argument in such a way that directly links the two issues (8–9). Similarly, counterarguments by Christopher Hill, among others, mistakenly mirror that same connection. In following the lead of Christopher Hill, those, like John Rumrich and Joseph Wittreich, who attempt to elaborate an account of Milton's heretical views continue to assume the unnecessary connection made by Hunter and Hill. See John P. Rumrich, "Milton's Arianism: Why It Matters," and Joseph Wittreich, "Milton's Transgressive Maneuvers: Receptions (Then and Now) and the Sexual Politics of *Paradise Lost*," both in *Milton and Heresy*, eds. Stephen B. Dobranski and John P. Rumrich (Cambridge, 1998), 75–92 and 244–66, respectively. See also the editorial introduction to that volume. In each of these more recent cases, the attitude toward the debate over *De Doctrina* reveals a failure to imagine that it is possible to insist upon Milton's (relative) heterodoxy while nevertheless remaining skeptical about the authorship of the treatise. But as each of those arguments inadvertently demonstrates, the evidence of Milton's heterodoxy is not limited to *De Doctrina*. Some of the objections raised by the essays in *Milton and Heresy* are taken up by Hunter in "Responses" and Sellin in "Further Responses."

4. Sellin, "John Milton's *Paradise Lost* and *De Doctrina Christiana* on Predestination," 50–51 (cf. 46–47). Sellin compares *Paradise Lost* 3.131–34 with the treatise, CM 14:90, 102 (YP 6:168, 175). My quotations from *Paradise Lost* are from *John Milton: Complete Poems and Major Prose*, ed. Merritt Y. Hughes (New York, 1957). English quotations from *De Doctrina* and Milton's prose are taken from *Complete Prose Works of John Milton*, 8 vols., ed. Donald M. Wolfe et al. (New Haven, 1953–82), hereafter designated YP and cited parenthetically by volume and page number in the text. References to the Latin texts are from *The Works of John Milton*, 18 vols., ed. Frank Allen Patterson et al. (New York, 1931–38), hereafter designated CM.

5. Stephen M. Fallon, *Milton among the Philosophers: Poetry and Materialism in Seventeenth-Century England* (Ithaca, 1991), 180–90. John P. Rumrich, in *Milton Unbound* (Cambridge, 1996), also picks up on Fallon's observation regarding Milton's use of allegory to display ontic privation (126–28, 179); however, Rumrich develops that point in importantly different directions from those indicated here. Rumrich's account of Chaos is often effective in countering some of the customary critical assumptions regarding Milton's materialism (e.g., pointing out the qualitative differences between the Satanic and Divine attempts to impose order on Chaos [124–27]). However, his description of Chaos as a quasi-hermaphroditic "feminine otherness" internal to God (145) is misleading for two reasons. First, his emphasis upon the "goodness" of Chaos obscures the fact that *Paradise Lost* clearly follows the biblical account of nature, by implying that Creation is unambiguously good in a way that Chaos is not. Second, by insisting that God, rather than Creation itself, is the opposing counterpart of Chaos (140–45), Rumrich risks imposing upon the epic a kind of gnostic dualism that is ethically inconsistent with the rest of the poem. For further discussion of Chaos in *Paradise Lost*, see also Catherine Gimelli Martin, "Fire, Ice and Epic Entropy," in *Milton Studies* 35, ed. Albert C. Labriola (Pittsburgh, 1997), 73–113. Both Rumrich and Martin describe Milton's emphasis upon indeterminacy in ways that are partially consonant with the present argument. At the same time, the distinction I make here between matter and Chaos must not be misunderstood as one more example of what Martin calls the "critical tradition that unself-reflexively associates disorder with evil" (107). Rather, I submit that the epic, while affirming the goodness of matter per se, nevertheless depicts chaos (the principle allegorically presented as the character "Chaos") as, in itself, literally not-a-thing—it is ontologically only a state of pure *potentia*. Thus, while absolute chaos does, in

this sense, stand completely apart from issues of moral good and evil, there remains within Milton's cosmology and ontology a clear link between a given rational creature's evil choices and a movement toward the chaos of unbeing—which is simply to say that Milton viewed sin as a kind of self-destruction. Both Rumrich and Martin, despite the great subtlety and learning that they bring to their consideration of Chaos, tend to obscure this moral dynamic that I take to be central to the epic.

The above essay by Martin presents part of the argument that she unfolds more fully in her recent book, *The Ruins of Allegory* (Durham, N.C., 1998). I concur with her attempt to distinguish Milton's aesthetic and philosophic position from the ascendant "neoclassical rationalism" of the Restoration (11; see also 178–79). However, the extent of Martin's emphasis upon Chaos tends toward a serious distortion of the epic. For example, she maintains that "Chaos also provides an imaginative bridge between the realms of physical and metaphysical causality" (165). In effect, Martin, like Rumrich, seems to substitute a gnostic Chaos for a Christian *Logos*. Similarly, although she does distinguish between the good of created indeterminacy and the evil of Satan's chaotic self-consumption (165), she fails to consider the necessary basis for that very distinction. Only by presuming that *caritas*, not Chaos, is the ultimate basis of creaturely freedom and ontic reality can Milton (or Martin) distinguish intelligibly between the two kinds of indeterminacy. Within Milton's cosmology, "reason also is a choice" (*PL* 3.108), not because chaotic indeterminacy is the root of goodness (as Martin implies), but because true *caritas* entails for rational creatures the indeterminacy of genuine freedom.

6. Fallon, *Milton among the Philosophers*, 127.

7. For a detailed response to Fallon's position see my essay, "'Matter' versus Body: The Character of Milton's Monism," *Milton Quarterly* 33 (1999): 79–85. In the following treatment of Milton's monism I incorporate part of my previous argument, which fully substantiates claims presented here only in brief.

8. Hunter insists that the *Artis Logicae* is irrelevant on this point because it "discusses the material causes of things but does not argue the question of how matter originates" (*Visitation*, 122); however, I submit that (notwithstanding the accuracy of Hunter's claim) the author of *De Doctrina* in the passage cited here directly echoes the logic text's treatment of the relation between form and matter (something even Hunter would expect from one of Milton's former students). Again, regardless of whether Milton is the original author of the theological work, the echoes of the logic text are clearly relevant to the argument of the doctrinal treatise. Even if we take such a view, however, it remains a point in question whether Milton would have agreed with the author of *De Doctrina* in applying the terms of causation from *Artis Logicae* to an account of originary first matter. This is precisely why I maintain that the epic narrative voice handles the chaotic state of first matter in the indirect (allegorical) way that it does. In his recent "Responses," Hunter insists that Raphael's "Scale of Nature" speech does not apply to pre-Creation chaos because "such unity must be restricted to the created cosmos" (33). On that point I agree: to be created at all is to exist—Raphael's concern in that context is with things that are. Hence he makes no mention of the pre-ontological status of matter. Thus the treatment of first matter in *Paradise Lost* does not explicitly contradict the treatise, so much as question the degree to which the condition of matter in a state of complete chaos can be intelligibly discussed using direct terms.

9. Fallon, *Milton among the Philosophers*, 102.

10. Regarding *De Doctrina*'s distinction between "substance" and "essence," see William B. Hunter, "Further Definitions: Milton's Theological Vocabulary," in *Bright Essence: Studies in Milton's Theology*, eds. W. B. Hunter, C. A. Patrides, and J. H. Adamson (Salt Lake City, 1971), 19–21.

11. Wendell Berry, "Poetry and Place," in *Standing by Words* (San Francisco, 1983), 104–5.

12. Erich Auerbach, *Mimesis: The Representation of Reality in Western Literature*, trans. Willard R. Trask (Princeton, 1953), 14–15.

13. Dennis Danielson, *Milton's Good God: A Study in Literary Theodicy* (Cambridge, 1982), 130.

14. Hunter, *Visitation*, 115. Cf. Thomas S. K. Scott-Craig, "The Craftsmanship and Theological Significance of Milton's *Art of Logic*," *Huntington Library Quarterly* 17 (1953): 1–16.

15. YP 8:234, as quoted and altered in Hunter, *Visitation*, 115–16.

16. Hunter, *Visitation*, 116.

17. John Carey and Alastair Fowler, eds., *The Poems of John Milton* (London, 1968), 573.

18. Biblical quotations are from the Authorized King James Version.

19. Barbara K. Lewalski, *Milton's Brief Epic: The Genre, Meaning and Art of Paradise Regained* (London, 1966), 7–9, 103.

20. Hunter, *Visitation*, 113–14.

21. Indeed, some recent critical attention is devoted specifically to the recovery of that less well-known textual record of those who claimed to discern the Arianism of *Paradise Lost* long before the discovery of *De Doctrina*. See Rumrich, "Milton's Arianism," 76–77, and Michael E. Bauman, "Heresy in Paradise and the Ghost of Readers Past," *College Language Association Journal* 30 (1986): 59–68. For a broader consideration of the possibilities concerning Milton's association with some of the most heterodox elements on the far left wing of the Reformation see Christopher Hill, *Milton and the English Revolution* (London, 1977).

22. Danielson, *Milton's Good God*, 132.

23. Hunter, *Visitation*, 148, 154–55. Cf. Campbell et al., "Final Report on the Provenance of *De Doctrina Christiana*," 104–10.

"SUBSTANTIALLY EXPRESS'D": MILTON'S DOCTRINE OF THE INCARNATION

John C. Ulreich

I T I S A T R U T H universally acknowledged—at least among Miltonists—that the relation between *De Doctrina Christiana* and Milton's poetry is problematic. The various points at issue resemble "those confused seeds which were impos'd on *Psyche* as an incessant labour to cull out, and sort asunder."[1] Although scholarship during the last century and a half has done much to illuminate the complexities of Milton's theology, and to enrich our understanding of its poetic function, we still lack a satisfactory model to account for the intricate relation between Milton's theological ideas and their poetic expression. Maurice Kelley's attempt to show "that the treatise and the poem agree in their theological doctrines" has generally been persuasive and fruitful, but it has certainly not won universal assent.[2] Crucial doctrines in the treatise remain extremely controversial in themselves, and even when due allowance is made for the differences between prose argument and poetic representation, the doctrines set forth in the treatise are not always obviously consistent with the poetry. Kelley's conclusion, that *Paradise Lost* and *De Doctrina* express essentially the same "fundamental corpus of belief," needs refinement, not only to register more precisely the "different and distinctive manners" (195) of poetry and prose, but also to account more adequately for the *development* of Milton's theological ideas as they are worked out and refined in his poetry.

This essay proposes that we might usefully conceive of Milton's theological development as a process of incarnation. From this perspective, Milton's epics—especially *Paradise Regained*—can be seen as "radiant image[s]" in which the doctrinal conceptions of the treatise are "substantially expressed" (*PL* 3.63, 140). Milton's "dearest and best possession" (YP 6:121) should not be read simply as a gloss on the poetry; rather, the treatise and the poems must be seen as interdependent: doctrines that inform the poetry are themselves completed, and redefined, by their poetic expression.

In attempting to define this process, I borrow Sidney's conception of poetry as a "delivering forth" of the poet's idea, a substantial embodiment of his imaginative activity. According to this hypothesis, the treatise represents an "*idea* or fore-conceit" that the poetry "figures forth,"[3] so that ideas formulated in prose are actualized in the concrete form of the poetry (*PL* 10.587). In other words, *De Doctrina*, taken as a whole, constitutes the "ground plot" for the "profitable invention" of Milton's last poems: the relatively abstract theological structure of the treatise *informs* the metaphoric energy of the poems, as their soul or first principle. Ideas conceived in the treatise, as theory, are concretely *embodied* in the poems as crucial sources of their imaginative life.

Employing this dynamic model, we can discern more clearly and fully the way in which treatise and poems complement each other, not simply as diverse expressions of a "fundamental corpus of belief" (Kelley, 195), but as an interrelation of body and spirit. As the theory is expressed—worked out experimentally—it is no doubt modified; at the same time, the concreteness of the poetry illuminates the theology and so enables us to grasp some of its deeper significance. More importantly, however, the idea itself provides a sort of conceptual model for interpreting the poetry, not as a prose abstract of poetic meaning, but as an informing principle. Treatise and poems are thus to be regarded, not as statement and embellishment, or theme and variations, but as soul and body, formal definition and material expression, wholly interdependent. And when we conceive this interrelation as a polarity—an interplay of contrary impulses rather than a multiplication of identities—we can better see the innovative character of Milton's poetic theology. His heresies— for such I take them to be: "after the way which they call heresy, so worship I the God of my fathers"[4]—appear not merely self-consistent but actively productive of new insight; his ideas are not simply heterodox, in the technical sense, but prophetic, and thus progenitive, because they create new doctrine. Whereas the treatise is grounded in revelation, the poetry constitutes a new revelation, by which revelation itself must be reinterpreted; from this fusion arises Milton's radical theology.[5]

It is in this fashion, I believe, that the doctrine of the Incarnation, briefly sketched in the treatise, informs the structure of Milton's epics, where the notion of progressive incarnation is embodied and realized. Milton's theory of the Incarnation itself, as set forth in Chapter 14 of *De Doctrina*, "Of . . . Christ the Redeemer" (YP 6:418–29), provides both an analogy for the poetic process and a case very much in point: notwithstanding its apparent obscurity, the doctrine sketched in the treatise, defined in terms of its Catholic antecedents and Protestant precedents, clarifies the meaning of the poetry, especially *Paradise Regained*. Conversely, the poetry reveals the deeper meaning of the doctrine.

THE GREATEST MYSTERY OF OUR RELIGION

Catholic Antecedents: Aquinas and Origen

Milton's conception of the Incarnation seems, on the face of it, heretical. He insists that Christ is formed from a "hypostatic union," not merely of "two natures," as the orthodox suppose, but "of two persons," divine and human (YP 6:423, 424). According to the doctrine promulgated by the Council of Chalcedon in 451, Christ is "known *in (of) two natures*"—not persons— "*without confusion, without conversion, without severance, and without division;* the distinction of the natures being in no wise abolished by their union, but the peculiarity of each nature being maintained, and both concurring in one person and hypostasis."[6] Now, Milton's affirmation that two modes of being, divine and human, are joined in the person of the Christ in such a way that each "remain[s] individually distinct" (YP 6:424) is perfectly orthodox. Where he departs from orthodoxy is in his insistence that the "mutual hypostatic union [*unio . . . hypostatica*)] of two natures [*naturarum*]" is necessarily a conjunction "of two essences [*essentiarum*], of two substances [*substantiarum*] and consequently of two persons [*personarum*]" (YP 6:423, 424; CM 15:268, 270). The orthodox view was formulated precisely to deny that the divine Logos was joined with the human *person* of Jesus. As H. A. Wolfson has observed, according to the creed of Chalcedon, "it is 'God the Logos' that constitutes the one person or the one hypostasis in Jesus; the humanity in him is only a nature."[7]

In order to define as clearly as possible the contours of Milton's heresy— to clarify the crucial terms (*nature* and *person*) and disentangle Milton's beliefs from the labels that have been attached to them—it is useful to have recourse to the arguments of scholastic philosophy. As Heiko Oberman has shown, "medieval scholasticism, primarily due to the incompatibility of Greek and Latin idiom, had to find its way through trial and effort back to the formulations of Chalcedon."[8] Oberman identifies "three distinct interpretations of . . . the bond between the two natures in Jesus Christ": (1) "the *assumptus* theory," according to which "not human nature, *humanitas,* but a human person, *homo,* is taken into the divine Person"; (2) "the *subsistence* theory," which holds that "two natures are carried by one *hypostasis*"; and (3) "the *habitus* theory . . . that the immutable God . . . dressed himself in the human nature as in a mantle" (251–52). The first and third theories were rejected by the church, on the grounds that they were tainted by Nestorian emphases, and the *subsistence* theory formulated by Aquinas eventually achieved orthodox status.

Milton's doctrine is clarified by its relation to all three theories. Although he frequently uses *habitus* similes in his earlier poetry,[9] he emphatically rejects the doctrine in the treatise: "The fact that Christ had a body shows that he was a real man" (YP 6:426). Milton's argument does show some affinity with the *assumptus* heresy, inasmuch as he insists that it is not possible to assume human nature (*naturam humanam*) without also assuming man (*hominem;* CM 15:266). At the same time, however, he insists that the union of the two natures was intrinsic rather than accidental, and hence indissoluble: "the Son of God . . . was made flesh and . . . is called and is in fact both God and man . . . θεάνθρωπος" (YP 6:424). Neither theory accounts satisfactorily for Milton's doctrine. Consequently, the distinctive features of his theory are most clearly seen in contrast with the orthodox view, as represented by Aquinas's formulation of the *subsistence* theory.[10]

According to Aquinas, "the union of the Word with man [is] a union of natures," not of persons: "two natures in the Word become one," so that "two [distinct] natures [divine and human] truly persist in Christ's one person." The closest analogy with this mystery is "the union of rational soul with the body. The analogy is not with the soul as the form of the body, for the Word's relation to human nature cannot be like that of form to matter, but with the soul as using the body as its instrument." We should not be misled by analogy, however, for "the Incarnation is a unique union, surpassing every communion known to us . . . a union in which human nature is taken into the person of the Word," so that "one simple divine Person subsists in two natures, divine and human."[11]

Milton's view of the Incarnation stands in flat contradiction to Aquinas's: "what a[n] absurd idea," he argues, "that someone should take human nature upon himself without taking manhood as well!" (YP 6:422) "Obviously the Logos became what it assumed, and if it assumed human nature, but not manhood, then it became an example of human nature, not a man. But, of course, the two things are really inseparable" (YP 6:422–23). If we were to suppose that "Christ's human nature never had its own separate subsistence [as a person], or . . . [that] the son did not take that subsistence upon himself: it would follow that he could not have been a real man, and that he could not have taken upon himself the true and perfect substance or essence of man" (YP 6:223). To avoid this absurdity, Milton argues, we must conclude that there is "in Christ a mutual hypostatic union . . . of two substances and consequently of two persons" (YP 6:424).[12]

Apart from this heterodox insistence that Christ was an actual union of two persons, not merely of two natures, Milton's discussion of "the greatest mystery of our religion" (YP 6:420) is surprisingly reticent. All that we can certainly know about the mystery of the *theanthropos* is "that the Son of God, our Mediator, was made flesh and that he is called and is in fact both God and man." And since "God has not revealed to us how this comes about it is much better for us to hold our tongues and be wisely ignorant" (YP 6:424). Milton then goes on to advance the startling proposition that "the opinion I have advanced here about the hypostatic union corroborates further the conclusion of my more lengthy discussion of the Son of God in the fifth chapter" (YP 6:424–25). The basis of this corroboration, however, is not immediately apparent. In Chapter 5 Milton had argued that the *persons* of the Father and the Son are wholly distinct: "the essence of the Father cannot be communicated to another person" (YP 6:225). "Two distinct things cannot be of the same essence. God is one being, not two" (YP 6:212). But if two (or three) persons cannot subsist in one being, how can one being, Jesus of Nazareth, be simultaneously two persons, both God and man? Milton would seem to have imported into his treatment of the Incarnation the very mystery he had sought to banish by rejecting orthodox Trinitarianism, "the bizarre and senseless idea that the Son, although personally and numerically distinct, was nevertheless essentially one"—not, to be sure, with the Father, but with the man Jesus (YP 6:212).

Moreover, Milton's ostensible distinction between *nature* and *person* is not strictly or consistently maintained. Though his rejection of the orthodox position is emphatic enough, he then goes on to speak as though the distinction were of no real consequence, inasmuch as "the two things [human nature and manhood] are really inseparable" (YP 6:423): "*nature* can mean nothing in this context except the essence itself," which is to say the person (YP 6:423). Milton is therefore content to speak of a "hypostatic union of two natures or, in other words, of two essences, of two substances and consequently of two persons" (YP 6:424). Given this concession to orthodox terminology, and his admonition to "let mysteries alone and not tamper with them" (YP 6:421), why does Milton go out of his way to invite the charge of heresy?

Milton's underlying purpose in all this would seem to be to deny that "the person who was made flesh must necessarily be the supreme God" (YP 6:425). This intention gives rise, not only to Milton's heterodox view of Christ's personality, but to an even more radical proposition, that the Incarnation is a twofold process: "the Logos became what it assumed,"[13] both God and man, first by uniting itself with the already human person of Jesus, and then by participating consciously and *voluntarily* in God's will (YP 6:416, 417). In other words, Milton's purpose in asserting the manhood of Christ would seem to be, not to deny that human nature is joined with Christ, but to affirm that humanity can be redeemed only through the individual choice of a fully independent human will. Here we begin to glimpse the deeper consistency, as well as the radical unorthodoxy, of Milton's position: if "the essence of the Son" were "the same as the essence of the Father," then "the Son could not have coalesced in one person with man, unless the Father had also been included in the same union—unless, in fact, man had become one person with the Father as well as with the Son, which is impossible" (YP 6:425). From this argument it would appear that Milton's anti-Trinitarianism in fact grew out of his radical opinions about the Incarnation, which were shaped in turn by his belief in the indispensable freedom of the human (as well as the divine) will. When Christ *voluntarily* fulfills the will of the Father, he does so not as an agency of the Father Himself but in his independent person as both "a real man" (YP 6:426) and as "God's beloved Son" (YP 6:425).

In effect, Milton rationalizes one mystery, the Trinity, in order to deepen the mystery of the Incarnation: no man can become one with the Father, but all men may become one with the Son, by participating *consciously* in "his death, burial and resurrection" (YP 6:544). Citing (*inter alia*) Colossians 2:9, "the whole fullness of the godhead dwells in him bodily," Milton argues that "*bodily* [*corporaliter*] ought to be interpreted as meaning *in reality* [*revera*]," and he consequently prefers to read "*fullness* [*plenitudo*] as *fulfilment* [*impletionem*]." Milton therefore takes the passage to mean "that the entire fulfilment of the Father's promises resides in, but is not hypostatically united with Christ as a man" (YP 6:419; CM 15:260). In other words, whatever Christ's nature is potentially, he becomes incarnate Word, not simply by embodying, but by *consciously* enacting the will of the Father. Thus, taking the word *body* to imply *reality*, we can conceive of the Incarnation as a twofold process in which what had been potential in the Son becomes actual in the human consciousness of Jesus.

Milton's understanding of the Incarnation as a conscious realization of God's will stands in stark contrast to the orthodox dogma. According to Aquinas, "the Word who was with God assumed flesh, not a man already existing," not in any sense "an individual man who became God": "Christ's humanity was like an instrument of his divinity" (*Theological Texts*, 282, 302). For Aquinas, as Thomas Gilby observes, the Incarnation "is the real embodiment of the Word in human history, an event which is physically effective as well as morally instructive."[14] Milton does not deny the physical reality of the event, but he is much more concerned with its moral and spiritual consequences than with any sort of "bodily" effect. For Aquinas, a sacrament is "the visible figure of invisible grace, bearing its likeness and serving as its cause"; by this means "the grace running from the Incarnate Word is admirably led along the channels of sense": Christ "come[s] through to men in bodily fashion" (*Theological Texts*, 350, 154, 354). For Milton, participation in the sacraments is wholly spiritual: "the mere flesh is of no use here," he argues, for "it is the Spirit which gives life and it is faith which feeds" (YP 6:553, 557).[15]

Milton's anti-traditional and anti-corporeal understanding of sacramental efficacy bears directly on his conception of the Incarnation. For Aquinas, "The Creature can be conjoined to God in three ways. First, by likeness only, when it reflects divine goodness but does not reach to the divine substance: this is the common causal presence of God in all things. Secondly, by reaching as well to God's substance through the activity of mind and heart . . . : this is the special presence of God in the soul by grace. Thirdly, by reaching to God's substance by its very being, not merely by its activity: this is God's presence in the Incarnation" (*Theological Texts,* 68).

For Milton there is no way in which the creature can be "conjoined to God": "the essence of the Father cannot be communicated to another person" (YP 6:225), still less to a created being. There are, however, two (not three) ways in which men may be called sons of God. First "by virtue of our very nature" (YP 6:495); Satan and other angels are also sons of God in this sense: "the Son of God I also am, or was" (*PR* 4.518). The second mode of sonship is by *adoption,* whereby "we become sons by a new generation and a new nature" (YP 6:497). These two forms of sonship resemble Aquinas's first two forms of participation, likeness and substantial activity; for Milton, there is no third. So, when the Word is "found / By Merit more than Birthright Son of God" (*PL* 3.308–9), Milton seems to imply that He has been *adopted* as God's Son, as if "by a new generation and a new nature." Aquinas, of course, denies that Christ could "be termed God's son by adoption, for he is begotten eternally by the Father" (*Theological Texts,* 156).

In effect, Milton has asserted an essential difference between Father and Son in order to minimize the difference between the Son and those who are regenerated as God's sons. His discussion of the Incarnation does not admit Aquinas's distinction between activity and being, *except* in connection with the relation between Father and Son. They share one substance—a substance in which man also participates through the Logos—but they are distinct in essence. The only union that Milton admits between the Son and the Father, other than their consubstantiality, is that "reaching . . . to God's substance through the activity of mind and heart," which Aquinas calls "the special presence of God in the soul by grace" (*Theological Texts,* 68). For Milton, that grace is common to all believers: "Christ has received his fulness from God . . . [just] as . . . we shall receive ours from Christ" (YP 6:273). In other words, as Christ has been adopted by God, so may we be adopted by Christ, becoming sons of God through the mediation of the Word. As Christopher Hill has observed, "Milton never emphasized Christ's humanity at the cost of denying his divinity—far from it; but he did stress the possibility of the unity of believers with Christ in sonship."[16] Christ and "the Father are one in the same way as we are one with him: that is, not in essence but in love, in communion, in agreement, in charity, in spirit, and finally in glory" (YP 6:220).

The heterodox implications of this analogy—Christ/God : humanity/ Christ—can be further illuminated by considering possible influences on Milton's formulation. William B. Hunter has shown that Milton's theory closely resembles, in some respects, "the heresy of Nestorius . . . that in Christ a divine person and a human person were joined." In Hunter's view, "Milton denied that human nature in general was the object of the Incarnation, affirming instead that only one individual was involved."[17] I think that Hunter overstates the problem, inasmuch as Milton holds that *manhood* and *human nature* are the same thing, and that *all* of redeemed humanity, "As from a second root shall be restor'd . . . And live in thee transplanted . . . Thir Nature also to thy Nature joyn; / And be thy self Man among men on Earth, / Made flesh" (*PL* 3.288, 293, 282–84). Indeed, as Barbara K. Lewalski has argued, "Milton's discussion of the actions of Christ after the hypostatic union assumes a unification much more complete and total than even the orthodox theory provides for."[18] The Incarnate Word speaks as one person, both divine and human: "Once his two natures [*naturae*] have coalesced hypostatically into a single person [*personam*], whatever Christ says of himself he must say it (unless he makes a distinction himself) not as if he possessed one nature or the other, but as a whole person speaking about a whole person" (YP 6:228; CM 14:228).

It would seem, therefore, that Milton's purpose in arguing for the coalescence of two persons was to assert, not that only one individual was joined to God, but that human nature is potentially capable of that union with divinity actually enjoyed by Christ's manhood, which was *his* human nature. For as Hunter himself goes on to observe, "the union of the elect with the Son is accomplished by each individual rather than by the common human nature of each." Indeed, Milton uses the same word, *coalescere,* to define both the Incarnation and the communion of "believers in the mystical body of Christ."[19]

Aquinas's objection to Nestorius brings Milton's doctrine into sharp relief: "The Nestorian conclusion was that the human person of Christ was distinct from the divine person. . . . This doctrine disagrees with the Holy Scriptures, which speak differently of Christ and of men in whom the Word of God dwells by grace" (*Theological Texts,* 288). Whether it be scriptural or not, Milton emphatically asserts the distinction of human and divine persons in Jesus at the same time that he denies Aquinas's distinction between Christ and other men in whom the Logos dwells. Though he does not deny the uniqueness of Christ, the distinction that Milton is chiefly concerned to draw is between Father and Son, not between the Son and men in whom grace dwells. Indeed, the complete indwelling of grace might be said to constitute a definition of the Incarnation, once *actual*—"in him all his Father shon, / Substantially express'd" (*PL* 3.139–40)—now *in body:* "Thir Nature also to thy Nature joyn" (3.282).

In effect, Milton seems to suggest that the Logos is incarnate in all redeemed souls. This doctrine, as it happens, resembles not so much the Nestorian heresy as the teaching of Origen. As Harry F. Robins has shown, Origen's heterodox theology is strikingly congruent with Milton's, and their theories of the Incarnation would seem to be no exception.[20] According to Origen, the Logos, who is the Son of God but is not Himself God the Father, assumes "a being that has a human soul and body": "The power and divinity of God come to dwell among men through the man whom God wills to choose and in whom He finds room."[21] In the Incarnation the Logos becomes (in Milton's words) "a real man" (YP 6:426): "The Son of God . . . took not only a human body, as some suppose, but also a soul, and one like our souls in nature, but like Himself in purpose and power, and such as could fulfill without turning all the wishes and dispensations of the Word."[22] If anything, Origen is more emphatic than Milton about the distinctness of Jesus's human person: the term "Son of Man" must always be "understood to refer to the Man in relation to Jesus" (*Exhortation* 35; 67). As Eugene de Faye observes, the Logos has "united to himself" not human nature but the individual humanity of "Jesus, the son of Mary"; "He loses nothing of his own nature through this union; he simply cohabits with Jesus and remains himself." At the same time, however, the union of the two persons is not a mere juxtaposition; it constitutes an "organic unity": "the man Jesus becomes transformed by contact with the Logos" so that "his mortal and his human soul become transmuted into divinity."[23] As far as it goes, this would seem to be a reasonably concise description of Milton's belief—closer to Milton, in fact, than the Nestorian heresy, which argues a mere juxtaposition of the two persons.

The two writers' affinity becomes even more apparent when we consider Origen's tendency to equate the Word incarnate with incarnations of the Word in other souls: "each member of the Church must pray that he may make way for the Father's will in just the same way that Christ made way for it, when He came to do His Father's will (cf. Jn. 4:34) and perfected it completely" (*On Prayer* 26:3; 135). This statement, it seems to me, constitutes a very useful gloss on Milton's suggestion that "Christ has received his fulness from God in the same sense as that in which we shall receive ours from Christ" (YP 6:273). For as Origen asserts, "it is possible for the one united to Him to become one Spirit with Him" (*On Prayer* 26:3; 135). Origen does maintain a distinction between Christ and other souls in whom the

Logos dwells: "we do not say that the Son of God was in [Christ's] soul the way He was in the soul of Paul or of Peter or of the other saints in whom Christ is believed to speak," for they were not "clean of defilement" as He was, whose soul "chose good before it knew evil" (*First Principles* 4:4; 209). But this distinction is less crucial than the likeness that Origen asserts between the Word Incarnate in Jesus and the incarnation of the Word in holy souls.

Where Aquinas asserts a single Revelation of the Word, Origen imagines repeated incarnations: "In each generation His Word descends into holy souls" (*Contra Celsum* 4:4; 186). Whatever good has happened among men, he argues, has occurred when "the divine Logos . . . has visited the souls of those who are able, even if but for a short time, to receive these operations of the divine Logos" (*Contra Celsum* 6:78; 392). The whole emphasis of Origen's Christology is upon every man's participation "in the Logos of God" (*Contra Celsum* 5:1; 264): "those who in many places teach the doctrine of Jesus rightly and live an upright life are themselves also called Christs by the divine scriptures" (*Contra Celsum* 6:79; 392). Or as Milton has it, the function of Christ's "mediatorial ministry is to shape us in Christ's image" through participation in his divinity (YP 6:450).

Protestant Precedents: Luther and the Radical Reformers

In view of the foregoing account, Milton's doctrine seems very close to that of Origen. Where Milton goes beyond Origen is in his suggestion that the Incarnation involves a twofold process: of actualization (the infusion of the divine person into the human) and embodiment (the realization of its divine potential by the human nature of Jesus). That which is potential in Jesus, his God-given substance, is actualized by a conscious incarnation of the Logos. For this radical development I have discovered no precedent among the early Church fathers. To find instructive analogues to Milton's thinking we must turn our attention to developments in Reformation theology. Three indications seem to me worthy of attention: (1) the popular belief that Christians actually embody the Christ; (2) the doctrinal understanding of Scripture itself as a sacrament, the spoken incarnation of God's word; and (3) the consequent spiritualization of Gospel narratives as foreshadowings of that which is to be born within us. The first and third ideas are found in the writings of Milton's radical Protestant contemporaries, Gerrard Winstanley and John Everard. The theological link between them, and between them and Milton, is Martin Luther's conception of preaching as a verbal sacrament.

An idea implicit in Scripture is that those who "receive . . . the divine Logos" are (in a sense) the Christ incarnate: All those who "submit [them]selves . . . unto the Lord . . . are members of his body, of his flesh, and of his bones" (Ephesians 5:22, 30). The understanding of this corporate metaphor as signifying an actual Incarnation of the Logos was especially characteristic of radical Protestant thinking in seventeenth-century England. The millenarian social Gospel of the Digger, Gerrard Winstanley, is a case in point. In *The Mysterie of God Concerning the Whole Creation,* Winstanley declared that "God now appears in the flesh of the saints." In *The Breaking of the Day of God,* he asserted that "the same spirit [which] filled Christ . . . should in these last days be sent into whole mankind." In *The Saints Paradice* he concluded that Christ is in everyone: "that perfect man . . . shall be no other but God manifest in the flesh."[24]

Milton would likely not have approved of Winstanley's secular allegorization of Scripture, but he did endorse the principle of Christian liberty that authorized Winstanley's imaginative re-interpretation of biblical themes and images: "men should be free not only to sift and winnow any doctrine, but also openly to give their opinions of it and even to write about it, according to what each believes" (YP 6:122). Milton also embraced the idea of divine sonship that grounds Winstanley's social theory: "Every creature . . . is a Son to the Father" (Winstanley, *The Breaking,* 131–32). In *Paradise Lost,* God's "accepted Son" looks forward to the time when "All my redeemed may dwell in joy and bliss, / Made one with me as I with thee am one" (11.46, 43–44). As Denis Saurat has argued, "Christ incarnates into a number of men, who become his mystical body; he is in each, he is in all, they are one in him. . . . Christ is the creator of Regenerated Man, is Regenerated Man: that part of God incarnated in the Elect."[25] According to *De Doctrina:* "The growth of the regenerate man . . . which relates to Father and Son is union or communion with the Father in Christ, the Son, and glorification in Christ's image. . . . It is from this union . . . with the Father and with Christ, and among the members of Christ's body themselves, that there comes into being that mystic body, the invisible church, the head of which is Christ (YP 6:498–99).

Like the metaphor of incorporation in Christ's mystical body, the doctrine that believers become sons of God is biblical. According to St. Paul, "As many as are led by the Spirit of God, they are the sons of God" (Romans 8:14). But the theological nexus that links that belief with the idea of the mystical body and with Milton's doctrine of the Incarnation is most clearly suggested by the Reformation understanding that the preaching of Scripture enacts a verbal sacrament, in which the Word is really present to whose who receive it with faith. By the proclamation of Scripture the Word becomes incarnate in the words of the preacher.

According to Martin Luther, the preaching of the Word is the Word: "I hear the sermon; but who is speaking? The minister? No, indeed! You do not hear the minister. True, the voice is his; but my God is speaking the Word which he preaches or speaks."[26] Luther's affirmation became an integral part of Calvin's systematic theology. Commenting on the Gospel of John, Calvin writes: "the Evangelist call[s] the Son of God *the Speech* [*Sermo*] . . . first, because he is the eternal Wisdom and Will of God; and, secondly, because he is the lively image of His Purpose; for, as *Speech* is said to be among men the image of the mind, so it is not inappropriate to apply this to God, and to say that He reveals himself to us by his *Speech.*"[27] This understanding of the Incarnate Word entails a major shift in sacramental predication, from the *elements* in which Christ's body and blood are manifested to the *words* by which Christ's presence is proclaimed. As Robert L. Entzminger has observed, in Calvin's theology, "only baptism and the Eucharist retain their sacramental character, and he shifted the locus of the union between God and the participants from the ceremony and its elements to the word which makes its meaning clear."[28]

Luther and Calvin attribute to preaching the efficacy of a sacrament, in which the Christ is really present to those who believe. Their understanding of the "real presence" became the general doctrine of Reformed theology, as it was formulated by Heinrich Bullinger in his *Confessio Helvetica Posterior:* "When this Word of God is proclaimed . . . [it is] the very Word of God"— *Praedicatio verbi Dei est verbum Dei.*[29]

As Heiko Oberman has shown, this "equation of the preached word with the Word of God" affirms the actual and "certain presence of the Word of God in the mouth of the preacher . . . the living authority and actualization of the Scriptures." For medieval Catholicism, the sermon is a preparation; its function is "to dispose the fallen Christian for the infusion of grace in the sacrament. . . . Only in the sacraments is communication between God and Man established." For the Reformers, however, the proclamation of the Word is "not a *preparation* for the encounter with the sphere of the holy but the *decisive* encounter with the Holy One himself. . . . Jesus Christ becomes present under the veil of the preached Word."[30]

For Protestants, therefore, preaching itself becomes a sacrament: like the visible Word, the audible Word becomes *actually present,* not according to "the medieval doctrine of tran-substantiation of the elements, but [according to] the apostolic doctrine . . . [whereby] the dispersed congregation is assembled and changed into the body of Christ" (Oberman, 227). In other words, that "real presence" of the Word experienced by Catholics in the transubstantial Eucharist would also, and especially, be experienced by Protestants in the hearing of the Word, so that the Word uttered becomes, in effect, the Word incarnate, "that mystic body . . . the head of which is Christ" (YP 6:499). As Oberman explains, "the administration of the Word itself is understood as a corporate action" in which "those who receive the promise of the Gospel with true faith are . . . changed into the body of Christ" ("Refor-mation," 227, 224, 227). Milton does not attribute such efficacy to preaching itself, but the logocentric theology of the Reformers presses directly upon Milton's notion of our communion with Christ as a "participation through the spirit" (YP 6:499). For *praedicatio* means not simply 'preaching' but 'procla-mation'; the real presence of the Word is communicated by "process of speech" (*PL* 7.178): *Praedicatio verbi Dei est verbum Dei.*

As Georgia B. Christopher has shown, the emphasis of Reformation theology on "encountering the Real Presence in biblical" texts profoundly influenced Milton's "belief in a 'verbal' sacrament."[31] By embracing the "analogy that Father and Son are related as 'speaker' and 'speech,'" Luther precipitated a radical transformation in "the locus of religious experience from visual symbol and ritual action to verbal action" (Christopher, 4). As a consequence of this shift, "God makes himself present to man," not so much through the consecrated elements of the Communion as through "the dy-namic processes of speech" (Christopher, 176). Accordingly, interpreting the sacred text becomes itself a sacramental act: the spoken word manifests "the *verbum reale*" of Scripture (Christopher, 102). Because "Christ [is] assumed to be present"—somehow incarnate—in "the verbal sign," the proc-lamation of that sign becomes "for Luther a de facto sacrament" (Christo-pher, 121).[32]

Now, inasmuch as Communion had been for Catholics the *sign* par excellence of the Incarnation itself, the shift of sacramental predication from bread and wine to *Verbum Dei* necessitates a reformulation of the terms in which the Incarnation must be imagined. And as I hope to show presently, the Lutheran conception of the *verbum reale* informs Milton's representation of the Son, not only in *Paradise Regained,* where the implications of Re-formed ideology are most fully worked out, but also in *Paradise Lost,* where the idea is only implied.

Even more striking than Luther's doctrine, however, is the typological image of Christ presented by Milton's fellow Englishman, John Everard, in his *Gospel-Treasury Opened.* Lewalski has explored the tendency of Protes-tant typology to shift its hermeneutic focus from the collective events of history to the individual process of spiritual self-discovery. As a consequence of this figural internalization, the antitypal fulfillment of Old Testament types came to be associated less with the incarnate Christ of the New Testament than with the spiritual life of the contemporary Christian, so that all types, including the antitype, Christ, came to be seen as "correlative types, re-capitulating the situation of Israel of old . . . in that they await afar off the millennial antitypical fulfillment of all the types."[33] Historically speaking, that fulfillment remains "afar off," but from the believer's point of view it is *now,* as one finds one's spirit transformed by the living presence of the Christ. Everard's writing strikingly illustrates this internalized typology. In his radically Protestant hermeneutic, even the words of Scripture, and the historical truth embodied in the letter of the New Testament, are only vehicles of the Spirit. "External Jesus Christ," he asserts, "is a *shadow,* a symbole, a figure of the *Internal:* viz. of him *that is to be born* within us. In our Souls."[34]

Milton presents an analogous understanding of Scripture in *De Doctrina:*

> We have, particularly under the gospel, a double scripture. There is the external scripture of the written word and the internal scripture of the Holy Spirit . . . engraved upon the hearts of believers, and . . . the pre-eminent and supreme authority . . . is the authority of the Spirit, which is internal, and the individual possession of each man. . . . [Indeed,] the Spirit which is given to us is a more certain guide than scripture, and . . . we ought to follow it.(Book 1, Chapter 30; YP 6:587, 589)

In accordance with this duality of letter and spirit, Christ's "prophetic function has two parts, one external and one internal. The first is the revelation of divine truth, the second the illumination of the mind" (YP 6:432). Those who have been thus illuminated by "the spirit [of] truth" possess within themselves "the mind of Christ" (583). In other words, the external Word of God "is a *shadow,* a symbole, a figure of the *Internal.*"

This seems to me a very apt description of the way Milton represents the Son in *Paradise Regained,* not as an image of the historical Jesus, but as a prefiguration, *once actual,* of that which may be *embodied* in our souls. And it is in *Paradise Regained,* I think, that we can see most clearly how Milton's theory of the Incarnation as a twofold process, actual in one Man, potential in all men, shapes, and is in turn shaped by, his imaginative experience of Christ.

By Proof th' Undoubted Son of God

In his brief epic, Milton makes it abundantly clear that, until the moment of his climactic self-revelation, Jesus thinks and acts as "meer man" (*PR* 4.535). But he is also the Son of God. Satan places the Son on the pinnacle in order to learn "In what degree or meaning thou art call'd / The Son of God, which bears no single sence" (4.516–17). Not even Satan's literal-mindedness can obscure Milton's sense that "All men are," in some sense, "Sons of God" (4.520). Milton's purpose is to explore the special sense in which Jesus is "pronounc'd the Son of God" (4.513). When he sets out to prove that Jesus is "th' undoubted Son of God" (1.11), he seeks not merely to demonstrate but to test the nature of Christ's sonship. "In what degree or meaning" is thus an even more urgent question for Jesus himself than it is for Satan. He knows that he is to be the "Saviour to mankind" (1.187), but he does not yet know how he is to fulfill that office; in fact, he does not fully know who he is. As he is led into the wilderness, he simply conforms his patient will to a divine impulse at work in him:

> And now by some strong motion I am led
> Into this Wilderness, to what intent
> I learn not yet, perhaps I need not know:
> For what concerns my knowledge God reveals.   (1.290–93)

Ultimately, of course, Jesus does need to know what God intends, and that self-discovery is the primary reason for the Father's allowing the Son to be tempted: "To exercise him in the Wilderness" so that he might "lay down the rudiments / Of his great warfare" (1.156–58). The man Jesus has given considerable thought to the various means by which the prophecies about him might be fulfilled. Having made the Law of God his "whole delight" (208), he had been wont, at one time, to muse upon "victorious deeds" (215), hoping "to subdue and quell o're all the earth / Brute violence and proud Tyrannick pow'r" (218–19); at another time he had held it "more humane, more heav'nly first / By winning words to conquer willing hearts, / And make perswasion do the work of fear" (221–23). When Jesus is able to perceive both alternatives as temptations, he is able to clarify his purpose. He rejects both action and contemplation, both physical and merely rational forms of power. His rejection of political power comes fairly easily, but in terms that open him more fully to a more subtle form of worldly temptation. The true kingly course, he argues, comes from self-mastery, through government of "the inner man" (2.477); the true function of earthly power is

> to guide Nations in the way of truth
> By saving Doctrine, and from errour lead
> To know, and knowing worship God aright
> Is yet more Kingly, this attracts the Soul,
> Governs the inner man, the nobler part.   (2.473–77)

But this ideal, however deeply it may reflect the Protestant humanist's desire for a reformation of society, remains essentially worldly—as Satan's next temptation plainly reveals. "Be famous then / By wisdom" (4.221–22), Satan urges him, "Ruling them by perswasion as thou mean'st" (4.230). Jesus immediately sees the trap: the "wisdom" that Satan offers is wholly secular, unrelated to man's real, spiritual place in the world as God's creature: those whose reason is directed to solely intellectual ends, or worse still to merely rhetorical ends, remain "Ignorant of themselves, of God much more" (4.310). The apparent harshness with which Christ rejects unredeemed philosophical wisdom should not blind us to the true wisdom he espouses. That wisdom derives from

"A spirit and judgment equal or superior" to any external knowledge (4.324). It comes only through participation in the Logos, who is the divine nature of Jesus. By asserting his receptiveness to that "Light from above" (4.289), the man Jesus brings himself into a more intimate, and more fully conscious, relationship with the Logos within him.

But Jesus's rejection of all worldly authority gives rise to Satan's perfectly reasonable question:

> Since neither wealth, nor honour, arms nor arts,
> Kingdom nor Empire pleases thee, nor aught
> By me propos'd in life contemplative,
> Or active, tended on by glory, or fame,
> What dost thou in this World?   (4.368–72)

In the merely human terms proposed by Satan, this question is unanswerable; it compels Jesus to find within himself the terms in which the question can be answered. And Milton's whole representation of Jesus, as perfect *man* beset by temptation, encourages his "fit audience" (*PL* 7.31) to search within themselves for a similar self-revelation. Milton's representation of the son is both "doctrinal and exemplary" (*The Reason of Church-Government;* YP 1:815). Satan's temptation of Jesus is exemplary for the reader because it is instructive for Jesus: he not only shows us how to resist temptation, he himself actively "increase[s] in wisdom" (YP 6:425). God "exercise[s]" Jesus in the wilderness so that "men hereafter may discern" what it means to be "perfect Man" (*PR* 1.154, 164, 166). And because Jesus is tempted as "meer man" (4.535), he demonstrates the "merit" that enables him "To earn Salvation for the Sons of men" (1.166–67).

Orthodox theology emphasizes the doctrine of vicarious atonement as a remedy for sin: "Unless [Christ] were God," Aquinas argues, "he could not have brought the remedy"; "God alone is of such infinite dignity that atonement can be complete in the flesh he assumes."[35] Milton also acknowledges this orthodox doctrine: Mankind will die,

> [Man] with his whole posteritie must die,
> Die hee or Justice must; unless for him
> Som other able, and as willing, pay
> The rigid satisfaction, death for death.   (*PL* 3.209–12)

In *Paradise Regained,* however, the doctrine of atonement is displaced by Milton's emphasis on the Son's exemplary function.[36] Origen argues that "Christ is set forth as an example to all believers, because just as he always 'chose good' even before 'he knew evil,' . . . so also each person either after a fall or after an error cleanses himself from stains by the example set forth."

So it is that "we may be made participants in the divine nature by imitating him."[37] In the same way, Milton emphasizes our *conscious* participation in the will of the Son; his example makes it possible for all men to obtain salvation, not by their works, but by manifesting the divine spirit in their works.

His belief in the Son's exemplary function, I think, leads Milton to assert the absolute humanity of Jesus. Reformation theology was inclined to emphasize the Pauline idea that, in becoming incarnate, Christ *emptied* himself of divinity: "though he was in the form of God, [Christ] did not regard equality with God as something to be exploited, but emptied himself, taking the form of a slave, being born in human likeness. And being found in human form" (Philippians 2:6–7).[38] Aquinas uses the Pauline text to argue against the Incarnation as a mere "indwelling by grace."[39] Origen, however, connects Christ's emptying himself with our "participation in the Son of God" and in the divine nature.[40] Milton's reading of this text is much closer to Origen's than to Aquinas's. He interprets the Son's emptying of Himself by conflating Philippians 2:7 with Luke 2:52 and John 21:17: "He could . . . both *increase in wisdom*, . . . after he had emptied himself, and *know everything*, . . . that is, after the Father had instructed him" (YP 6:425). Milton's idea, I believe, was that the Logos initially incarnate in Jesus had been emptied of its divinity, so that the man Jesus grew in knowledge, as a man and without divine self-knowledge, until his reason was finally perfected by the instruction of the Father.

In *De Doctrina* Milton had declined to speculate about whether Christ, "after his incarnation . . . retained a two-fold intellect or a two-fold will" (YP 6:425). But Milton's argument that the Word incarnate united two *persons* would seem to imply a distinction of wills in the man who was also God. Origen (again interpreting Philippians 2:6–8) suggests the form in which such a twofold will might be conceived: by "humbling himself and becoming obedient to death," the man Jesus becomes able to receive the power of the Logos, who then *assumes* "the Man . . . when he had been made that power's own."[41]

Paradise Regained allows us to experience the operation of such a twofold will. Emptied of his divinity, Jesus is tempted as perfect man, fully able to withstand temptation as man. As Lewalski has argued, the fusion of the two natures in Christ "is not achieved by commingling and confusing the two natures, but rather . . . by an emptying out by the divine nature of that which properly belongs to itself as divine, so that what is left to operate in the new person is the human element, the human understanding and will."[42] Jesus's conscious human will is fully obedient to the divine will, but that will is as yet operating in him only unconsciously, as a "strong motion" to which he submits, voluntarily but without any knowledge of its purpose (1.290). Borrowing Origen's terminology, we might say that Jesus becomes obedient to the divine will by submitting himself to death. Only when that submission is complete does Jesus become fully conscious of the divine nature in him, with which he thereby becomes united. Jesus is brought to the pinnacle of the temple by Satan in order that he might discover who he really is. Satan believes that he has created an impossible dilemma, in which either standing (proudly secure) or falling (through weakness) will destroy the Son of Man. Instead, Jesus shows his "Progeny" by discovering and revealing himself to be the Son of God: "To whom thus Jesus: also it is written, / Tempt not the Lord thy God, he said and stood" (4.554, 560–61).

In speaking the Word once again, Jesus is not asserting Godhood. Rather, he is expressing his absolute trust in the Father, whom he will not tempt. That final submission, even unto death, enables the Logos to reveal itself in and to him. As Arnold Stein has said, "The Flesh becomes word. Christ says it, and then becomes it."[43] Throughout the poem, until his final self-realization, which is also an epiphany, the Son remains "meer man" (4.535)—perfect man, to be sure (that is the mystery of the Logos *actual* within him), but merely human, and only potentially divine. The expression "Son of God" remains "Allegoric" (4.390), for Jesus as well as for Satan, until Jesus *enacts* the divinity hidden in his human person. As Robert Entzminger has observed, Jesus "fully realizes the significance of himself as the Incarnate Word"; the paradox he speaks "restores to language the possibility of expressing divinity."[44] That expression, the embodiment of what had been merely actual, is what Milton means by incarnation. When the Son of Man says "Tempt not the Lord thy God," he expresses the Logos; in doing so he becomes, consciously, the Son of God, and so both God and Man, *theanthropos*. The realization of that consciousness *is* the Incarnation: the Word becomes flesh when he utters it. *Praedicatio verbi Dei est verbum Dei incarnatum.*

Freely We Serve, Because Wee Freely Love

If we can perceive the doctrine of a twofold incarnation as informing the action of Milton's brief epic, we can equally well use the poetry to interpret the doctrine. *Paradise Regained* may be said to *embody* the difficult notion that the Word empties Himself of divinity in order that he might first become perfect man. (In the process of perfecting himself, Jesus must also purge himself of ordinary human weakness, which he does by resisting the temptations of his flesh, his human nature.) Much as the Son is first begotten and then manifested ("This day I have begot whom I declare," *PL* 5.603), so also the Logos is first begotten, in the Son of Man, and then manifested as the Son of God, once actual, now in body. As Robins has argued, "in *Paradise Lost,* upon the occasion of the metaphorical begetting, the invisible Logos is manifested as the visible Son."[45]

Through the Son's poetic embodiment Milton seeks to reveal the fundamental identity between his human nature and our own. His rejection of the orthodox view, that Christ was only a union of two natures, arises from his conviction that the Incarnation must become a conscious realization within each Christian soul, individually and personally. Human nature is not redeemed in us unless we choose to redeem it. Just as "the Logos became what it assumed . . . the true and perfect substance or essence of man" (YP 6:422–23), so perfect man becomes a substantial expression of that Word. The Incarnation must be consciously realized and enacted by Milton's fit audience, so that what was made historically actual in Jesus of Nazareth, as a prefiguration of that which is to be born within us, becomes also embodied in us. This conscious and voluntary intimacy between our two natures compels Milton's insistence upon the union of two persons in Christ. For just as the human person of Jesus had received the Logos, by realizing Him within himself, so must everyone become the conscious vehicle of that divine Word. In this way Milton struggles to realize in himself, and to make it possible for us to realize, that "we shall receive our [fullness] from Christ" in the same way that "Christ has received his fulness from God" (YP 6:273).

Accordingly, Milton embraces, on a deeper level, the very mystery that he had seemed to rationalize in his discussion of the Trinity. "Two distinct things cannot be of the same essence. God is one being, not two" (YP 6:212). Nonetheless, Christ is a union "of two persons" in one person, "both God and man. . . . We do not know how it is so," and so we must remain "ignorant of things which God wishes to remain secret" (YP 6:424). But we can know *that* it is so, from our conscious embodiment of the divinity that is actual within us. That, I believe, is the central mystery of the Incarnation as Milton conceived it, the voluntary apotheosis of man in the *theanthropos*.

This doctrinal singularity, the conviction that incarnation is a conscious process, brings into focus several of Milton's otherwise confusing heterodoxies—(1) his anti-Trinitarianism, (2) his belief in creation *ex Deo* rather than *ex nihilo,* (3) his anti-sacramentalism, (4) his mortalism, and (5) his radical understanding of Christian liberty. In brief, Milton holds that: (1) the Father and Son are two distinct and unequal persons; the Son does not share the "essence" of the Father and is not co-eternal with Him (YP 6:211–12). (2) God creates "not out of nothing but out of himself" (YP 6:310). (3) Participation in the sacraments is purely spiritual, an act of "understanding and will" (YP 6:547). (4) When someone dies, "the whole man dies," not just the body (YP 6:400). (5) Under the new covenant, "all the old covenant, in other words the entire Mosaic law, is abolished" (YP 6:525–26).

These doctrines are not necessarily incoherent, but they are certainly heterogeneous, and their consistency is not obvious from any traditional perspective. At first glance, Milton's views about the union of two persons in the Incarnation seem to contradict his belief in the impossibility of such a (con)fusion in the Godhead. This problem is compounded by Milton's teaching that, although Father and Son do not have the same essence, they both share the divine substance of the Father (YP 6:209).[46] Indeed, all creation must share this substance, since everything is created out of God, who is "the source of all substance" (YP 6:308). Moreover, Milton's restriction of the sacraments to a purely spiritual efficacy seems inconsistent with his philosophical monism, and especially with his insistence that soul and body are inseparable and his consequent mortalism: "the whole man dies . . . body, spirit and soul" (403). Finally, his radical antinomianism is not obviously supported by his other beliefs—least of all, perhaps, by his insistence in *Paradise Regained* that the Son fulfills the letter of obedience (to the moral law) as well as the spirit, even "though love / Alone fulfill the Law" (*PL* 12.403–4).

Arthur E. Barker has persuasively located one source of philosophical consistency in Milton's "conviction of the unity of soul and body in the human individual." Milton "could not accept the common distinction between soul and body . . . because it did not suit with his view of human nature. Man was created in the image of God 'not only as to his soul, but also as to his outward form.'" Barker shows that Milton's theory of the Incarnation is grounded in the same first principle: "the union of the two natures in Christ" was indissoluble, so that "he died in his divine as well as human nature." Barker's analysis is intended to develop "the effect of Milton's monism on his interpretation of Christian liberty."[47] In this he has succeeded admirably. It is easy to see, for example, that Milton's philosophical monism is firmly rooted in his mortalist conception of the human being as "intrinsically and properly one and individual . . . not double or separable: not, as is commonly thought, produced from and composed of two different and distinct elements, soul and body" (YP 6:318).[48] This conception is also consistent with Milton's belief that "Christ's two natures add up to a single person": "one Christ, one ens, and one person is formed from [a] mutual hypostatic union of two natures" (426, 423).

As far as Barker is concerned to press his investigation, his analysis is sound. But since we are here occupied with "abstruse matters . . . beyond the scope of . . . his study," it may be useful to reverse the polarity of his argument, by suggesting that Milton's understanding of Christian liberty was the logical ground of his monistic theory of the Incarnation—"monistic," that is, in the sense that two natures of the same *kind,* though differing in degree, are *consciously* united in the person of the God-Man. For when we ask *why*

Milton conceived of human nature as he did, according to Hebraic rather than more traditional Christian formulations, it becomes possible to see his conception of the Incarnation as the ground of his other heterodoxies.[49]

The fore-conceit that unites these otherwise diverse doctrines is Milton's conviction that our communion with Deity is, in fact, an Incarnation of the Divine Logos, in whom we participate voluntarily and consciously. Before all else, Milton's God *chooses* to create, out of himself and through his first-begotten Word, "of all Creation first, / Begotten Son, Divine Similitude" (*PL* 3.383–84). "The Son existed in the beginning," Milton argues, "under the title of the Word or Logos"; "he was the first of created things, and . . . through him all other things, both in heaven and earth, were afterwards made" (YP 6:206). Although Milton seems to equivocate about whether the Word was *begotten* or *created*,[50] on one crucial point he is unambiguous: "This particular Father begot his Son not from any natural necessity but of his own free will." For Milton, "God always acts with absolute freedom" (YP 6:209). The only constraint on that freedom is the limitation that God imposes on himself when he begets, or creates, his Word. By choosing to create, out of himself, that which is other than himself, God discovers himself by bringing to light that which had been dark, even within himself. As Joan Malory Webber has argued, "the act of creating something not oneself is a way of bringing about self-consciousness, and [in *Paradise Lost,* at least, if not in *De Doctrina*] Milton portrays God as enduring this experience, subject to the same limitations or requirements that beset other conscious beings."[51] The first stage of incarnation occurs as self-discovery, when the Father expresses himself, and thereby knows himself, in the Son who is His "radiant image," in whom "all his Father shon / Substantially expressed" (*PL* 3.63, 139–40). Thereafter, the whole process of creation is the conscious realization of God's "great idea" (7.557), the substantial expression of his goodness in the process of becoming incarnate, once actual now in body. Creation, in other words, is the process by which God comes to know Himself.

Many of Milton's most radical beliefs proceed directly from this first principle of voluntary self-discovery. His apparent anti-sacramentalism, for example, is grounded in his conviction that true communion with Christ demands "both understanding and will" (YP 6:547). This radically Protestant view is defined, on the one hand, by his conviction that God always creates "not out of nothing but out of himself" (310), and, on the other hand, by his insistence that body and spirit are one: "one first matter all, / Indu'd with various forms, various degrees / Of substance . . . Till body up to spirit work" (*PL* 5.472–74, 478). As body is transformed into spirit, created beings become more *substantial,* "more refin'd, more spiritous, and pure, / As neerer to him plac't or neerer tending" (475–76). As a consequence, the divine substance out of which (*ex Deo*) all things have been created becomes more fully realized. The formative principle that shapes this process is consciousness— the self-realization of animate life in human self-awareness:

> flowrs and thir fruit
> Mans nourishment, by gradual scale sublim'd
> To vital Spirits aspire, to animal,
> To intellectual, give both life and sense,
> Fansie and understanding, whence the Soul
> Reason receives, and reason is her being.   (482–87)

From this perspective, Milton's belief that sacramental efficacy is spiritual rather than material does not contradict his assertion that body and soul are one substance. They are "of kind the same," but they differ in *degree* (490): "spirit, being the more excellent substance . . . contains within itself . . . the inferior [material] substance; in the same way as the spiritual and rational faculty contains the corporeal, that is, the sentient and vegetative faculty" (YP 6:309). And so it is that participation in a sacrament always requires a conscious act of will: "that living bread which, Christ says, is his flesh, and the true drink which, he says, is his blood, can only be the *doctrine* which teaches us that Christ was made man in order to pour out his blood for us" (YP 6:553; emphasis mine).

Finally, the conviction that "both understanding and will are requisite" (YP 6:547) for true faith grounds Milton's radical understanding of Christian liberty: "Not only the ceremonial law but . . . the whole Mosaic law is abolished by the gospel" (530–31)—including the moral law. Orthodox Protestants held that Christ's sacrifice had abolished only the ceremonial and civil portions of the law; the moral law was still binding on Christians. Moreover, as Kelley points out, for the orthodox, "Christian liberty . . . is limited to the spiritual life of believers, and has no bearing on civil and political matters. In contrast, Milton . . . argues that Christ's sacrifice abrogated the total Mosaic law . . . and bestowed on believers a complete Christian liberty that frees them from . . . civil or ecclesiastical coercion in religious matters."[52] Mankind's inalienable, God-given freedom is a fundamental principle in Milton's writings from first to last. In *Areopagitica,* a human being is "a reasonable creature, Gods Image," and "when God gave [Adam] reason, he gave him freedom to choose, for reason is but choosing" (YP 2:492, 527). So also in *De Doctrina:*

Christian Liberty . . . [pertains] chiefly to the gospel. . . . This is so, first, because truth exists chiefly under the gospel, John i. 17: *grace and truth are present through Jesus Christ,* and truth liberates, viii. 31, 32: *if you remain in my word . . . you will know the truth, and the truth will make you free,* and viii. 36: *so if the son liberates you, you will really be free.* Secondly, because the peculiar gift of the gospel is the Spirit and : *where the Spirit of the Lord is, there is liberty,* II Cor. iii. 17.

Christian Liberty means that Christ our liberator frees us from the slavery of sin and thus from the rule of law and of men . . . so that . . . we may serve God in charity through the guidance of the spirit of truth. (YP 6:536–37)

In *Paradise Regained,* therefore, the Son fulfills the moral law, not by subscribing to any of its prescripts, nor yet by carrying out explicit instructions from his Father, but by obeying "the spirit of truth." In doing so he recovers for fallen human beings, not merely the operation of "Conscience, or right reason," which exists to some degree "even in the most evil men" (YP 6:132), but the full blessing of that rational liberty with which human beings had been endowed by the Creator: "God left free the Will, for what obeys / Reason, is free, and Reason he made right" (*PL* 9.351–52). The Son obeys the Father out of Love, as do all creatures who *choose* to obey Him: "freely we serve, / Because wee freely love, as in our will / To love or not" (5.538–40). Love, freely chosen and expressed, "refines / The thoughts, and heart enlarges, hath his seat / In Reason, and . . . is the scale / By which to heav'nly Love [we may] ascend" to a knowledge of God (8.589–92).

Attaining to that knowledge is the first principle of Milton's theology: "The end . . . of learning is to repair the ruins of our first parents by regaining to know God aright, and out of that knowledge to love him, to imitate him, to be like him" (*Of Education; YP* 2:366–67). That mimetic knowledge is also the essence of what Milton means by incarnation: the process of self-discovery whereby "God with man unites" (*PL* 12.382). As Hill has argued, "all angels and men can ultimately attain oneness with God through Christ if they love and trust the Father as perfectly as the Son does. This eventual unity of all creation under the Son will lead to the final abdication of Christ's kingly power when God shall be all in all."[53] Humanity's original God-likeness is fully restored by realizing God within ourselves—as Jesus did when he submitted himself wholly to the will of the Father. "Redemption is that act by which Christ . . . redeemed all believers at the price of His own blood, which he paid voluntarily" (YP 6:415–16). Milton's theory of redemption is defined, not by a doctrine of vicarious atonement, but by the principle of Christ's *voluntary* self-sacrifice, in which the regenerate *choose* to participate. Much as Christ "willingly performed, and still performs all those things through which . . . salvation . . . [is] attained" (YP 6:430), so too those who voluntarily accept "the benefits of Christ's incarnation," participate, sacramentally and consciously, in his "death, burial and resurrection" (YP 6:553, 544). And this spiritual participation constitutes the ground of Christian Liberty: "Christ writes the internal law of God on the hearts of believers through his Spirit, and leads them as willing followers" (YP 6:535).

The University of Arizona

NOTES

I am grateful to Janel Mueller and John Shawcross for their detailed and provocative responses to a much earlier version of this essay; to William B. Hunter and Heiko Oberman for their many constructive suggestions; to Kari Boyd McBride and Peter E. Medine for their help and encouragement; and to Albert Labriola for his wise and scrupulous editorial guidance.

1. *Areopagitica,* in *Complete Prose Works of John Milton,* 8 vols., ed. Don M. Wolfe et al. (New Haven, 1953–82), vol. 2, 514. Unless otherwise noted, all quotations of Milton's prose are taken from this edition and are hereafter cited parenthetically in the text as YP, with volume and page number. The Latin text of *De Doctrina Christiana* is quoted from *The Works of John Milton,* 18 vols., gen. ed. Frank Allen Patterson et al. (New York, 1933), vols. 14–17, ed. James Holly Hanford and Waldo Hilary Dunn; hereafter cited parenthetically in the text as CM, with volume and page number. All quotations of Milton's poetry are from *The Complete Poetry of John Milton,* ed. John T. Shawcross (Garden City, N.Y., 1971 rev. ed.) and are cited parenthetically in the text.

2. Maurice Kelley, *This Great Argument: A Study of Milton's De Doctrina Christiana as a Gloss upon Paradise Lost* (Princeton, 1941), 192. Until recently, the basic validity of Kelley's conclusions has been accepted, with qualifications, even by scholars who have questioned the unanimity of doctrine between treatise and poems. As William B. Hunter, Jr., observed in his article "Incarnation," in *A Milton Encyclopedia,* 12 vols., ed. William B. Hunter, Jr., John T. Shawcross, John M. Steadman, Purvis E. Boyette, and Leonard Nathanson (Lewisburg, 1978–86), vol. 4, 101, "For Milton's mature understanding of this dogma, the major statement is *CD.*" Recently, however, Hunter has questioned Milton's authorship of the treatise. In *Visitation Unimplor'd: Milton and the Authorship of De Doctrina Christiana* (Pittsburgh, 1998), he concludes that "so many of Milton's genuine ideas are at odds with those in *DDC* that he could not have been its author unless he were the most incoherent thinker in history" (153). Hunter's arguments have not gone unchallenged. For example: Stephen B. Dobranski and John P. Rumrich, eds., *Milton and Heresy* (Cambridge, 1998) reject Hunter's philosophical arguments and conclude that "*De doctrina* expresses Milton's thought and convictions . . . more fully and centrally than any other single work in the accepted canon" (10). Barbara K. Lewalski, "Milton and *De Doctrina Christiana:* Evidences of Authorship," in *Milton Studies* 36, ed. Albert C. Labriola (Pittsburgh, 1998), 223, concurs: "The evidence for Milton's authorship of *De Doctrina Christiana* seems to me to reach well beyond a reasonable doubt." I find Lewalski's arguments generally persuasive. For the present, however, it seems safest to accept the conclusions of Gordon Campbell, Thomas N. Corns, John K. Hale, David Holmes, and Fiona Tweedie, "The Provenance of *De Doctrina Christiana,*" *Milton Quarterly* 31 (October, 1997): 67–117: As we have it, the treatise "was a working manuscript under revision by Milton"; "Some parts of the manuscript show more evidence of Miltonic composition than others"; consequently, "The relationship of *De Doctrina Christiana* to the Milton oeuvre must remain uncertain" (110). Therefore (and in agreement with Hunter) in the present state of our ignorance, it would still be "dangerous to develop as 'Milton's' any arguments found only in [the treatise] and not supported by the canonical writings" (Hunter, *Visitation,* 153). I have tried to circumvent this danger by

reading back and forth between treatise and the poetry, not wishing to claim for the treatise any point of doctrinal singularity that could not be supported by direct inference from the poems themselves.

3. Sir Philip Sidney, *An Apology for Poetry or The Defence of Poesy,* ed. Geoffrey Shepherd (London, 1965), 101, 124.

4. Acts 24:14, cited by Milton, YP 6:124. Unless otherwise noted, all biblical quotations are from the Authorized Version of 1611 and are cited parenthetically in the text.

5. Although I have reformulated his hypothesis to incorporate *De Doctrina,* my understanding of Milton's theology as a progressive revelation is indebted to Joseph A. Wittreich's conception of *Paradise Lost* and *Paradise Regained* as epic prophecies, as formulated in *Visionary Poetics: Milton's Tradition and His Legacy* (San Marino, 1979): inasmuch as "every new prophecy is an interpretation of what it succeeds and a vision requiring and receiving interpretation from the works it inspires" (88), Milton's "diffuse epic is a focusing of the orthodoxies that *Paradise Regained* proceeds to demolish; the brief epic is a formulation of a new system of religion, more perfect and enduring than the one it supersedes" (208–9).

6. Quoted from Philip Schaff, *History of the Christian Church,* 8 vols. (Grand Rapids, 1972–75), vol. 3, 745–46. The orthodox position is affirmed in the Thirty-nine Articles in *The Book of Common Prayer* (London, 1971), 388, Article Two: "The Word of the Father . . . took Man's nature . . . so that two whole and perfect Natures, . . . the God head and Manhood, were joined together in one Person, never to be divided, whereof is one Christ, very God, and very Man."

7. Harry Austryn Wolfson, *The Philosophy of the Church Fathers, Volume I: Faith, Trinity, Incarnation* (Cambridge, Mass., 1956), 372.

8. Heiko Augustinus Oberman, *The Harvest of Medieval Theology: Gabriel Biel and Late Medieval Nominalism* (Cambridge, Mass., 1963), 252–53.

9. E.g.: In "On the Morning of Christs Nativity," the Son chooses "a darksom House of mortal Clay" (14). In *A Mask,* the Attendant Spirit "take[s] the weeds and likeness of a swain" (84).

10. Milton uses Zanchius to distinguish his view from "the orthodox position" (YP 6:421–22) and "to demonstrate the sheer vacuity of the orthodox view" (423), but Aquinas's arguments afford a clearer perspective on the issues. In selecting Aquinas to represent "orthodoxy," however, one must proceed with caution. Even as late as the seventeenth century, the triumph of Thomistic realism over the nominalism of Duns Scotus was uncertain; Milton implies that the latter had as much (or as little) authority as the former when he lumps them together in the *Areopagitica,* speaking of "our sage and serious Poet *Spencer*" as "a better teacher then *Scotus* or *Aquinas*" (YP 2:516). As Oberman has pointed out to me (in a letter dated November 24, 1998), "the evidence [discussed in *The Harvest*] strongly suggests that Milton followed the interpretation of Duns Scotus," and that he was "as entitled as Aquinas to be regarded as an orthodox teacher."

11. *St. Thomas Aquinas: Theological Texts,* ed. and trans. Thomas Gilby (London, 1955), 282, 285, 286, 290–91, 292.

12. CM 15:270: *fit itaque naturarum, id est, essentiarum, substantiarum adeoque necessario personarum in Christo duarum hypostatica utrinque unio.* Although he had earlier (in Chapter 5) been concerned to distinguish *essentia* and *substantia,* Milton here seems to take them as synonyms.

13. YP 6:422; according to the Latin text, CM 15:268, "*id factus est quod assumpsit*" ["was made that which it/he assumed"].

14. *Theological Texts,* 275. According to Aquinas, the Eucharist, "in which *Christ is really present* [through the transubstantiation of the elements], is the culmination of all the other

sacraments in which his power is shared" (368; emphasis mine). Because sacraments are the instruments of the Word Incarnate, it is "fitting . . . that divine virtue should continue to work invisibly in them through visible appearances" (354).

15. *On Christian Doctrine, Book One, Chapter 28*: "Of the External Sealing of the Covenant of Grace." Milton insists that participation in a sacrament must be spiritual. Of Christ in the Eucharist he says, "not teeth but faith is needed to eat his flesh" (553). He is equally explicit about the efficacy of Baptism: "we are not saved by that outward baptism which washes away merely the filth of the flesh, but, as Peter says [1 Peter 3:21], *by the obligation of a good conscience*" (545). For a discussion of the sharp contrast between Milton's "anti-sacramentalism" and Aquinas's view that Christ "come[s] through to men in bodily fashion" (*Theological Texts*, 354), see John C. Ulreich, Jr., "Milton on the Eucharist: Some Second Thoughts about Sacramentalism," in *Milton and the Middle Ages*, ed. John Mulryan (London and Toronto, 1982), 32–56.

16. Christopher Hill, *Milton and the English Revolution* (Harmondsworth, 1977), 302.

17. Hunter, "Milton on the Incarnation: Some More Heresies," *JHI* 21 (1960): 349–69; rpt. in and qtd. from Hunter, C. A. Patrides, and J. H. Adamson, eds., *Bright Essence: Studies in Milton's Theology* (Salt Lake City, 1971), 131–32, 140.

18. Barbara Lewalski, *Milton's Brief Epic: The Genre, Meaning, and Art of Paradise Regained* (Providence, 1966), 153.

19. Hunter, "Milton on the Incarnation," 140.

20. Harry R. Robins, *If This Be Heresy: A Study of Milton and Origen* (Urbana, 1963), argues "that . . . the doctrine of Origen . . . differs in few major respects from the doctrine of Milton" (16).

21. Origen, *Contra Celsum* 4:5, ed. and trans. Henry Chadwick (Cambridge, Engl., 1953), 187. Further quotations from this edition are cited parenthetically in the text.

22. Origen, *First Principles* 4:4; in *Origen: An exhortation to Martyrdom, Prayer, First Principles: Book IV, Prologue to the Commentary on the Song of Songs, Homily XXVII on Numbers*, ed. and trans. Rowan A Greer (New York, 1979), 208. Further quotations from this collection are cited parenthetically in the text.

23. Eugene de Faye, *Origen and His Work*, trans. Fred Rothwell (London, 1926), 105–6.

24. Winstanley, *The Works of Gerrard Winstanley*, ed. G. H. Sabine (Ithaca, 1941), 114, 166–68, 225; qtd. in Hill, *Milton and the English Revolution*, 299.

25. Denis Saurat, *Milton: Man and Thinker* (London and New York, 1925; rpt. New York, 1970), 174, 176. Saurat also notices the voluntary nature of our participation in "one greater Man" (*PL* 1.4), which is "material," like our genetic inheritance from Adam "by the continuity of physical generation" (174), but which becomes effectual, as a "second creation," only "through the will of the creatures" (179).

26. Martin Luther, *Werke, Kritische Gesamtansgabe*, 68 vols. (Weimar, 1883 ff.), vol. 47, 229; qtd. and trans. by Heiko Oberman, "Preaching and the Word in the Reformation," *Theology Today* 18 (1961): 16–29; rvsd. as and qtd. from "Reformation, Preaching, and *Ex Opere Operato*," in *Christianity Divided: Protestant and Roman Catholic Theological Issues*, ed. Daniel J. Callahan, Heiko A. Oberman, and Daniel J. O'Hanlon, S.J. (New York, 1961), 232.

27. John Calvin, *Commentary upon John's Gospel*; in *Calvin's Commentaries*, 45 vols. (Grand Rapids, 1948–59), vol. 34, 26.

28. Robert L. Entzminger, *Divine Word: Milton and the Redemption of Language* (Pittsburgh, 1985), 12.

29. Bullinger, *Confessio Helvetica Posterior*, vol. 1, 4, in Philip Schaff, ed., *The Creeds of Christendom*, 3 vols. (New York, 1882), vol. 3, 237–38.

30. Oberman, "Reformation Preaching," 233–34, 224–25.

31. Georgia B. Christopher, *Milton and the Science of the Saints* (Princeton, 1982), 12–13.

32. It is worth noting, in this connection, that Origen had also asserted the sacramental value of the Scriptures. As Rowan A. Greer has observed (*Origen,* 12), Origen looked "upon converse with the Written Word as sacred, and as much deserving of reverence as converse with the consecrated elements [of the Eucharist]."

33. Barbara Lewalski, *Protestant Poetics and the Seventeenth-Century Religious Lyric* (Princeton, 1979), 130–31.

34. John Everard, *The Gospel Treasury Opened,* 2 vols. (London, 1657), vol. 1, 55.

35. Aquinas, *Theological Texts,* 279, 310.

36. Saurat, *Milton: Man and Thinker,* 178, was perhaps the first to observe that "Vicarious atonement is no Miltonic conception, and that is why the crucifixion plays so small a part in his conception of human destiny." Hill, *Milton and the English Revolution,* 286, also remarks on Milton's "abandonment of traditional ideas of Christ's atonement" and links this heterodoxy with his anti-Trinitarianism.

37. Origen, *First Principles* 4:4, in *Origen,* ed. Greer, 209.

38. I quote this text from the New Revised Standard Version; the Authorized Version is somewhat obscure: "made himself of no reputation" (Philippians 2:7). The Greek text reads "ἑαυτὸν ἐκένωσεν, ["emptied himself"]. Milton's interpretation of this passage is consonant with Origen's view that the Logos "restored the form of a servant to the form of God . . . and called it back to that fulness from which it had emptied itself . . . just as a person receives the adoption of sons by participation in the Son of God" (*First Principles* 4:5, in *Origen,* ed. Greer, 210). The bearing of *kenosis* theology on Milton's poetic practice has been skillfully traced by Michael Lieb, "Milton and the Kenotic Christology: Its Literary Bearing," *ELH* 37 (1970), 342–60.

39. Aquinas, *Theological Texts,* 288.

40. Origen, *First Principles* 4.5, in *Origen,* ed. Greer, 210.

41. Origen, *On Prayer* 26.4; in *Origen,* ed. Greer, 135.

42. Lewalski, *Milton's Brief Epic,* 158. Cf. Hill, *Milton and the English Revolution,* 286: "The *De doctrina* emphasizes that the human Jesus has emptied himself of divine understanding and will: *Paradise Regained* shows him uncertain and in some respects ignorant until his moment of self-realization."

43. Arnold Stein, *Heroic Knowledge: An Interpretation of Paradise Regained and Samson Agonistes* (Minneapolis, 1957), 128. Lewalski's analysis supports Stein's reading of Jesus's "notoriously ambiguous" response: on one level, "the words refer . . . to Christ himself, indicating that he is now given to understand, at this climactic moment, the full meaning of his divine sonship—his nature as the Image of the Father" (*Milton's Brief Epic,* 316).

44. Entzminger, *Divine Word,* 103.

45. Robins, *If This Be Heresy,* 116. The passage in question (*PL* 5.603) is a notorious crux; the assumption (shared by most modern scholars) that the Son's begetting is "metaphorical" cannot simply be taken for granted. Almost no one has accepted Saurat's reading of *begot* as referring to the creation of the Son, and most scholars incline toward a metaphorical understanding of the passage; Shawcross, for example, believes that the passage represents, "not the creation of the Son, but his anointing as king" (*Complete Poetry,* 357, n.39). But Albert C. Labriola has argued persuasively for a literal begetting of the Son as an angel, in " 'Thy Humiliation Shall Exalt': The Christology of *Paradise Lost,*" in *Milton Studies* 15, ed. James D. Simmonds (Pittsburgh, 1981), 29–42: "As Saurat argues, the Son is 'created' at the begetting. But his divine nature is not being originated; only an angelic nature and form are being assumed . . . [and thus the connection that Hunter sees] between the events of eternity and time . . . is more fully affirmed by the recognition that the Son 'really' becomes an angel in Book V, for the two begettings—the first in eternity, the second in time—show the continuing humiliation of the deity, first as an angel, then as a man" (32–33). Further confirmation for an incarnational reading

of this passage is suggested by Richard S. Ide, "On the Begetting of the Son in *Paradise Lost*," *SEL* 24 (1984): 141–55. I agree especially with Ide's understanding that "the event on earth analogous to the begetting [of the divine Son in heaven] would seem to be the Incarnation, not the Resurrection" (143).

46. God "was in a real sense Father of the Son, whom he made of his own substance. It does not follow, however, that the Son is of the same essence as the Father" (YP 6:209).

47. Arthur E. Barker, *Milton and the Puritan Dilemma* (Toronto, 1942), 318–19.

48. For an illuminating discussion of the inextricable connection between Milton's mortalism and his monism, which he aptly calls "animist materialism," see Stephen M. Fallon, *Milton among the Philosophers: Poetry and Materialism in Seventeenth-Century England* (Ithaca, 1991).

49. In Genesis, according to the NRSV, "the LORD God . . . breathed into his nostrils the breath of life; and the man became a living being" (2:7; the AV has "living soul"). According to the *New Oxford Annotated Bible*, ed. Bruce M. Metzger and Roland E. Murphy (New York, 1991), 4, "Human nature is not a duality of body and soul; rather God's *breath* animates the dust and it becomes *a living being* or psycho-physical self."

50. In *De Doctrina* Milton argues that "to Adam, formed out of the dust, God was creator [*opifex*] rather than Father; but he was in a real sense [*proprius*] Father of the Son" (YP 6:209; CM 14:186). A little earlier, however, he had spoken of the Son as "the first of created things [*rerum creatarum primum*]" (YP 6:206; CM 14:180). The apparent terminological confusion is perhaps an artifact of translation, since Milton distinguishes, not between "created" and "begotten," but between *making* and *producing*: God *formed* Adam from the dust, *ex pulvere facti* ("having been made"), whereas he *brought forth* the Son from his own substance, *ex substantia eius producti* ("having been produced"; CM 14:186).

51. Joan Malory Webber, *Milton and His Epic Tradition* (Seattle, 1979), 112.

52. Kelley, vol. ed., *On Christian Doctrine*, YP 6:520, n.1.

53. Hill, *Milton and the English Revolution*, 286.

MORAL PRAGMATISM IN THE THEOLOGY OF MILTON AND HIS CONTEMPORARIES, OR *HABITUS* HISTORICIZED

Paul Cefalu

I N *THE RETURN OF EDEN* Northrop Frye defined Milton's conception of radical liberty as a force that "arrests the current of habit and of the cause-effect mechanism."[1] Frye's assumption that freedom in *Paradise Lost* requires an awareness and questioning of beliefs that may have been previously governed by unreflective habit finds its warrant in *Areopagitica's* dictum "reason is but choosing," which Frye expands into a thesis that, he believes, attests to Milton's commitment to ethical rationalism: "There is a parallel distinction between rational action and action which has no vision to guide it. The latter is mindless, habitual, mechanical action, the action based on tradition, precedent, custom, the doing of what has been done before because it has been done before."[2] From Milton's critique of custom in *Areopagitica* and the divorce tracts, Frye extrapolates Milton's conception of ethical humanism in *Paradise Lost*. Despite slight variations in focus, much recent criticism, following Frye's example, has suggested that because Milton viewed the rational pursuit of non-absolute truths as iconoclastic freedoms, he therefore viewed mechanical repetition and habit as authoritarian constraints.[3]

In the following pages I will argue that previous discussions of Milton's views on habit have failed to draw an important distinction between the role of habit in matters of belief, on the one hand, and its role in ethical conduct, on the other hand. Milton and many of his contemporaries held that habituation is indispensable in guiding ethical conduct, in spite of the dulling effects it can have on the process of dialectical intellection. In his poetry and prose, Milton promotes a pragmatic model of ethical self-management, according to which ethical agents rationally commit themselves to act habitually and automatically, at least as a short-term strategy in the pursuit of salvation. The process of ethical habituation that Milton endorses, along with Pascal, Richard Baxter, John Tillotson, and Robert South, among others, converges with at least one modern ethical theory, William James's pragmatic "will-to-believe" argument, which holds that moral agents are permitted to act "as if" they believed in God and unprovable fundamentals of theodicy.[4] The centrality in Milton's work of this paradoxical ethic of willful habituation has been overlooked by critics who have focused strictly on Milton's handling of the binary relationship between reason and faith. The seventeenth-century preoccupation with a third term, habit, helps us to understand a historically idiosyncratic ethic of conduct that is founded upon an interplay of reason, habit, and faith, in which habit mediates an initiating rational choice and the eventual acquisition of pure faith.

In terms familiar to seventeenth-century theologians, Milton's moral pragmatism is an ethic of intrapersonal compatibilism—a phrase I will use in order to distinguish it from both poles of the reformation opposition between compatibilism and libertarianism. Intrapersonal compatibilism redescribes the compatibilist God–subject relationship—in which God provides the necessary cause behind an individual's second, freely chosen action—as an intrapersonal, self–self relationship. According to intrapersonal compatibilism, the moral agent, in making a determining, rational decision to act nonrationally and habitually in future ethical affairs, commits himself or herself to automatism, in a process analogous to the compatibilist argument that God commits the individual to determinism. I will argue, against recent criticism, that although Adam and Eve develop morally in Eden, their development is governed by this two-step process of rational choice followed by unreflective conduct, so that there are no tensions between Milton's Irenaean or "soul-making" theodicy and the self-regulation of behavior by habit and custom. As moral pragmatists, Adam and Eve are permitted to undergo the reflexes of faith, instrumentally binding themselves to God, until maturity can provide them with firm knowledge of God's ways and pure or formed faith.

While I will argue that Adam and Eve are educated in the virtues of rational choice accounting, I will not suggest that Milton was a precocious historical materialist or that *Paradise Lost* enacts a logically unfolding drama of the rise of individual freedoms. The Milton industry continues to interpret *Paradise Lost* as a systematic, historically transitional text, in which Milton, as a Whiggish philosopher of history, incorporates into his mimetic epic bourgeois ideals and anticipatory liberalism. For example, in his recent work on Milton's revolutionary politics John Rogers concludes that by the close of Book Twelve, "Adam and Eve are released from the subjection to hieratic divinity . . . we have represented before us the birth of the individual with her seemingly autonomous subjectivity."[5] Like most transitionalist readings of *Paradise Lost*, Rogers's reference to the "birth of the individual" suggests that, from the perspective of nostalgic worldviews and ideologies— authoritarian politics, philosophical animism and neofeudal economics— Adam and Eve's radical freedom and rational choosing is historically specific.

As I argue in the following pages, Adam and Eve are given the freedom to act in radically unconstrained ways, but Milton's allowance for rational choice need not be read as an anticipation of bourgeois liberalism or neo-Smithian economizing. Because transitionalist readings inevitably view Milton as either a political allegorist or a systematic theologian, they underplay Milton's identity as, above all, a poet, spiritually contracted to write an epic poem depicting the conduct of mimetic characters. When Milton endows Adam and Eve with the capacity to maximize rationally, he simply offers an intuitively understandable depiction of the conduct of individuals who have not yet internalized a set of clearly articulated beliefs and constraints.

The larger aim of this paper is to historicize the late-seventeenth-century conception of habit. During the past decade, Pierre Bourdieu's practice theory has figured importantly in interpretations of Chaucerian theories of subjectivity, Elizabethan courtesy theory, Renaissance conceptions of popular culture, and, most recently, in a provocative article by Fred Hoerner, Milton's conception of custom as represented in *Paradise Lost*.[6] While all of this criticism has offered insightful applications of practice theory to early modern texts, none has evaluated Bourdieu's theory of *habitus* against the many medieval and early modern theories of *habitus* that figure centrally not only in the philosophy of Aquinas, Scotus and Ockham but also in the sermons of William Ames, Richard Sibbes, Richard Baxter, and John Tillotson, and in the philosophy of Descartes, Pascal, Malebranche, Hobbes and Locke. A proper historicization of early modern views of habit will help us to see that most of Milton's ethical writings viewed habit favorably, and that his ethical vision in *Paradise Lost* is a product of the mid- to late-seventeenth-century belief that ritualized, often unreflective conduct could provide a safeguard against the despair caused by theological voluntarism and occasionalism.

THE SEVENTEENTH-CENTURY WILL-TO-BELIEVE ARGUMENT

Milton's critics have often argued that Milton shared with Richard Baxter a Puritan commitment to justifying the ways of an authoritarian God to recalcitrant sinners. Stanley Fish invokes Baxter's *Saint's Everlasting Rest* (1650) in support of his thesis that Milton's God is an entrapping and chastising presence in *Paradise Lost*, in keeping with Milton's presumptive theodicy.[7] C. A. Patrides argues that Milton shared a number of Baxter's orthodox views, as exemplified by, for instance, a belief in the forensic and retributive nature of the contract between God and the Son regarding the Son's sacrifice.[8] Because discussions of the Milton-Baxter affiliation have centered on doctrinal similarities, less attention has been given to Milton and Baxter's converging ethical views, perhaps because Baxter's practical works in general have been neglected.[9] Below is a brief introduction to the ethical writings of Baxter and his mid- to late-seventeenth-century contemporaries, which in many respects exemplify Milton's moral pragmatism.

In his practical writings, Baxter lays out a systematic ethical program that gives a prominent role to habit in ethical affairs. In Baxter's view, habits play a fundamental role in setting conduct on a rightful path, conduct which need not be consciously directed or evaluated once firmly rooted habits have programmed the individual to act ethically:

> The intending of God's glory or our spiritual good, cannot be distinctly and sensibly re-acted in every particular pleasure we take, or bit we eat, or thing we use; but a sincere, habitual intention well laid at first in the heart, will serve to the right use of many particular means. As a man purposeth at his first setting out to what place he meaneth to go, and afterwards goeth on, though at every step he think not sensibly of his end; so he that devoteth himself to God . . . will carry on small particulars to that end, by a secret, unobserved action of the soul, performed at the same time with other actions, which only are observed. . . . As the accustomed hand of a musician can play a lesson on his lute, while he thinks of something else: so can a resolved Christian faithfully do such accustomed things as . . . labouring in his calling, to the good ends which he (first actually, and still habitually) resolved on, without a distinct remembrance and observable intention of that end.[10]

Baxter believes that habit is a controlling faculty which, after having been developed properly, exercises more influence over an agent's actions than divine inspiration, reasoned motivation, or passional response. The confirmed believer is so proficient in his habits of faith that Baxter compares him to an expert laborer whose unthinking proficiency in a craft allows him the freedom to contemplate worthy objects and ideas while he works: "A weaver, a tailor, and some other tradesmen, and day-labourers, may do their work well, and yet have their thoughts free for better things, a great part of the day: these must contrive an ordinary way of employment for their thoughts, when their work doth not require them."[11]

Baxter also finds value in permitting individuals who are gradually assimilating the tenets of faith to accept religious doctrine without the proper knowledge thereof, until proper understanding can unfold the mysteries one has accepted and practiced unknowingly: "Though your religion must not be taken on trust, there are many controverted, smaller opinions that you must take upon trust, until you are capable of discerning them in proper evidence." Baxter's practical and functional ethics aim to promote ease and fluidity in moral conduct: "By the faithful practice of these directions, obedience may become, as it were, your nature; a familiar, easy, and delightful thing: and may be like a cheerful servant or child, that waiteth for your commands, and is glad to be employed by you." One suspects that his Puritan forebears would have contended that Baxter comes dangerously close in these exhortations to permitting moral mechanism, wherein moral agents can programmatically act in an ethical manner without full awareness of the implications of their conduct.

Baxter's moral pragmatism derives in part from his frequent reactions against affective inwardness, which for an earlier Puritan tradition (William Perkins, Richard Sibbes, and William Ames, for example) often involved an anxious process of self-watchfulness. Throughout his writings, Baxter warns against excessive inward scrutiny: "A Christian indeed is more in getting and using his graces, than in inquiring whether he have them; he is very desirous to be assured that he is sincere, but he is more desirous to be so: and he knoweth that even assurance is got more by the exercise and increase of grace than by the bare inquiry we have it already."[12] Baxter suggests that a preoccupation with the state of one's soul can even be sinful: "small excesses of fleshpleasing" are lesser sins than "excessive scrupulousness," wherein a "man should daily perplex his mind about scruples, about every bit he eats, whether it be not too pleasing or too much; and about every word he speaks, and every step he goes, as many poor, tempted, melancholy persons do; thereby disabling themselves, not only to love, and praise and thankfulness, but even all considerable service."[13] Baxter's moral philosophy is of a piece: he replaces a self-conscious inward turn with an exhortation to act responsively and efficiently; the surest means to preclude the disabling lethargy following from self-scrutiny is to allow habits efficiently and even mechanically to guide the regenerate to moral progress.

Despite Baxter's formal alliance with late-seventeenth-century nonconformity, versions of his views on ethical habituation are expressed by a range of late-seventeenth-century theologians nominally grouped under the banner of high church Anglicanism and latitudinarianism.[14] Baxter's writings do not fall neatly into any denominational category such as Puritan nonconformity, which during the later decades of the seventeenth century found adherents in John Howe, John Owen, William Bates, Robert Barclay, and John Bunyan. Nonconformists promote the erection of a primitive church of Presbyters and a "reconstruction of individualism" as an alternative to Episcopalian uniformity and anti-enthusiasm.[15] While Baxter sympathizes with Puritan nonconformists and mainstream Puritans of the early seventeenth century, including Perkins, Sibbes and Preston, whom he calls "our old, solid divine" in *The Saint's Everlasting Rest* (1650), he also shows, in his autobiography, appreciation of the writings of moderate Anglicans, including Joseph Hall and Ussher.[16] He also expresses respect for latitudinarians such as Wilkins, Tillotson, Stillingfleet, and Nest, most of whose sermons he attended and appreciated in the 1660s: "Ordinarily I went to some parish church, where I heard a learned minister that had not obtruded himself upon the people, but was chosen by them, and preached well (as Dr. Wilkins, Dr. Tillotson, Mr. Nest, etc.), and I joined also in the common prayers of the church."[17] As Isabel Rivers says, "The respect in which Baxter was held by moderate Anglicans is evidenced by the fact that in 1660, when a moderate church policy for a short time seemed possible, Charles II made him one of his chaplains. . . . And his respect for the latitudinarians, especially Wilkins ('a lover of mankind, and of honesty, peace and Impartiality and Justice'), Tillotson, Whichcote, and Stillingfleet, emerges at several points in his autobiography."[18]

Baxter and his latitudinarian contemporaries believe that orthodox Calvinism underestimated the role of ethical training and holy living in the acquisition of faith. Latitudinarians such as Edward Stillingfleet, Robert South, Isaac Barrow, and John Tillotson, among others, argue that scripture contains only a few self-evident principles or saving truths, and that in place of an undue concern with mystery and sacrifice, ministers and lay persons should preoccupy themselves with matters of pastoral discipline.[19] Tillotson, a contemporary of Baxter and Milton, expressed a similar belief in the indispensability of custom in guiding proper conduct: "custom bears a huge sway in all humane actions. Men love those things and do them with ease to which they have become long inured and accustomed." Like Baxter, he realizes that steadiness of purpose can operate beneath the level of discursive awareness and rational proof, as long as it follows from an initiating commitment to believe and act properly:

Not that we are obliged always actually to think upon [salvation]; but to have it frequently in our minds, and habitually to intend and design it, so as to make it the scope of all our endeavors and actions, and that everything we do be either directly in order to it, or some way or other subservient to this design . . . like the term and end of a man's journey, towards which the traveler is continually tending, and hath it always habitually in his intention, tho' he doth not always think of it every step that he takes, and tho' he be not always directly advancing and moving towards it, yet he never knowingly goes out of the way . . . if our mind be once fixed and resolved, that will determine and govern all our motions, and inspire us with diligence, and zeal, and perseverance in the prosecution of our end.[20]

For Tillotson, as for Baxter, the "habitual intention" once implemented requires negligible additional management—as if both theologians argue a kind of internalized or personalized deism, modeling the self as a clock or similar mechanism that, once set properly by a foundationally rational act, remains perfectly operative and self-governing. In a Eucharist sermon preached at Westminster Abbey, Robert South, who usually occupied a position more conservative than his latitudinarian contemporaries on doctrinal points, draws an analogy between individual ethical maintenance and mechanistic functionalism:

> Common experience shows that the wisest of men are not always fit and disposed to act wisely. . . . They have a . . . standing ability of wisdom and eloquence within them, which gives them an habitual sufficiency for such performances . . . [but] the most active powers and faculties of the mind require something besides themselves to raise them to the full height of their natural activity: something to excite, and quicken, and draw them forth into immediate action. . . . [Like] the having of wheels and springs, though never so curiously wrought, and artificially set, but the winding of them up, that must give motion to the watch . . . we must add actual preparation to habitual.[21]

The causal relationship South underlines between "actual" and "habitual" preparation conforms to the procedure Baxter and Tillotson describe of setting habitual conduct to work by a prior momentous rational decision or series of rational decisions. Moral pragmatism does not involve an ongoing disposition to act with practical wisdom, according to classical ethics, nor is such pragmatism an integral feature of mid-century notions of ethical rationalism, which, for moderate Anglicans like Chillingworth and John Hale, held that the light of reason itself helped the individual to make deductions and reach conclusions about theological fundamentals.[22]

In an influential article on the role of habit in late-seventeenth-century theology, Paul Alkon argued that Aristotle's theory of *hexis* or moral habituation influenced the moral theories of South, Tillotson, William Law, and Samuel Johnson. Alkon, rightly noting the many references to habit throughout latitudinarian sermons, concludes that South and Tillotson, for instance, place Aristotle's familiar advice that moral virtue is acquired through practice and repetition in a "thoroughly Christian context of otherworldly concern by stressing the supernatural and scriptural benefits of actively cultivating virtuous habits."[23] While Alkon cites a number of passages in which latitudinarian views on habit are consistent with Aristotelianism, he fails to point out the fundamental differences between Aristotelianism and late-seventeenth-century moral pragmatism, differences that range beyond the basic pagan–Christian tension running throughout the sermons.

In the above passages, the preachers argue that a series of momentous rational choices guide the will to bind the moral agent to habitual, non-rational action. For Aristotle, prudence or practical wisdom, the product of ethical habituation, is an improvisational capability to act virtuously in contingent situations.[24] All of the theologians cited above recommend in some cases unthinking action in pursuit of spiritual ends, a process which Aristotelian virtuosity militantly disallows. Because Aristotelian *hexis* provides practical skills which can be applied in novel situations, it assumes that intense self-awareness, clarity, and reasoned choice precede virtuous action. In contrast to Aristotelian *hexis,* seventeenth-century moral pragmatism assumes that habituation relieves the burden of evaluation and re-evaluation at every moment, that an application of hardened conduct itself can provide ethical guidance and the eventual acquisition of faith.[25]

Late-seventeenth-century moral pragmatism shares much with Blaise Pascal's influential account of habit, as related in his notes on the wager concerning the existence of God. After arguing that the decision to believe in God is justified because of the potential gains in the afterlife if, in fact, God does exist, Pascal imagines a question posed by his skeptical interlocutor: "yes, but my hands are tied and I cannot speak a word. I am being forced to wager and I am not free, they will not let me go. And I am made in such a way that I cannot believe. So what do you want me to do?"[26] After responding that his interlocutor's inability to believe stems from his servitude to the passions, Pascal recommends that rather than futilely multiplying arguments and proofs, his interlocutor should carry on like those who act "as if they believed, having masses said, etc. This will make you believe quite naturally, and according to your animal reactions."[27] Pascal believes that purer versions of belief and faith will eventually follow if his skeptic agrees to act obediently, in spite of the skeptic's uncertainty regarding God's existence. When Pascal resorts to the nascent principles of decision theory and probabilistic reasoning, he aims neither to prove the existence of God nor even to convince his readers to make a willful decision to believe in God. He simply argues that obedience is worthwhile given the utilities presented by the wager. As Ian Hacking writes, Pascal realizes that "one cannot decide to believe in God. One can decide to act so that one will very probably come to believe in God."[28]

For Pascal, the existence of God cannot be deduced by an exercise of pure reason or elaborate metaphysical proofs. Such misleading proofs are the product of dogmatism, particularly rational deism, which assumes that the rational faculty can probe the rational principles of nature and divine law. Pyrrhonist skepticism, however, at the other extreme from dogmatism, is atheistical in negating the existence of God in the absence of contrary proofs. In place of dogmatism and unmethodological skepticism, Pascal believes in the efficacy of discrete rational choices, choices that are self-undermining because they are based on probability calculations that yield governance to habitual conduct: "In the end, we have to resort to custom once the mind has seen where the truth lies, to immerse and ingrain ourselves in this belief, which constantly eludes us."[29] Pascal realizes that the "last proceeding of reason is to recognize the fact that an infinity of things are beyond it."[30] As Jean Mesnard writes, "On the path to the affirmation of God, reason can help us take the first steps and, from the moment that it exerts itself correctly, all of its resources can be usefully employed without reservation and distrust," but "the affirmation of God demands the submission of reason." As Pascal says, "Nothing conforms so much to reason as this disavowal of reason."[31]

English latitudinarian sermonists of the 1660s through the 1680s frequently made pragmatic and probabilistic arguments similar to those of Pascal. Consider Tillotson's claim: "If there be no God the case of the Religious man and the Atheist will be alike, because they will both be extinguished by death and insensible of any further happiness or misery. But . . . if there is a God . . . where shall the wicked and ungodly appear? What can they expect but to be rejected by him whom they have renounced, and to feel the terrible effects of that Power and Justice which they have despised? So that tho' the arguments on both sides were equal, yet the danger is not so. On the one side there is none at all, but 'tis infinite on the other."[32] As Henry Van Leeuwen says of this passage, Tillotson, "using a wager argument similar to that of Pascal . . . argues that if Christianity is false the believer will lose only some of the baser pleasures of life, whereas if it is true that there is a God and future rewards the atheist will lose his soul for eternity."[33] Jeremy Taylor uses a Pascalian argument in order to explain the problems of obeying God, rather than the more foundational problem of believing in God's existence. Taylor writes in *Unum Necessarium* (1655): "the first cause of an universal impiety is, that at first God had made no promises of heaven. He had not propounded any glorious rewards, to be as an argument to support the superior faculty against the inferior, that is, to make the will choose the best and leave the worst, and to be as a reward for suffering contradiction."[34]

Before we turn to a discussion of Milton's ethical views and *Paradise Lost* in the context of the above themes, I will further define the role of reason in seventeenth-century moral pragmatism by drawing a distinction between reasonableness and rational choice. As John Rawls notes, moral philosophers frequently argue that a person who acts reasonably considers the effects that his or her actions will have on the well-being of larger communities of reasonable agents. An agent who acts rationally, on the other hand, is concerned primarily with personal utility, and acts in accordance with probability calculations and economic preferences. The outcome of a rational choice may have desirable ethical consequences, but such consequences are incidental to the initial rational commitment. As one commentator writes, "knowing that people are rational we do not know the ends that they will pursue, only that they will pursue them intelligently. Knowing that people are reasonable, where others are concerned, we know that they are willing to govern their conduct by a principle which they and others can reason in common."[35] The moral pragmatist relates rational choices to reasonableness as a means to an end. By rationally committing oneself to habitual conduct, a decision that itself is a means to future personal gains, he or she will eventually acquire a reasonable end of true belief and ethical certainty.

The therapeutic ethical strategy I have been describing departs significantly from both poles of the Reformation opposition between compatibilism and libertarianism. Seventeenth-century compatibilists argued that beliefs in determinism and free will are not mutually exclusive, since God is the first cause by which persons act contingently and freely. Seventeenth-century anticompatibilists, as Dennis Danielson notes, argued that free will requires causal indifferency, "according to which, in a given moral choice, necessary conditions exist that allow the agent to choose one way or the other."[36] Thus the anticompatibilist Walter Charleton argued that "the nature of Liberty Elective seems radically to consist in that Indifference, in respect whereof the Faculty called free, may or may not be carried on towards any particular object."[37] Charleton believed that anticompatibilists reject causal indifferency, although they do not assume causal compulsion: "The Elect are therefore Free, because they do their Good works Libently, or Willingly; and likewise, that the Reprobate are also Free, because they do their Evil works Libently."[38] As Danielson remarks, "according to the compatibilist view, one is responsible for the evil one does, because it is done willingly, though necessarily."[39]

The pragmatic ethic of habituation can be described as a form of anthropological or intrapersonal compatibilism. Pragmatists relocate the originating cause of practical-ethical, everyday conduct, analogous to what compatibilists term the godly "prenominating cause," internally within the moral agent. Libertarianism does not follow this foundational act or series of acts, since the efficient act of self-management then binds the will to act in accordance with whatever beliefs, standards, and goals to which one has committed oneself. Moral agents, guided by a range of instructional sources—education, scripture, natural law—create themselves as efficient moral beings. In the pages below, I argue that in *Paradise Lost* Adam and Eve are placed in the precarious prelapsarian situation of experiencing all of the elements of the pragmatic ethic except for one essential component, the rational decision to commit themselves to the nonrational guidance of habit. Prelapsarian Adam and Eve are compatibilists who need to transform themselves into intracompatibilists. They exhibit the kind of habitual but not automatic or mechanical ethic recommended by late-seventeenth-century moral doctrine, but they have been denied the option of choosing a life of mostly unreflective nonchoosing. How Milton has them resolve their ethical quandary will be the subject of the rest of this essay.

MILTON'S MORAL PRAGMATISM

Drawing on the foundational work on the Fall by N. P. Williams and John Hicks, Dennis Danielson has distinguished two early Christian accounts of man's ethical stature, the Augustinian or "maximal" view and the Irenaean or "minimal" view. According to the Augustinian position, Adam and Eve are ethically perfect upon creation; moral progress is a postlapsarian phenomenon.[40] According to the Irenaean position, Adam and Eve are ethically imperfect upon creation; only gradually, through a process of trial and error, do they realize their preordained likeness to God. According to this "soul-making" theodicy, the "one who has attained to goodness by meeting and eventually mastering temptation, and thus by rightly making responsible choices in concrete situations, is good in a richer and more valuable sense than would be one created ab initio in a state . . . of virtue."[41] Danielson argues that *Areopagitica*'s vindication of trial by contraries is consistent with Irenaean rather than Augustinian theodicy. According to Danielson, when Milton claims that "God sure esteems the growth and compleating of one vertuous person, more than the restraint of ten vitious," Milton is suggesting that "Adam must not be a puppet."[42]

Other critics have found a similar ethic of soul-making in Milton's critique of custom and habit in his prose writings. John Rumrich, the most outspoken critic of the "invented" Milton, argues that for Milton, "truth was a goal to be worked toward, rather than an accomplished set of beliefs. How should we reconcile the vision of Milton as a preaching narrator with the voice that, in *The Doctrine and Discipline of Divorce,* allegorized custom or tradition as the puffed-up countenance of monstrous error? Milton's conviction that submission to external interpretive authority undermines true virtue was fundamental to his disenchantment with the 'ordinary' Christians of his time. . . . Sources often cited as background for Milton's pedagogical method and message, however, recommend automatic, habitual, unreasoning response to trial and temptation."[43]

Neither Rumrich nor Danielson is willing to attribute to Milton a pro-habit ethical system that is personally initiated, rationally motivated, and largely self-governing. Although Rumrich argues for an iconoclastic Milton and Danielson for a theocentric Milton, both critics draw an overly simplified opposition between freedom to choose and habit, when habit may very well be the most desirable outcome of free choices. In the passage quoted above, Rumrich makes unwarranted inferences from Milton's abhorrence of institutional practices to Milton's conception of "pedagogy" (which may or may not include institutionalization), to Milton's recommendation for alleviating "trial and temptation." Surely practices of ethical habituation can be essential to moral conduct even if such conduct is neither monitored by Presbyterianism nor recommended by the "authoritative interpretation of revelation."

Areopagitica's Irenaenism remains mostly on the level of diagnosis and exhortation, and as such it cannot explain the precise nature of Adam and Eve's practical-moral education in a mimetic epic like *Paradise Lost*. As a polemical text, *Areopagitica* does not describe how ethical agents act on a daily basis, how discrete acts of trial by contraries can be organized into a larger ethical framework, or how classical and Christian virtues can be acquired and retained. Irenaenism is a teleological ethical system that posits the final cause of creaturely existence but does not offer practical, everyday advice on how an individual's behavior can be regulated. In addition to a few remarks regarding trial by contraries, Irenaeus's ethical commentary in *Against Heresies* is limited to general observations like the following: "[God planned that] man, passing through all things, and acquiring the knowledge of moral discipline, then attaining to the resurrection from the dead, and learning by experience what is the source of his deliverance, may always live in a state of gratitude to the Lord. . . . Now it was necessary that man should in the first instance be created; and having been created, should receive growth; and having received growth should be strengthened; and having been strengthened should abound."[44] Irenaeus fails to discuss precisely how man is able to acquire moral discipline.

If we turn briefly to Milton's views on custom we will not find evidence that Milton abhorred ethical habituation in the way that he did certain traditional beliefs and superstitions. In *Doctrine and Discipline of Divorce*, he denounces custom because it "puffs up unhealthily a certain big face of pretended learning, mistaken among credulous men for the wholesome habit of soundness and good constitution, but is indeed no other than that swoln visit of counterfeit knowledge and literature, which not only in private mars our education, but also in public is the common climber into every chair."[45] Milton does not offer here anything more than a critique of custom from the vantage point of epistemology. Such a criticism of traditional or "counterfeit" modes of thinking does not suggest that unreflective practical conduct is equally stultifying. In fact, Milton draws a *distinction* in the passage between custom and habit when he suggests that custom is often mistaken for the "wholesome habit of soundness and good constitution." Unfortunately Milton does not elaborate his appreciation of habit, but he clearly believes that habit and custom are not identical.

In *Of Reformation*, Milton refers approvingly to Cyprian's Seventy-fourth Epistle on the subject of custom: "neither ought Custome to hinder that Truth should not prevaile, for Custome without Truth is but agednesse of error" (YP 1.561). In the prefatory comments to *The Reason of Church-*

Government, Milton justifies his project by invoking Plato's belief that a "well-tempered discourse . . . would so incite, and in a manner charm, the multitude into the love of that which is really good, as to embrace it ever after, not of custom and awe, which most men do, but of choice and purpose, with true and constant delight" (YP 1:747). In these references and those of the divorce tracts, customs originate from sources external to the individual. The administration of customary thinking is never a private affair from its inception. As does power in Foucault's sense, custom traverses and insinuates itself into persons, hence the coupling of personification and action verbs used to track its movements. Often custom is objectified, the focus of our "awe," but it more often travels and finds its terminus by "visiting" and "climbing" its way into our belief systems. Custom so conceived bears little resemblance to the process of habituation described by moral pragmatism, which is implemented purposefully by an individual's rational decisions.

One passage that links Milton's ideas on faith (and implicitly habit) with the tradition of late-seventeenth-century moral pragmatism appears in Book One, Chapter 20, of *De Doctrina,* in Milton's discussion of implicit faith: "Implicit faith, which sees not the objects of hope, but yields belief with a blind assent, cannot possibly be genuine faith, except in the case of novices or first converts, whose faith must necessarily be for a time implicit, inasmuch as they believe even before they have entered upon a course of instruction" (YP 6:338). That Milton finds implicit faith neither uncommon nor unacceptable (if not ideal) is shown by the list of exemplary implicit believers he compiles from biblical history: "such was that of the Samaritans. John xi. 31. and of the disciples, who believed in Christ long before they were accurately acquainted with the many articles of faith. Those also belong to this class, who are slow of understanding and inapt to learn, but who nevertheless believe according to the measure of their knowledge, and striving to live by faith, are acceptable to God" (YP 6:338).

Milton's account of implicit faith would parallel moral pragmatism exactly if Milton also had written that the act of yielding is itself a rational choice to admit reason's impotence in the absence of further instruction. This further criterion can be assumed in Milton's account, given the hymns to reasonableness which are found elsewhere in *De Doctrina.* As Richard Strier has pointed out in a rigorous discussion of Milton's ethical rationalism, *De Doctrina's* anti-Calvinism emphatically stresses the role of deliberative reason under all conditions. Strier has compiled a series of comments from *De Doctrina* showing Milton's commitment to ethical rationalism. Milton remarks, for example, that if Trinitarian arguments are to be convincing they must be based on "reasonable, and not absurd notions which are utterly alien to all ways of thinking" (YP 6:222). Milton argues further that predestination is false because it is "repulsive and unreasonable" (YP 6:164), and that "everyone is provided with sufficient innate reason for him to be able to resist evil desires by his own efforts" (YP 6:186).[46] As Strier writes, Milton's "conception of freedom is entirely a conception of deliberation and choice."[47]

How can we reconcile the ubiquitous call in *De Doctrina* to act deliberatively with the same text's own admission that first converts can act justifiably following a nonrational, blind assent to believe? Is such a novice pardoned, during her formative stages of religious education, from prudential conduct? The only way to make sense of the logic of *De Doctrina* is to assume that Milton has in mind a pragmatic argument: the novice, not fully instructed in matters relevant to the acquisition of pure faith, can still act reasonably by making a rational decision to trust uncertain doctrine. I will argue below that in *Paradise Lost* Adam and Eve, despite their keen acquisition of scientific knowledge and self-knowledge, remain novices in matters of faith and ethical conduct.[48]

ADAM AND EVE'S FALL FROM REASONABLENESS TO RATIONAL CHOICE

In her essay "Innocence and Experience in Milton's Eden," Barbara Lewalski draws an analogy between Adam and Eve's cultivation of the garden and their development of a virtuous "paradise within." After noting that Edenic growth tends toward wildness and so requires constant maintenance, Lewalski writes:

> The poem's garden imagery identifies Adam and Eve not only as gardeners but also as part of the Garden: they too are 'planted' by God, expected to grow and perfect themselves through cultivation, and to bear appropriate fruits. . . . Adam and Eve . . . have natures capable of a prodigious growth of good things, but which require constant pruning to remove excessive or unsightly growth, constant direction of overreaching tendencies, constant propping of possible weaknesses, and also, one supposes, further cultivation through art.[49]

Throughout the essay Lewalski collapses distinctions between the knowledge and progress that Adam and Eve are to attain—the growth of human society or the knowledge of astronomy, for example—and Adam and Eve's moral development. Except for one command by God to Adam—"govern well thy appetite, lest sin / Surprise thee" (*PL* 7.546–47)[50]—Lewalski cites no compelling evidence suggesting that the analogy between external and internal "labor" concerns specifically moral progress rather than biological, historical, or scientific progress. Nor does Lewalski explain in any detail the association she seems to make between virtue and progress in general. During key moments, rather than show Adam and Eve's linear development in virtue, Lewalski refers to Milton's ideas on morality that appear in texts other than

Paradise Lost. Thus she quotes *Areopagitica* on the importance of "temper-
ing virtue" to support her claim that the only security from Satan is "watchfulness and constant growth in virtue and wisdom."[51]

The passages Lewalski does invoke in order to draw out the analogy
between the cultivation of the garden and Adam and Eve's self-initiation have
nothing to say about the construction of virtuous character. She cites, for
instance, as evidence of the cultivation of a "paradise within," the following
passage from Book Five: "They led the vine / To wed her Elm; she spous'd
about him twines / Her marriageable arms, and with her brings / Her dow'r th'
adopted Clusters, to adorn / His barren leaves" (5.215–19). Lewalski writes of
this passage that "Eve has been identified as a 'vine' with tendrils clustering
about Adam, and she is to solace his loneliness, bring him progeny, cleave to
him."[52] Lewalski offers a beautiful gloss on these lines. But she cannot discuss
its ethical implications, since the passage has nothing to say about moral
perfection. In another instance, after discussing Adam and Eve's sexual relations, their need to deepen their knowledge of astronomy, and Raphael's
remark that all things "body up to spirit work, in bounds / Proportion'd to each
kind" (5.478–79), Lewalski writes, "By means of such departures from the
expected, primal man's nature is shown to be complex and constantly developing, not simple and stable. Each new situation in Milton's Eden is an opportunity to grow in wisdom, virtue, and perfection."[53] She uses the term virtue so
generally that it is emptied of meaning. One wants from Lewalski a fuller
account of the relationship between virtue and science, virtue and sexual
consummation, virtue and perfection, and virtue and wisdom.

Lewalski's most curious conflation of knowledge and ethics occurs when
she invokes Socratic ethics in order to describe Adam's realization that he
should seek to acquire practical rather than cosmological knowledge: "Now
he announces himself a committed humanist, and like Socrates proposes to
'descend': from speculation about the heavens (whether angelic warfare, or
creation, or planets) and seek the 'prime wisdom,' namely, 'That which before us lies in daily life'—in Socratic terms, self-knowledge, ethics (8.193–
94)."[54] Adam's decision to focus on matters of "daily life" rather than cosmological issues does not necessarily reflect his acquisition of self-knowledge
and a Socratic ethic. Adam makes a case in these passages for what Charles
Taylor has described as the seventeenth-century "affirmation of ordinary
life," according to which a commitment to acquiring useful knowledge replaces unprofitable curiosity regarding God's voluntaristic nature (a world-
view which Taylor himself says is incompatible with Socratic ethics).[55] Such
an affirmation of ordinary life does not assume "self-knowledge" necessarily;
indeed, it in many ways served to relieve the burden of intensely experienced
affective individualism. More important, a commitment to learning useful

knowledge is not a sufficient condition for Socratic virtue, which denies incontinence and requires objective knowledge of good and evil. If Adam and Eve possessed such objective or scientific knowledge of good and evil in Eden, then what point would the Tree of Knowledge and the Fall possibly serve?

There is, I think, an alternative way of explaining the role of Edenic labor, one which avoids making generalizations about Adam and Eve's moral progress but does not deny the importance of their education in science and cosmology. In Book Four, after relating to Eve God's prohibitions concerning the Tree of Knowledge, Adam tells her that, "God hath pronounc't it death to taste that Tree, / The only sign of our obedience left. . . . Then let us not think hard / One easy prohibition. . . . But let us ever praise him . . . following our delightful task to prune these growing plants, and tend these Flow'rs" (4.427–38). Have Adam and Eve made a rational decision not to "think hard one easy prohibition"? What, as Jeremy Taylor asks, are the gains and losses of such obedience? There are no future gains in the sense that Adam and Eve stand to acquire something more than what they already have been given (they have not yet been told that they can ascend the scale of nature should they remain obedient, an important condition which I discuss below). Of course, what they would retain is "all this happiness" (4.417) and "Dominion giv'n / over all other Creatures" (4.430–31), but Adam performs no weighting procedures indicating that he understands the possibility of losing such goods should they disobey. He argues that since they already have such goods, obeying one easy prohibition cannot be so difficult. The distinction is a fine but I think essential one. Adam does not make a rational calculation to obey based on an evaluation of his interests. He makes a decision to obey based on his sense of the proper gratitude and duty owed toward God. His experience of happiness makes obedience easier; it does not motivate his obedience in the same way that one's abstention from alcohol, for instance, might be motivated by a desire to remain healthy or to retain a job.

What does seem more self-interested is Adam's fear of death, but his comments on death are so confused as to make any attribution of rationality to his obedience unwarranted. He tells Eve of the Tree of Knowledge: "planted by the Tree of Life, / So near grows Death to Life, whate'er death is, / Some dreadful thing no doubt; for well thou know'st / God hath pronounc't it death to taste that Tree" (4.424–27). Adam does not say that death is dreadful and God has said as much; he says that death is dreadful *because* God has said as much. This ranks among the most transparently voluntaristic comments in the entire poem. It is reminiscent of Ockham's well-known revision of Aquinas's naturalistic ethic. While Aquinas had argued that God demands x because x is good, Ockham argued that x is good simply because

God demands x. God might have substituted anything for "death" in his prohibition, and Adam would have simply re-inserted the substitution in his template of a remark: "x is some dreadful thing no doubt."

If, for argument's sake, we suppose that the pair does make a considered decision to obey the prohibition, does this imply that they act in accordance with the tenets of theological pragmatism? To the extent that they make rational decisions to act for the most part unreflectively, they still will have met only two of the three criteria for pragmatism. What justifies a rational decision to act nonrationally is the assumption, included in Baxter, Pascal, and Milton's views on the subject, that over time agents will come to understand clearly matters previously taken on blind faith. This is precisely what is omitted from Adam and Eve's decision scenario, since God does not suggest that they will eventually acquire a deeper understanding specifically of the Tree of Knowledge and the prohibition. Since they do not factor the promise of firmer knowledge into their original decision to act habitually, their conduct does not meet the criteria of moral pragmatism; without such a promise, obedience is diluted of rationality.

From the assumption that Adam and Eve's conduct up to this point meets only the second criterion of moral pragmatism—moderate reflectiveness in the face of limited knowledge (excluding any rational decision to obey)—we can see that the first call to labor in Book Four partly serves a benign means of distraction. Adam says to Eve, "Then let us not think hard / One easy prohibition. . . . But let us ever praise him . . . following our delightful task / To prune these growing plants, and tend these Flow'rs" (4.427–38). Here and elsewhere Adam's abrupt turn from epistemological questioning to the immediacy of physical labor allows him to fix his attention on a manageable and non-speculative pursuit. Lewalski fails to remark on the arbitrariness of Adam's first invocation of gardening, which is introduced as a non sequitur from his immediately preceding narration of God's prohibitions. Edenic labor often provides a distraction that allows Adam and Eve to avoid inquiring about unanswerable questions. Rather than recall a scheduled responsibility, Adam seems to happen upon the prospect of ritualized labor.

Adam and Eve's conduct throughout Books Four and Five oscillates between distraction and moderate reflectiveness. If Adam first suggests to Eve that labor will redirect their attention away from God's dispensations, Eve then suggests to Adam that his decrees alone can bind her unthoughtful obedience:

> My Author and Disposer, what thou bidd'st
> Unargu'd I obey; so God ordains,
> God is thy Law, thou mine: to know no more

> Is woman's happiest knowledge and her praise.
> With thee conversing I forget all time,
> All seasons and thir change, all please alike   (4.635–40).

Eve expresses here almost a parody of the doctrine of learned ignorance. Rather than reasonably deriving her conclusion to bind herself unarguingly to Adam, she allows a simple awareness of chained commandments to govern her conduct: "I will act as Adam acts because Adam acts as God commands." Should we say that such a resignation furthers Eve's moral progress?

Following Eve's narration of her dream in Book Five, Adam attempts to calm her by offering a brief lesson in faculty psychology and the role of fancy in self-deception, and he assures her that images of evil in one's mind "may come and go" (5.118). But then rather than give Eve time to respond and allow a dialogue to follow, Adam quickly reminds her of the work at hand: "And let us to our fresh imployments rise" (5.125). The conjunction "and" is curious, since the natural word to mark the syntactical turn in Adam's speech should be "instead," or "rather." Adam's full comment is, "Be not disheart'nd then, nor cloud those looks / That wont to be more cheerful and serene / Than when the fair Morning first smiles on the World, / And let us to our fresh employments rise" (5.122–25). The use of "and" rather than a more appropriate transition allows Adam to finesse the call to labor in the groves, which are alluringly suffused with "the choicest bosom'd smells" (5.127). Adam might as well have waved an apple, or any other enticement that might have helped to press back into Eve's unconscious the images of her dream. Here again, the call to labor serves as an efficient means of distractive pleasure. Lewalski hurries over the passage when she remarks, "In the moral climate of Milton's Eden, Eve's virtual experience of evil no doubt creates new tensions within her but by making her so much more aware of evil's true nature, it could greatly enhance her ability and her determination to shun the actual experience."[56] But of course the episode does not enhance Eve's ability to shun the actual experience. Rather, Milton's decision not to allow Eve the time to respond to Adam, to ruminate on his advice, to think for herself in a reasoned dialogue, all converge to make her that much more susceptible to the actual temptation.

Adam and Eve's ethic of unreflection is represented not only in their timely moves toward labor but also in the tableau which models their unity in devotion. The narrator notes that on one occasion before praying, Adam and Eve "both stood, both turned" (4.720), and upon completion of their devotions, they lay their troublesome disguises "straight side by side" (4.741). Their conduct is also perfectly synchronized in Book Five when they perform their Orisons without meditation or rehearsal: "Unmeditated, such prompt eloquence / Flow'd from thir lips" (5.149–50). "Unmeditated" is a suggestive word choice in this description. To say that one meditates or not when pray-ing would seem to refer to a practice occurring (or not occurring) during the actual event of praying. The narrator, however, suggests that meditation, if it had occurred at all in this context, would have begun prior to the praying, as if meditation has a causal rather than constitutive relationship to the conduct. Adam and Eve's devotions just break into sound, seemingly without motiva-tion. There is certainly something endearing about the spontaneity of Adam and Eve's behavior. Because they pray "in various style" (5.146), they should not be described as automata. But there is also something unsettling about the limits Milton puts on their ability to self-consciously coordinate their own actions.

Adam and Eve at this point seem to meet many of the criteria for morally pragmatic behavior. Their conduct is mostly unreflective, although not entirely mechanical, in keeping with the recommendations of Baxter and his contemporaries; it is predictable, disciplined, and sufficiently routine, but not slavishly practiced. But their behavior has never been fixed by a self-consciously rational act or set of acts, and so may not be sufficiently resolute, enabling them to withstand perverse turns of the will. Of course, part of the reason that such formative prior moments are not represented is that, given the myth bequeathed to Milton, Adam and Eve have no extended past lives. This is no small problem when it comes to representing the long and arduous processes by which pre-modern ethical agents learn how to act ethically. And it helps to explain, as I discuss in detail later, why Raphael painstakingly narrates the War in Heaven as a means of preventing the pair's apostasy.

Lewalski argues that, during his expostulation with God in Book Eight immediately following his creation, Adam begins a process of growth that is governed above all by his use of a "discourse of reason": "By discourse of reason he [Adam] works out the fact that he is not self-generated, and that he ought to discover and adore his creator, so he asks the creatures (not yet knowing they are mute) who he is, and who his maker is."[57] The lines actually read, "Fair Creatures, tell, / Tell, if ye saw, how came I this, how here? / Not of myself; by some great Maker then" (8.276–78). Adam's immediate answer to his own question gives the impression that, despite the reflexive pronoun, somehow his own voice and the creatures' response have been fused into one intuitively clear response, as if the answer is so obvious that the question never had to be asked in the first place. To say, as Lewalski does, that Adam undergoes such an illumination by "discourse of reason" misleadingly implies that much more ratiocination is at play than what the lines suggest. Adam, of course, does later show his gifts for ratiocination when he makes his plea to God for a mate, but his reasoning is focused neither on God's prohibitions nor on his decision to commit himself to such prohibitions.

During their otherwise benign rituals, Adam and Eve reveal that they have not simply deferred a rational inquiry as to God's unrevealed ways; rather, they have deferred an otherwise self-imposed rational choice *not* to explore God's ways. Adam thrusts himself into habitual labor just as Eve unquestioningly accepts Adam's decisions on the pair's behalf. The problem is not in their not asking but in their thrusting without having first made a considered decision not to ask. The term "choice" to describe prior willing, deliberation, or reasoning behind their conduct is conspicuously missing throughout these exchanges. This is what makes so curious the double reference to choice when Eve decides to prepare an eclectic meal for Raphael: "She turns, on hospitable thoughts intent / What choice to choose for delicacy best, / What order, so contriv'd as not to mix / Tastes" (5.332–35). Given how committed Eve has been thus far to unchosen actions and beliefs, there is a certain pathos in her obsessiveness about choosing what to serve for dinner. Eve's overchoosing in relation to a domestic triviality suggests that if the relationship between choice and habit is not proportionably dispensed, rationality, which, according to moral pragmatism, needs to decide upon its own impotence, immeasurably lingers and follows rather than precedes habit. The limitations in acting unreflectively without having rationally committed oneself to unreflection surface when Adam confesses to Raphael that his "constant thoughts" are not necessarily unswerving: "Yet that we never shall forget to love / Our maker, and obey him whose command / Single, is yet so just, my constant thoughts / Assur'd me, and still assure: though what thou tell'st / Hath past in heaven, some doubt within me move" (5.550–54). Since Adam's "constant thoughts" do not have assured staying power in the absence of a prior commitment to thinking constantly, his knowledge of another's fall from heaven partially undermines his own faith.

We can begin to see more clearly the problems of both the Irenaean view that Adam and Eve need to develop into morally responsible adults and the Augustinian view that they are morally perfect adults while in Eden. While the Irenaean school cannot make sense of Adam and Eve's intuitive knowledge of devotional practices and the spontaneity of their obedience, the Augustinian school cannot convincingly argue that, in the absence of clear deliberation about means and ends, Adam and Eve are perfectly ethical agents upon creation (at least not according to any acceptable criteria for moral excellence figuring in the history of moral doctrine). As I have been suggesting, moral pragmatism helps resolve a number of these difficulties, and helps integrate rather than dichotomize what Richard Strier has set up as, on the one hand, the ethical rationalism of *De Doctrina* and, on the other hand, Adam and Eve's spontaneous prelapsarian obedience and generosity.[58] Whether we describe spontaneous obedience as virtuous or not, it can only be considered sufficiently virtuous if it meets *De Doctrina's* criteria for virtue, that is, if it is combined with effective and binding practices of rational deliberation. The pragmatic ethic is the only normative ethic that allows for the integration of a minimum of reason with a maximum of instinctive obedience. And, as I suggest below, the processes by which Adam and Eve come to add such rationality to their spontaneity help to explain the events that lead up to the Fall.

The first step Adam and Eve take toward properly acquiring the pragmatic ethic occurs during the separation scene. Critics have failed to notice Adam and Eve exercise two very different types of reason throughout this scene. I have already mentioned the analytical distinction between reasonableness and rational choice, the former describing an ongoing disposition and willingness to act ethically, the latter an occurrent, mostly instrumental practice of private choosing based on probability calculations (the latter is more properly described as pragmatically ethical rather than ethical as such). During the separation scene, Eve insists on exercising rational choice, while Adam insists on exercising reasonableness. Eve tells Adam: "Let us divide our labours, thou where choice / Leads thee . . . while I . . . find what to redress till Noon: / For while so near each other thus all day / Our task we choose, what wonder if so near / Looks intervene and smiles, or object new / Casual discourse draw on, which intermits / Our day's work brought to little" (9.214–24). Given the probability that cooperative work brings too great a chance of interruption, Eve motions compellingly that the potential gains in fellowship will be offset by the potential losses in efficiency. Adam then defines cooperation and fellowship as man's distinguishing marks of reasonableness: "for smiles / from Reason flow, / To brute deni'd. . . . For not to irksome toil, but to delight / He made us, and delight to reason join'd" (9.239–43).

Eve displays in this exchange moral pragmatism writ small by making a rational case for committing herself to nonreasonable conduct, conduct which does not immediately involve discourse, curiosity, or mutuality. The encounter during the separation scene is one of the most formative and educational experiences in Adam and Eve's moral development; it instructs the pair (although Adam does not immediately realize this) in the importance of assessing a situation, weighing alternatives, and acting deliberately in pursuit of a long-term goal. No model of behavior like this one has been represented up to this point, and it anticipates the type of choice Eve will make when she is tempted by Satan. Only when Eve's conduct is evaluated out of the immediate context of the poem and the context of the history of moral philosophy does Eve seem to deserve the blame which Adam and legions of interpreters have heaped upon her.

Upon encountering Satan during the temptation scene, then, Eve has already assimilated the structural features of moral pragmatism. Whether she will decide to act obediently or not will be determined by a cost-benefit analysis. Before looking at the temptation scene I would like to remark on a passage on the Fall already quoted above, from Jeremy Taylor's *Unum Necessarium* (1655). Taylor writes that "the first cause of an universal impiety is, that at first God had made no promises of heaven, He had not propounded any glorious rewards, to be as an argument to support the superior faculty against the inferior, that is, to make the will choose the best and leave the worst, and to be as a reward for suffering contradiction."[59] Taylor believes that when faced with a decision to obey God, any rational person must resort to basic principles of decision theory and moral consequentialism. Since, as Taylor insists, God offered Adam no "recompense" for abstention, it is "no wonder that when Adam had no promises made to enable him to contest his natural concupiscence, he should strive to make his condition better by the devil's promises."[60]

Taylor's interpretation of Adam's behavior as rationally justifiable—a calculated decision to indulge—can be applied to Eve's conduct during the temptation scene. Eve seems ready to stake blind obedience in God but fails to understand the gains that would accrue were she to remain obedient and the losses that would ensue were she to commit herself to the serpent. The gains of disobedience are clearly proffered: a "happier life" (9.697) and "knowledge of good and evil" (9.697), and the chance to become "A Goddess among Gods, ador'd and serv'd / By Angels numberless, thy daily Train" (9.547–48). Significantly, such considerations appeal, as the narrator says, to Eve's "reason" (9.738), again suggesting that Eve at this point thinks pragmatically and calculatingly. On the other side, the potential losses if Eve forsakes God amount to death, but it is not clear that Eve has any settled notions of what death might entail. All God has told her (through Adam) is that she should neither eat nor touch the fruit, "lest ye die" (9.663), only a direful prospect if Eve understands the seriousness of death in the first place. As I have already noted, that neither she nor Adam feels any real dread of death at this point is shown by Adam's remark that although he has no clear notion of death, it is "some dreadful thing no doubt" (4.426). Satan exploits Eve's ignorance when he says, "whatever thing Death be" (9.695). Eve, of course, will later ruminate on death (9.758–73), but only after her lapse does she make any attempt to define death: "And Death ensue? then I shall be no more" (9.827). Given such utilities for and against God, at this point the serpent's gambit looks highly attractive.

It is more difficult to determine what Eve believes she would gain if she remains obedient, or, in the absence of any future compensations, whether she weighs the value of what she already has against Satan's offers. Raphael has already suggested to the pair what might be interpreted as a future gain should they remain committed to God. Raphael tells Adam that, should he and Eve remain obedient, their "bodies may at last turn all to spirit, / Improv'd by tract of time, and wing'd ascend / Ethereal, as wee" (5.497–99), to which Adam responds, "Well hast thou taught the way that might direct / Our knowledge, and the scale of Nature set / From centre to circumference, whereon / In contemplation of created things / By steps we may ascend to God" (5.508–12).

Why doesn't Eve remind herself of the promised ascent? What are the values Adam and Eve place on such a promise? Importantly, Milton never suggests that the ascent is considered by the pair to be a gain or achievement that might be desirable in itself. The extent to which Adam values Raphael's promise needs to be weighed against the substance of the question he poses just following his words cited above: "can we want obedience then / To him . . . Who form'd us from the dust, and plac'd us here / Full to the utmost measure of what bliss / Human desires can seek or apprehend?" (5.514–18). If we assume that Adam believes the ascent is valuable because it will enhance his and Eve's happiness, then we cannot make sense of his comment that he and Eve already possess the "utmost measure of bliss" while in Eden. It is difficult to interpret the future ascent as an event that might motivate their obedience, since they fail to see how their level of Edenic happiness can be matched by an alternative or future state of affairs. If Adam were a bit more outspoken he might respond to Raphael by asking, "If I fail to remain obedient and so lose the chance to ascend to God, will I still be able to remain with Eve in Eden?"

But this still leaves unresolved why Eve fails to consider the possibility of having to forsake Edenic life if she disobeys God. Why doesn't she recall Raphael's narrative of the War in Heaven? We need, I think, to assess the impression that the events of the War in Heaven have on Adam and Eve's obedience. Adam's comments just before and just after he has learned the details of the War in Heaven provide the clearest test case of *Areopagitica*'s claim that virtue is learned from knowledge of vice. The claim is momentarily called into question when Adam, upon learning merely that disobedience is possible, begins to question his own constancy: "what thou tell'st / Hath past in Heav'n, some doubt within me move" (5.553–54). If the claim is to be validated, Satan's example should dissuade Adam and Eve from apostasy. That Raphael's narrative does not achieve its desired effect is of course proven by the Fall itself. The important question is whether Adam and Eve fail to appreciate the analogy between Satan's disobedience and their own potential disobedience, or whether, despite their having understood the analogy the pair lapses because supervening influences offset the otherwise effective power of the analogy to bind their obedience. I think that the former is the case, that something internal to the strategy behind the analogy fails, and that such a failure is implicit in Adam's response to the events of the War in Heaven. Adam tells Raphael:

> Great things, and full of wonder in our ears,
> Far differing from this World, thou hast reveal'd
> Divine interpreter, by favor sent
> Down from the Empyrean to forewarn
> Us timely of what might else have been our loss,
> Unknown, which human knowledge could not reach:
> For which to th' infinitely Good we owe
> Immortal thanks, and his admonishment
> Receive with solemn purpose to observe
> Immutably his sovran will, the end
> Of what we are   (7.70–80).

Adam's emphasis on the distance separating the War in Heaven and Edenic life—"far differing from this world"—has the effect of straining the relevance of Satan's disobedience to his and Eve's potential disobedience, widening the applicability of Satan's act of "too high aspiring" (6.899) to his and Eve's much less dramatic act of obeying or disobeying their one easy prohibition.

Adam then thanks Raphael specifically for forewarning him and Eve "timely of what might else have bin our loss" (7.74). If we assume that the object of "forewarn" (7.73) is roughly equivalent to "the possibility of falling as Satan fell," and that "our loss" refers to Adam and Eve's possible fall, the line can be paraphrased as, "to forewarn us of the possibility of falling as Satan fell, which would have been our loss (would have happened to us, too) had you not mentioned the events." Here, as in his earlier determination not to "think hard / One easie prohibition" (4.432–33), Adam undergoes very little deliberation and weighing of alternatives.[61] The use of the contrary-to-fact conditional suggests that Adam's reaffirmed obedience is achieved simply upon his hearing the details of Satan's fall, as if Raphael's narration serves as an extended speech act carrying sufficient weight to bind Adam's obedience. Adam does not say, "Now that I have learned of the events of the War in Heaven, I understand the penalties of disobedience and rewards of obedience; therefore I desire and plan to act accordingly." His response is something like, "Now, Raphael, that you have narrated the events of the War in Heaven, you have made unlikely the possibility of my (our) apostasy." That Adam undertakes negligible decision-making before responding is reflected in his final claim to obey immutably God's "will" (7.79), which he suggests is equivalent to what he and Eve "are" (7.80). Whatever small measure of ratiocination Adam has applied is undercut by his act of yielding rational autonomy to God's authority. Adam begins his response by emphasizing the distance between heavenly and earthly matters; he then simply acknowledges that his awareness of Satan's fall has changed his future course. He completes his response by affirming that his and Eve's wills are absorbed by God's will. It is no wonder that Raphael's calculated exposition does not achieve its intended effect.

If we return to Eve's conduct during the temptation scene, we can better understand, assuming that Raphael's narration is at least as influential on Eve's conduct as on Adam's, why she fails to imagine any lesser punishment after she has convinced herself that death will not follow from her indulgence. Eve's inability to reflect rationally on the possibility of losing Eden reinforces my argument that her experiences up to this point have been largely unreflective. That she does not introduce into her mental accounting the possibility of expulsion during this crucial moment suggests both that she has not experienced her Edenic existence in any dynamic way, and that she has only begun to assess her own behavior in any rational manner.

If, during the separation scene, Eve discovers the efficiencies of rational choice accounting, during the temptation scene she puts into practice what she has learned. If, as I have been arguing, Eve's rational choosing is a positively formative step insofar as it is a constituent feature of the pragmatic ethic (the other feature is habituation), then it follows that the Fall is logically necessary in order for Eve (and Adam) to develop their moral identities. Only after the Fall will they learn the benefits and costs of obeying or disobeying God. The events leading up to the Fall are instrumental in introducing the pair to the importance of rational choice, so that after the Fall they will be able to apply their rational choices on God's behalf but not simply at his behest. Their disobedience and the Fall are necessary as a means of instructing the pair as to the structure of rational choice that will eventually help them atone for the Fall and act obediently. The Fall is not as much fortunate as it is instrumentally necessary. Michael's biblical exegesis of Books Ten and Eleven, to which we now turn, does not morally regenerate Adam and Eve as much as provide them with useful knowledge on which to make a decision to bind themselves to God. Since they already know *how* to act ethically, Michael's purpose is largely to teach them *why* they should act ethically.

THE "EDUCATION" OF ADAM AND EVE:
A PRAGMATIC INTERPRETATION OF BOOKS TEN AND ELEVEN

In an attempt to save Books Eleven and Twelve of *Paradise Lost* from C. S. Lewis's comment that they amount to an "untransmuted lump of futurity," critics have called attention to Michael's moral education of Adam.[62] While most recent criticism has assumed that Michael achieves what he sets out to do, that he not only instructs Adam as to the future of mankind but helps Adam acquire virtue and pure faith, I will offer a much different interpretation of Adam's "education." Michael's examples are valuable to Adam not because they teach him patience and virtue but because they provide him with knowledge of the past and the future, as well as instrumental information regarding the consequences of believing or not believing in God. This knowledge of consequences will then convince Adam to stake belief in God, after which he will resume the manner of living that he and Eve enjoyed while in Eden, according to routine and habit, from which pure or "formed" faith will eventually follow.

Michael first introduces his educative narrative in Book Eleven by assuring Adam that he will "learn / True patience, and to temper joy with fear / And pious sorrow, equally inur'd / By moderation either state to bear, / Prosperous or adverse: so shalt thou lead / Safest thy life, and best prepar'd endure / Thy mortal passage when it comes" (11.360–66). The ethical strategy seems to be the classical (pre-Hellenistic) one of governing the passions by acquiring temperance through a process of "inuring" or habituation. Such a moral regimen should help Adam cope with the chilling notion that, as the Cain and Abel episode suggests, he must eventually "return to native dust" (11.463). Adam, however, misinterprets the education in temperance as Stoic in nature, responding to Michael's admonition to "observe / The rule of not too much" (11.530–31) with a promise to accept life's "cumbrous charge" (11.549). Michael corrects him by assuring him it is acceptable to "live well" rather than resignedly, offering in place of Stoic withdrawal what seems like the Aristotelian acceptance of external goods. The difficulty of learning how to cope with death, however, pales in comparison with the difficulty of learning how to cope with the prospect of eternal torment. Contemplating the endless woe that is to be his lot following his introduction of sin, Adam resumes despair; during the episode of the flood, however, he is informed of Christ's ransom, and he gains comfort in the thought that sainthood for the regenerate will replace eternal suffering on Judgement Day.

One of the differences between Book Eleven and Book Twelve is that in the former book Michael helps Adam cope with the consequences of sin that will affect his own earthly future, but in the latter book he confronts Adam with the consequence of sin that will affect the larger political community. The virtue Michael recommends is in both books temperance, but in Book Twelve, in his exposition of the Tower of Babylon episode, Michael identifies virtue with reason: "inordinate desires / And upstart Passions catch the Government / From reason, and to servitude reduce / Man till then free . . . sometimes Nations will decline so low / From virtue, which is reason" (12.87–98). As the focus shifts from Adam's strategies for coping with death to the worldly sins of ambition and tyranny, Michael suggests that the moral strategy Adam has been taught of inuring himself to pain is of a different order from the manner of governing passions in everyday political situations. Michael offers in his account of Nimrod only a diagnostic account of the subversion of reason by tyranny without offering any humanistic therapy for the overthrow of virtue defined as reason. Rather than instruct Adam on how tyranny such as Nimrod's can be avoided, Michael instead directly invokes Abraham's leadership into Canaan, emphasizing one of Abraham's famous displays of blind faith: "He straight obeys, / Not knowing to what Land, yet firm believes: / I see him, but thou canst not, with what Faith / He leaves his gods" (12.126–27).

By this point Michael has presented Adam with just two general models of behavior, each of which should be evaluated for its relative moral salience. In the first case Michael presents Adam with a grim situation and a resolution Adam cannot rationally refuse: acquire temperance in order to cope with anxieties about death. Importantly, the strategy is not properly Aristotelian, since a temperate Adam will not as much be fulfilling any telos or final cause as he will be acquiring a means-end strategy for alleviating the fear of death. This is a good example of a rational choice model of conduct. In the second case, Michael presents Adam with a series of equally grim situations about the world in which the overthrow of reason by the passions can only be redressed given the kind of blind faith in God exemplified by Abraham. What is the relationship between the two models of conduct? Does one displace the other? Will Adam's rational self-management lead to tyranny like Nimrod's, which then would require a full abdication of reason to a submission of faith and hope? Has Milton folded into the narrative a basic opposition between reason versus faith, pagan versus Christian morality?

There are, I think, two satisfactory answers to these questions, both converging with the principles of moral pragmatism. The first is that Adam's exercise of rational choice in acquiring temperance is related to Abraham's faith as a short-term goal is related to a long-term goal, or as a second-order goal is to a first-order goal. Adam, like Abraham, should commit himself to God in a nonrational way, carrying out all of God's decrees, but he should also apply a dialectic of reason and habit in matters of daily, practical conduct. Moral pragmatism is restricted to Adam's everyday conduct but can be trumped by God's intervention. The goal of acquiring temperance in order to provide comfort from the fear of death, for example, will yield to divine mandate, such as leading one's people into Canaan, or (alas) binding one's only son at God's behest. In this sense, Michael has separated morality from theology, since Adam's moral pragmatism has very little to do with his faith in God.

To understand the second way of explaining the narrative instruction up to this point we must first think about Abraham's significance in biblical history in more detail. Popularized modern conceptions of Abraham as the exemplar of irrational submission to God owe much to Kierkegaard's interpretation of the binding of Isaac. For Kierkegaard, Abraham, the "knight of faith," is permitted to act unethically—ignoring the Kantian imperative to treat all individuals as ends and not means—when acting in obedience to a divine call. If one focuses solely on the binding of Isaac, however, one neglects the fact that Abraham is tested ten times according to the Genesis tradition, and that his motives involve more than just an expression of his love of God. When Abraham pledges obedience to God in all cases except for the binding of Isaac, he assumes future gains for himself and his followers, including the prospect of fathering kingly descendants (Gen. 15) and the settling of Canaan. As a means to inspire obedience, early modern commentators on Genesis customarily point out the long-term benefits of Abraham's commitments. In *Prototypes out of the Booke of Genesis* (1640), William Whately writes, "thus you see, how worth the while it is to serve, feare, and obey God, what abundant blessings he grants, what honour and fame even after death. . . . Hee will give you the inheritance of life eternall, as sure as he did to Abraham."[63] Commentators also realize that, given his preoccupation with the beneficial consequences of faith, Abraham's other-regarding conduct could easily transform into self-centeredness, as when he decides to prostitute Sarah to Pharaoh for fear of death (Gen. 12). Calvin admits that "although they are rash judges, who entirely condemn this deed of Abram, yet the special fault is not to be denied, namely that he, trembling at the approach of death, did not commit the issue of the danger to God, instead of sinfully betraying the modesty of his wife."[64] Useful supplements to these early modern accounts are remarks by modern commentators noting that throughout Genesis Abraham acts as a skilled bargainer, as when he negotiates the salvation of sinners during the Sodom and Gomorrah episode.[65] Karl-Josef Kuschel writes, "If we look closely at Abraham's way we discover that his faith is quite a complex one. There is no trace of blind readiness to follow, of an irrational act of the will, of the obedience of an automaton. Abraham's faith is . . . made up of quite different ingredients: there is a touch of doubt and a touch of cunning, a touch of anxiety and a touch of risk-taking with his God; a touch of wordless obedience and a touch of canny haggling."[66] John Donne, who would have agreed with much of Kuschel's comment, wrote in a 1627 sermon that, although Abraham's conduct is ultimately defensible, "Abraham was bold, when he could conceive such an imagination, that God would destroy the righteous with the wicked, or that the Judge of all the earth should not doe right."[67]

Given the complex motives behind his pledges to God, Abraham acts as a moral pragmatist in much of his conduct, except for the binding of Isaac (since Isaac's death would mark the demise of Abraham's lineage and contradict God's promise that Abraham's descendants would rule future nations). Michael, of course, makes no mention of the Isaac episode, but focuses only on Abraham's deliverance out of Egypt, noting that "he [Abraham] straight obeys, / Not knowing to what Land, yet firm believes" (12.126–27). Given, however, that the sum total of Abraham's conduct accords more with a consequentialist and pragmatic ethic than it does blind faith, and given the instructions that Michael has earlier given to Adam regarding temperance as a means to cope with the inevitability of death, it is more likely that Abraham's "faith" reinforces rather than undermines Adam's moral pragmatism (or would have been understood as such by early modern readers). Interpreted in either of the two ways I have presented—that Abraham represents an example of faith which has priority over Adam's means-end ethic, or that Abraham represents an extension of that means-end ethic—up to this point the only practical model of behavior Adam has internalized is one of moral consequentialism.

I think that it can be further argued that the structure of Adam's moral education is mostly completed with the invocation of Abraham and the quest toward Canaan. What follows Michael's account of Abraham's faith is a series of references to the protoevangelium and a doctrinal lesson on the relationship between law and gospel. Michael's account of the displacement of Old Testament legalism by justification by faith is routinely Pauline, although his final admonition to embrace Christ "by faith not void of works" is sufficiently ambiguous regarding the temporal and causal relationship between faith and works. The lessons in Christology that follow the invocation of Abraham do not continue Adam's lesson in morality as much as begin his lesson in theology.

Critics of *Paradise Lost* have often claimed that Adam acquires not only classical and Christian virtue but also what Calvin describes as "formed" faith by the end of Michael's paraphrase. After detailing what he describes as the progressive moral education of Adam, Lawrence Sasek concludes that "the last two books present a drama in which Adam is molded into an example of Christian fortitude. They dramatize the final stage in Adam's development, which has proceeded from innocence, through sin, through reconciliation with God, to a full knowledge and acceptance of the justice of God's judgements."[68] Sasek fails to reconcile Adam's so-called moral regeneration and appreciation of human sinfulness with Adam's felix culpa epiphany in Book Twelve. Sasek evades the tension by arguing that Adam is not at all articulating felix culpa as "any reasoned theological view of the consequences of sin" but rather as an "emotional reaction to the final triumph of good." Sasek believes that Adam cannot really be justifying his sin because Adam's final words regarding his education are "Henceforth I learn, that to obey is best" and "suffering for Truth's sake / Is fortitude to highest victorie / And to the faithful Death the Gate of Life" (12.561–71).

Sasek argues too readily that Adam's final sentiments on obedience are irreconcilable with Adam's having a reasonable understanding of the fortunate fall. If pressed hard enough, Adam could assert that he is ready to obey God without exception, even though at this point he is only committed to the idea that the beneficial consequences will offset the pernicious effects of sin. Given what I have suggested above regarding the instrumentalization of Adam's belief, Adam's articulation of the fortunate fall shows that he is not knowledgeably contrite, but that he has acquired simply an awareness of the expediency of obeying God. Adam further reveals his confusion when he wavers from unsupported optimism in his premonition of felix culpa to a gratuitous worry that the Son's resurrection will abandon the faithful: "who then shall guide / His people, who defend? will they not deal / Worse with his followers than with him they dealt?" (12.482–84). Louis Martz, puzzling over Adam's despair, writes, "the strange thing is that there is nothing at all in Milton's account of the redemption to evoke this sort of pessimistic query. On the contrary, the question of how many shall believe is left entirely and deliberately open, while the tone of optimism and victory dominates."[69]

Strange indeed, but only if one assumes that Adam has been progressively absorbing fine points of doctrine, which his shift between optimism and pessimism suggests is unlikely. Readers like Sasek seem hastily optimistic when they dismiss Adam's confusions as emotional outbursts and accept that Adam fully understands what he thinks and says about doctrinal matters, or that he even believes what he says. Throughout the first half of Book Twelve, Adam repeatedly misses fundamental points of Michael's lesson, asking questions that he might have answered himself. For instance, Adam fails to understand why so many laws and rites will be established by God for His own people: "So many laws argue so many sins / Among them; how can God with such reside?" (12.283–84). After Michael elaborates the relationship between Mosaic law and gospel, Adam wonders when and where he will be able to see the heroic fight between God and the serpent: "say where and when / Thir fight, what stroke shall bruise the Victor's heel" (12.384–85). Finally, after having blundered and been corrected twice, Adam makes the biggest mistake of all, wondering whether he should repent of sin or rejoice that "much more good thereof shall spring" (12.476). Should we describe these outbursts as late stages in Adam's moral education? Adam is like a small child, eagerly listening to a homiletic bedtime story written for young adults. The most the child can do at this stage is either to project his imaginative re-creations on the characters and plots, or to distill a ponderous moral exemplum into its most provocative aspects. I think that Martz's comment on Adam's exultation at the ending of the Flood (11.874–78) is appropriate to Adam's final comments on his own education: Adam's closural statement sounds like nothing more than a "cry placed in Adam's mouth."[70] The only claim Adam makes that we can be sure he understands is his reference to death, which has preoccupied him all along, and about which he has learned that "to the faithful Death the Gate of life" (12.572).

That Adam has not yet acquired faith or virtue is clearly expressed in Michael's final admonition to "add / Deeds to thy knowledge answerable, add Faith, / Add Virtue, Patience, Temperance, add Love" (12.581–83). Michael's insistence that Adam must "add faith" to knowledge is overlooked in Barbara Lewalski's otherwise illuminating essay on the structural patterns of Books Eleven and Twelve. Lewalski describes the distinction Milton draws in *De Doctrina* between "implicit" and "saving faith." Implicit faith, as I have noted above, "sees not the objects of hope, but yields belief with a blind assent" (YP 6:338). Saving faith is defined as "a full persuasion operated in us through the gift of God, whereby we believe, on the sole authority of the promise itself, that whatsoever things he has promised in Christ are ours, and especially the grace of eternal life" (YP 6:338). Lewalski, using terms similar to Sasek's, argues that Michael's prophecy "is to lead Adam from the 'blindness' of implicit faith to the true vision of 'saving faith.' "[71] Lewalski adds that when Adam acknowledges Christ as his redeemer, he "demonstrates that his faith is now fully matured."[72]

But a review of Adam's conduct suggests that Milton holds a theory of saving faith whose criteria Adam does not fully meet by the close of Michael's prophecy. In the terms outlined in *De Doctrina,* Adam can move from blind assent to a "full persuasion" if he acquires knowledge of Christ's promises, the most important being knowledge of future salvation, "eternal life." Nothing in this definition assumes that at such a stage Adam will have acquired virtue, that he will have become regenerated, or even that he will have met the Reformation criteria for pure faith, as distinguished from the scholastic criteria for faith. While Reformation theories of faith require that the agent add emotional commitment to intellectual assent, scholastic theories of faith require that the agent merely assents to believe in God.

Milton's claim that proper belief is "full persuasion" suggests a neo-scholastic account of saving faith, since one can be fully persuaded by certain doctrine without also being emotionally committed or nonintellectually attached to such doctrine. Since Milton does not hold a stronger version of faith than the intellectualist version presented in *De Doctrina,* and since Michael tells Adam that he must eventually "add faith" to his "answerable knowledge" (which Lewalski fails to acknowledge), Milton is suggesting that Adam has not acquired "full persuasion" of God's promise regarding his salvation. If Adam is to carry on in an ethically effective manner after Michael's exhortation, his conduct will be governed by a measure of belief resting between "blind assent" and "full persuasion."

Eve will of course learn all of the knowledge which Adam has learned, but her statement of her position prior to having heard Adam's exposition suggests that whatever Adam tells her at this point will have little bearing on her settled convictions. Her commitment to acting according to God's decrees derives more from an awareness of the long-term benefits of doing so rather than from a non-instrumental grasp of fundamentals. She describes her final uplift as a "consolation yet secure / I carry hence . . . by mee the Promised Seed shall all restore" (12.620–23). Her commitment is to a shadowy premonition of the protoevangelium; her pledge of devotion is not even to God but rather to Adam, who to her is "all things under Heav'n" (12.618).

Adam and Eve's education never extends further than what Milton describes in *De Doctrina* as the "secondary species of repentance," according to which "a man abstains from sin through fear of punishment and obeys the call of God merely for the sake of his own salvation. . . . This kind of repentance is common to the regenerate and to the unregenerate"(YP 6:325). About ten years after Milton had written *Paradise Lost,* Robert South remarked in a sermon that "in the actions of duty . . . there is not a sufficient motive to engage the will of man in a constant practice of them . . . this complacency of mind upon a man's doing his duty, on the one side, and that remorse attending his neglect of it . . . on the other, are so far from excluding a respect to a *future recompence,* . . . that they are principally founded in it" (italics mine).[73] Richard Hooker had anticipated much of Milton and South's interpretation of moral consequentialism in the *Laws,* where he argued that only after sanctification do persons abandon an ethic of instrumentality: "Whereas we now love the thing that is good, but especially in respect of benefit to us; we shall then love the thing that is good, only or principally for the goodness of beauty itself."[74]

If Adam and Eve leave Paradise convinced of little more than the "future recompences" that will accrue from a commitment to God, we can assume that their moral "progress" is somewhat circular, and that after their expulsion they will resume the life they had led while in Eden, the difference being that they will have gained enough knowledge of future happenings to more firmly commit themselves to act in accordance with whatever knowledge they have learned of God. This circularity is suggested in the resemblances between Eve's consolation by the protoevangelium in Book Twelve and her and Adam's similar consolations near the beginning of Book Eleven, just prior to Michael's intervention. After Adam asserts that his memory of God's promise that Eve's "Seed shall bruise our Foe" (11.155), Eve recognizes that she is graced with "the source of life" (11.169). It is not inconceivable that Adam will repeat to Eve a version of his prelapsarian sentiment, "let us not think hard" (4.432) the way that lies ahead, and that Eve will interrupt their conversation with a version of her comment in Book Eleven, "But the Field / to labour calls us now with sweat impos'd" (11.171–72). This would mark the resumption of what I described earlier as an ethic of distraction, whereby Adam and Eve both before and (predictably) after the Fall govern their daily lives routinely, without thinking much about God's dispensations, and with the goal of "inuring" themselves to distress and the acquisition of temperance. Whether they will eventually acquire a "paradise within" is an open question, not an established fact.

As I have noted above, the logical starting point for an analysis and understanding of Adam and Eve's conduct is the presumption of rationality. From this foundational premise, the structure and logic of their conduct fall naturally into place. Since such rationality is not historically specific, we should not assume that it is exercised in the service of any political or religious ideology. If we must argue that Milton is a systematizer and *Paradise Lost* a "logical epic," then the most we can assert with confidence is that Milton, faced with the burden of filling in the empty spaces of the Genesis presentation of Adam and Eve's conduct, strove to make their conduct understandable and believable. Their conduct is not necessarily specific to a particular political affiliation such as Royalism or Independency, or to a religious denomination such as Puritanism, Conformism, or even Protestantism. To what extent, then, do Milton's political, religious, and scientific allegiances converge to inform the nature of Adam and Eve's ethical characters? Only to the extent that such ideological positions do not conflict with the presumption of rationality that dictates Adam and Eve's conduct both before and after the Fall. As a well-trained, highly self-conscious poet, Milton exercised meticulous control over the formal and aesthetic aspects of his craft. But when he constructed the logic of Adam and Eve's conduct, Milton could partially abdicate inventive craftsmanship and draw upon an intuitive understanding of the nature of rational choice.

Lafayette College

NOTES

I would like to thank Michael Fixler, Albert Labriola, Anna Siomopoulos, and Richard Strier for their helpful assistance with this essay.

1. Northrop Frye, *The Return of Eden* (Toronto, 1965), 96.

2. Ibid., 96.

3. See John Rumrich, *Milton Unbound: Controversy and Reinterpretation* (Cambridge, 1996) and Dennis Danielson, *Milton's Good God: A Study in Literary Theodicy* (Cambridge, 1982). For a discussion of iconoclasm in Milton's prose writings, see Lana Cable, *Carnal Rhetoric: Milton's Iconoclasm and the Poetics of Desire* (Durham, 1995). For a discussion of Milton's views on custom in *Paradise Lost*, see Fred Hoerner, " 'Fire to Use': A Practice-Theory Approach to *Paradise Lost*," *Representations* 51 (1995): 94–117.

4. See William James, "The Will to Believe," in *William James: Pragmatism and Other Essays* (New York, 1963).

5. John Rogers, *The Matter of Revolution: Science, Poetry, and Politics in the Age of Milton* (Ithaca, 1996), 176.

6. Bourdieu's practice theory figures importantly in H. Marshall Leicester, *The Disenchanted Self: Representing the Subject in the Canterbury Tales* (Berkeley, 1990); Frank Whigham, *Ambition and Privilege: The Social Tropes of Elizabethan Courtesy Theory* (Berkeley, 1984); Peter Stallybrass and Allon White, *The Politics and Poetics of Transgression* (Ithaca, 1986); and Hoerner, " 'Fire to Use': A Practice-Theory Approach to Paradise Lost."

7. Stanley Fish, *Surprised by Sin: The Reader in Paradise Lost* (New York, 1967), 12.

8. C. A. Patrides, *Milton and the Christian Tradition* (Oxford, 1966), 137–38.

9. For an overview of critical discussion linking Baxter and Milton, see Rumrich, *Milton Unbound*, 28–34.

10. N. H. Keeble does devote a chapter to Baxter's ethics, but his focus is mostly on Baxter's relationship to casuistry. See N. H. Keeble, *Richard Baxter: Puritan Man of Letters* (Oxford, 1982).

11. Richard Baxter, *Christian Ethics* in *The Practical Works of The Reverend Richard Baxter,* 23 vols., ed. William Orme (London, 1830), vol. 3, 101–2.

12. Richard Baxter, *Christian Ethics*, in *Works*, vol. 2, 203.

13. Richard Baxter, *The Character of a Sound, Confirmed Christian*, in *Works*, vol. 8, 435.

14. Richard Baxter, *Christian Ethics*, in *Works*, vol. 2, 203.

15. For a discussion of Baxter's relation to Puritan nonconformity and latitudinarianism, see Isabel Rivers, *Reason, Grace, and Sentiment: A Study of the Language of Religion and Ethics in England, 1660–1780* (Cambridge, 1991).

16. Nigel Keeble, *The Literary Culture of Nonconformity* (Athens, 1987), 24.

17. *The Autobiography of Richard Baxter,* ed. J. M. Lloyd Thomas (1696; London, 1925), 190.

18. Rivers, *Reason, Grace, and Sentiment,* 100.

19. For a good account of the complexities of the latitudinarian position, see Gerard Reedy, *Robert South (1634–1716): An Introduction to His Life and Sermons* (Cambridge, 1992), ch. 6.

20. John Tillotson, *Sermons on Several Subjects and Occasions,* 12 vols. (London, 1742), vol. 6, 155.

21. Robert South, *Sermons Preached Upon Several Occasions,* 4 vols. (Philadelphia, 1844), vol. 1, 326.

22. See C. F. Allison, *The Rise of Moralism: The Proclamation of the Gospel from Hooker to Baxter* (New York, 1966).

23. Paul Alkon, "Robert South, William Law, and Samuel Johnson," *SEL* 6 (1966): 499–528. Gerard Reedy has recently described Alkon's article as a seminal contribution to our understanding of the influence of Aristotelian ethics on South and his contemporaries. See Reedy, *Robert South (1634–1716): An Introduction to His Life and Sermons,* 27.

24. Aristotle writes of moral habituation, "Moral goodness . . . is the result of habit, from which it has actually got its name, being a slight modification of the word ethos. The fact makes it obvious that none of the moral virtues is engendered in us by nature, since nothing that is what it is by nature can be made to behave differently to habituation." *Nicomachean Ethics* 2.1 ([Penguin Books, 1976], 91).

25. With the emergence of fourteenth-century voluntarism, ethical goodness was no longer describable as part of natural law, as it had been for Aquinas, and hence moral laws were thought to depend on the arbitrariness of divine will. Although most voluntarists drew the familiar distinction between God's *potentia absoluta* and *potentia ordinata,* with the suggestion that God generally obeys his own decrees, ethical goodness was no longer interpretable as part of natural order or the divine essence. An individual's conscience and sense of right reason served as a compromise to revealed moral law, and the individual's practical conduct was governed by the will in tandem with the sensitive appetite. The great difficulty was to explain how habitual goodness could be located in the power of the individual will and how the will itself could mediate the direction of the sensitive appetite. Frederick Copleston writes, "if we indulge the sensitive appetite in a certain direction, a habit is formed, and this habit is reflected in what we can call a habit in the will. . . . On the other hand, it remains in the will's power to act against habit and inclination, even if with difficulty, because the will is essentially free." *A History of Philosophy,* 9 vols. (New York, 1963), vol. 3, 115.

26. Blaise Pascal, *Pensées* 45.680 (trans. Honor Levi [Oxford, 1995], 155).

27. Ibid., 156.

28. Ian Hacking, *The Emergence of Probability* (Cambridge, 1975), 66.

29. Pascal, *Pensées,* 148.

30. Pascal, *Pensées* 4.267, in *Oeuvres de Blaise Pascal,* 14 vols., ed. by Leon Brunschvicg (Paris, 1904), vol. 13, 196; cited in Jean Mesnard, *Pascal,* trans. Claude and Marcia Abraham (Alabama, 1969), 35.

31. Ibid., 4.272; cited in Mesnard, *Pascal,* 41. The novelty of Pascal's wager is that he neither sets reason against faith, gives primacy over faith, nor even gives directly causal precedence to faith. Reason simply binds the will by orienting the will to habitual action, a process which imitates or undergoes the reflexes of faith, but which does not describe in any case a state of pure faith. Pascal leaves the manner in which salvation eventually grows out of the habitual performance of works largely unaddressed, focussing instead on the extent to which the reflexes of faith will provide firm belief in God's existence. For Pascal, as for the English moral pragmatists described above, ethical practice is oriented toward providing assurance of God's existence and dispensations, even though such an end is secured through the intermediate stage in which the will is bound by unreflective conduct.

32. Cited in Henry G. Van Leeuwen, *The Problem of Certainty in English Thought (1630–1690)* (The Hague, 1963), 46.

33. Ibid., 46.

34. Jeremy Taylor, *Unum Necessarium* (1655), in *The Whole Works of the Right Reverend Jeremy Taylor,* 10 vols. (London, 1861), vol. 7, 276. The parallel between Pascalian ethics and English latitudinarianism has been well documented by Robert Todd Carroll, who begins his book on Edward Stillingfleet's philosophy with an explication of Pascalian skeptical rationalism. Arguing about precisely what knowledge nonconformist and latitudinarian sermonists had of Pascal is, I think, an unnecessary exercise in any case; the ethical model I have been describing was so prominent during the period that Richard Swinburne has described moral pragmatism as one of the three most historically influential theories of the relationship between reason and faith that had been promoted up until the eighteenth century. Swinburne distinguishes three historical accounts of faith: the Thomistic, the Lutheran-Calvinist, and the mid-seventeenth-century pragmatist. According to Aquinas's intellectualist and propositionalist model, faith entails only a "belief-that" God exists. The Lutheran view of faith adds to the Thomistic practice of "believing-that" a trust in God: "The man of faith . . . does not merely believe that there is a God (and believe certain propositions about him)—he trusts him and commits himself to him." Swinburne writes that, according to the third model of faith, the pragmatic version, "one can act in assumptions which one does not believe. To do this is to do those actions which you would do if you did believe. In particular, you can act on the assumption not merely that God, whom you believe to exist will do for you what you need or want, but also on the assumption that there is such a God (and that he has the properties which Christians have ascribed to him). . . . Although Pascal did not hold that acting-as-if was the essence of faith, he saw it as a step on the road." Swinburne's argument is important because it shows, as Taylor's comments above do, that the Pascalian argument can be applied to practical matters of obedience and not only to ontological questions regarding God's existence. See Richard Swinburne, *Faith and Reason* (Oxford, 1981), 104–25.

35. See W. B. Sibley, "The Rational versus the Reasonable," *Philosophical Review* 62 (October, 1953): 554–60, cited in John Rawls's *Political Liberalism* (New York, 1996), 36. See also Danielson, *Milton's Good God,* 134.

37. Danielson, *Milton's Good God,* 134–35.

38. Ibid., 135.

39. Ibid., 135.

40. Two influential Augustinian interpretations of prelapsarian perfection can be found in A. J. A. Waldock, *Paradise Lost and Its Critics* (Cambridge, 1966) and C. S. Lewis, *A Preface to Paradise Lost* (Oxford, 1961).

41. Cited in Danielson, *Milton's Good God,* 170.

42. Ibid., 173.

43. Rumrich, *Milton Unbound,* 33.

44. The citations are taken from Book Three, Chapter 20, and Book Four, Chapter 38, of *Against Heresies,* in *Writings of Irenaeus,* trans. Alexander Roberts and W. H. Rambaut (Edinburgh, 1880).

45. *Complete Prose Works of John Milton,* 8 vols., ed. D. M. Wolfe et al. (New Haven, 1953–82), vol. 2, 223; hereafter cited parenthetically in the text as YP, with volume and page number.

46. These three passages from *De Doctrina* are cited in Richard Strier, "The Ubiquity of the Ethical, or, Why Milton's Eden Is Better than His Heaven," 3–4, in paper delivered at the 1998 Newberry Library Seminar, Chicago.

47. Ibid., 5.

48. The discussion of implicit faith in *De Doctrina* places Milton in the tradition of late-seventeenth-century moral pragmatism. I am not arguing that Milton had Pascalian pragmatism in mind when he conceived of Adam and Eve's moral identities, although Catherine Gimelli

Martin has recently demonstrated some startling convergences between Milton and Pascal's views on a range of subjects from cosmology to pragmatic faith. Moral pragmatism was so well diffused throughout the period that Milton may have assimilated it from Baxter, Taylor, Tillotson, or any number of contemporary English writers who were not committed to an orthodox Calvinist belief in double predestination and theological voluntarism. For Milton's understanding of Pascalian skepticism, see Catherine Gimelli Martin, " 'Boundless the Deep': Milton, Pascal, and the Theology of Relative Space," *ELH* 63 (1996): 45–78.

49. Barbara Lewalski, "Innocence and Experience in Milton's Eden," in *New Essays on Paradise Lost,* ed. Thomas Kranidas (Berkeley, 1971), 93.

50. All quotations from *Paradise Lost* are from *John Milton: Complete Poems and Major Prose,* ed. Merritt Y. Hughes (New York, 1957) and will be cited parenthetically in the text, with book and line number.

51. Lewalski, "Innocence and Experience in Milton's Eden," 96.

52. Ibid., 94.

53. Ibid., 100.

54. Ibid., 113.

55. See Charles Taylor, *Sources of the Self: The Making of the Modern Identity* (Cambridge, 1989), particularly 218–19, where Taylor distinguishes classical ethics, including Socratic ethics, from Christian morality.

56. Lewalski, "Innocence and Experience in Milton's Eden," 103.

57. Ibid., 100.

58. Strier, "The Ubiquity of the Ethical," 28–30.

59. Jeremy Taylor, *Unum Necessarium* (1655), 276.

60. Ibid., 277.

61. Adam's reference to "our loss" can just as appropriately be taken to refer to something desirable which the pair might not be able to acquire if certain conditions do not obtain. Interpreted in this sense, "what" might still refer to the possibility of falling as Satan fell, but the line could be differently paraphrased as "to forewarn us of the possibility of falling as Satan fell, knowledge which otherwise would have gone unapprehended by us or lost on us (our loss)." While the first paraphrase sounds intuitively more plausible, the second gains plausibility in context, since the lines immediately following Adam's comment emphasize the distance between Raphael's knowledge and human knowledge: "Unknown, which human knowledge could not reach." If we read the passage according to the second paraphrase, we have very little basis on which to assume that Adam intuits a direct parallel between Satan's conduct, his own, and Eve's.

62. See, for example, George Williamson, "The Education of Adam," in *Milton: Modern Essays in Criticism,* ed. Arthur E. Barker (New York, 1965), 284–307; Gerald J. Schiffhorst, "Patience and the Education of Adam in *Paradise Lost,*" *South Atlantic Review* 49 (1984): 55–63; and Mary Ann Radzinowicz, " 'Man as a Probationer of Immortality': *Paradise Lost* XI–XII," in *Approaches to Paradise Lost: The York Tercentenary Lectures,* ed. C. A. Patrides (Toronto, 1968), 31–51.

63. William Whately, *Prototypes or the Primarie Precedent Presidents out of the Booke of Genesis* (London, 1640), 135.

64. John Calvin, *Commentaries on the First Book of Moses, Called Genesis,* 2 vols. (Michigan, 1984), vol. 1, 360. For further discussion of Renaissance conceptions of Abraham, see Arnold Williams, *The Common Expositor: An Account of the Commentaries on Genesis: 1527–1633* (Chapel Hill, 1948), ch. 8.

65. As Silvano Arieti says of Abraham's conduct during the Sodom and Gomorrah episode, "Abraham . . . has the boldness or, if you will, the temerity to speak and argue with God. Abraham's

attitude shows not only his compassion and desire to help his fellow man but also his feeling of entitlement to argue with God. Even the authority of God should not be unquestioningly accepted." Silvano Arieti, *Abraham and the Contemporary Mind* (New York, 1981), 112.

66. Karl-Josef Kuschel, *Abraham: A Symbol of Hope for Jews, Christians, and Muslims* (London, 1995), 26.

67. *The Sermons of John Donne,* 10 vols., ed. Evelyn M. Simpson and George R. Potter (Berkeley, 1965), vol. 8, 347.

68. Lawrence A. Sasek, "The Drama of *Paradise Lost,* Books XI and XII," in *Milton: Modern Essays in Criticism,* ed. Arthur E. Barker (New York, 1965), 347.

69. Louis Martz, *The Paradise Within: Studies in Vaughan, Traherne, and Milton* (New Haven, 1964), 163–64.

70. Ibid., 154.

71. Barbara Lewalski, "Structure and the Symbolism of Vision in Michael's Prophecy, *Paradise Lost,* Books XI and XII," *Philological Quarterly* 42 (1963): 30.

72. Ibid., 30.

73. Robert South, *Sermons Preached Upon Several Occasions,* vol. 3, 143. South invokes as an example of the necessity of moral consequentialism Mark 10:29–30: "There is no man, that hath left house, or brethren . . . for my sake, and the gospel's, but he shall receive an hundred fold now in this time, and in the world to come eternal life" South interprets this passage as follows: "So that we see here the antecedent smoothed over, and recommended by the consequent; duty and reward walking hand in hand; the riches of the promise still overmatching the rigours of the precept."

74. Richard Hooker, *Of the Laws of Ecclesiastical Polity,* Book One, in Richard Hooker, *Of the Laws of Ecclesiastical Polity,* ed. Christopher Morris (London, 1963), 204.

A SECOND DEFENCE:
MILTON'S CRITIQUE OF CROMWELL?

Robert Thomas Fallon

THE LIVES OF Oliver Cromwell and John Milton were fatefully linked. Cromwell, by virtue of his wartime achievements, was the dominant figure in England's early experiment with a republican form of government, initially as the first among equals under the rule of Parliament, later as the first above all, the Lord Protector of the English Republic. John Milton achieved a degree of fame during those years as well, though not as a poet. After the execution of Charles I in January 1649, Parliament promptly declared itself the ruling body of England in his stead and elected from among its members a Council of State, to which it delegated, while retaining strict control, certain executive functions of government. Soon after its initial meetings the Council appointed Milton its Secretary for Foreign Tongues, or Latin Secretary, as the position was called, and entrusted him with responsibility for translating its correspondence with the states and cities of Europe into the Latin that was the traditional language of international discourse. Since most of the crowned heads of those states were reluctant to recognize the legitimacy of a body so presumptuous as to decapitate a king, correspondence was not overly time-consuming at first, so Milton was employed in a variety of other functions, as diplomat, censor, translator at ambassadorial audiences (also conducted in Latin), and propagandist for the new and uncertain regime. In this last capacity he composed long polemic tracts in defense of the Republic and earned himself an international reputation as an ardent advocate of regicide.

Milton labored at these tasks for three years until in February 1652 his fading eyesight failed him completely. He remained at his post, however, with diminished duties, translating long treaties and occasional state letters. The years following his blindness were turbulent indeed. On 20 April 1653, backed by a file of soldiers, Oliver Cromwell dissolved the English Republic's ruling body, referred to somewhat disrespectfully as the "Rump" Parliament. He then convened a Council of Officers whose chief function was to arrange for the election of a successor to the Rump. The new Parliament, which finally met on 4 July, was composed of men whose names were submitted by the Congregational churches of each county, hence its name, the "Nomi-

167

nated" Parliament, or as it was rather derisively called, the "Barebones," after one of its more vocal and bizarre members. This body was fatally split on the question of state support of the church; and it finally foundered on the issue, dissolved itself on 12 December, and urged Cromwell to assume the mantle of government. Thus began the rule of the Lord Protector of England, who with the support of a loyal army presided over his country with an authority that was monarchical in all but name until his death almost five years later.

Milton remained as Latin Secretary to the new regime but in the reorganized government he was no longer responsible to the Council of State. For most of the Protectorate he was answerable to the reinstituted office of secretary of state, held by the able John Thurloe, Cromwell's closest and most trusted advisor. In the performance of his duties, therefore, Milton labored but two administrative levels removed from the Lord Protector himself.[1] The surviving records of the time indicate that during this time of transition he had little to labor over, there being, for example, but two state letters dated over a fifteen-month period from February 1653 to June 1654 among his published papers.[2] One task he was set to, however, was a reply to a virulent Royalist attack on the English Republic titled *The Cry of the Royal Blood to Heaven Against the English Parricides*, a condemnation of the regicide castigating Cromwell, John Bradshaw, who presided over the king's trial, and Milton himself, who had achieved an international notoriety for his earlier *Defence of the English People*. Milton's tract, *A Second Defence of the English People*, appeared in May 1654, some five months after the inaugural of Cromwell's Protectorate rule.

It is this last document that concerns us here, particularly in what it reveals about the poet's judgment of the Lord Protector. Oliver Cromwell is anathema to modern Miltonists. To them he represents everything a liberal academic deplores—a military dictator who dissolved an elected assembly, dismissed its executive body, and backed by a standing army imposed a single person rule on his nation. Milton scholars hope fervently, and write confidently, that the poet shared their distaste for such a figure. One biographer insists that Milton considered Cromwell "a tyrant and a thug."[3] Others are less inflammatory but confident that he "felt certain reservations about committing himself to the Protectorate regime,"[4] that he was "uneasy" and "dissatisfied" with it,[5] and, further, that he expressed his "reservations" in *A Second Defence*, at times quite "straightforwardly."[6] The work includes, it is said, a "coded criticism"[7] of Cromwell in which the poet attempts to "admonish and warn"[8] the Protector for assuming power in the state.[9]

The problem is that Milton never said anything of the kind, so those intent upon dissociating the poet from the government he served search out his writings for scattered passages, isolate them from their textual and historical context, and point to them as proving the case.[10] There is nothing new about this activity. Literary scholars and historians have pursued the theme of Milton's discontent with Cromwell for more than a century—even David Masson suggested that the poet had "reservations" about the Protectorate[11]—but postmodern theory has provided scholars with a fresh array of hermeneutic implements with which to update the contention.

Advocates of this "coded criticism" must perforce ignore what Milton actually said about Cromwell in *A Second Defence,* a fifteen-page defense and praise of the Lord Protector extravagant in its accolades (YP 4:662–72). He lauds Cromwell's character—"Commander first over himself, victor over himself, he learned to achieve over himself the most effective triumph" (YP 4:668)—and his military prowess—"He soon surpassed well-nigh the greatest generals both in the magnitude of his accomplishments and in the speed with which he achieved them" (YP 4:667). He goes on to applaud Cromwell's assumption of the title of Protector: "You suffered and allowed yourself, not indeed to be borne aloft, but to come down so many degrees from the heights and be forced into a definite rank, so to speak, for the public good. . . . You, the liberator of your country, the author of liberty, and likewise its guardian and savior, can undertake no more distinguished role and none more august" (YP 4:672). In a burst of rhetoric, Milton concludes:

Cromwell, we are deserted! You alone remain. On you has fallen the whole burden of our affairs. On you alone they depend. In unison we acknowledge your unexcelled virtue. No one protests save such as seek equal honors, though inferior themselves, or begrudge the honors assigned to one more worthy, or do not understand that there is nothing in human society more pleasing to God, or more agreeable to reason, nothing in the state more just, nothing more expedient, than the rule of the man most fit to rule. All know you to be that man, Cromwell! (YP 4:671–72)

♞

A reading of *A Second Defence* leaves the impression of a multi-colored quilt of concerns. The tract is, first of all, a defense of the regicide, since the purpose of *Cry* was to condemn that act. But Milton patched into *A Second Defence* other matters that had little to do with the execution of the king. *Cry* concluded with a separate chapter that attacked Milton personally, characterizing him viciously as "a dark pettifogger, pure corruption and poison, filth soaked with black blood, an unnameable buffoon" with "an empty, hollow head, such a stupid and doltish head" (YP 4:1079–80); and in reply the poet frequently digresses to defend his reputation, to include a twelve-page account of his life. Further, he strikes back at Claude Salmasius, whom he had already "destroyed," as he put it, in his first *Defence,* at Alexander More, whom he erroneously believed to be the author of *Cry,* and at Adrian Vlacq, who published it.

Milton stitched into the quiltwork of *A Second Defence* further matters that were only remotely connected with the death of the king. In keeping with his perception that God wished the "noble deeds" of the founders of the Republic to be "worthily praised and extolled, and that truth defended by arms be also defended by reason" (YP 4:553), he included passages honoring a number of figures who had been prominent in the struggle against the crown, Cromwell chief among them.[12] He closed with advice to the recently installed Lord Protector and a peroration to his "fellow countrymen," in which he warns them against backsliding from the cause of freedom.

A glance at the background of *A Second Defence* may help explain the quiltlike quality of the text. It was commissioned by the government, according to Milton; and though the exact publication date is not known, it was obviously some time after the appearance of *Cry* in August 1652 (YP 4:767). Milton had been preparing a reply to the anticipated rebuttal by Salmasius, whom he had excoriated in his first *Defence;* but that gentleman died in August 1653 with the rebuttal unfinished, and Milton turned his attention to *Cry.* Included in the material he was collecting for his reply was a Latin poem satirical of Salmasius, which he says he "had in readiness for the long-awaited edition of the famous book" (YP 4:580–81). The remark suggests that the poem was not the only passage he had prepared for the projected reply, that he had more material at hand; and unwilling to waste all that labor, he then incorporated it into *A Second Defence,* which may explain why he dwells at such length, and with such invective, on a Salmasius who was by then many months dead. The first twelve pages of the tract, for example, would have been equally appropriate for the abandoned work.

Something should be said about the timing of the work's composition. By early 1653, official demands on Milton's time and energies had diminished markedly. Because of his blindness, he had been forced to relinquish responsibility for many of the customary activities of the Latin Secretary; and, as mentioned, the number of state letters he was asked to translate had dwindled to a trickle. To all appearances he languished in his office, a state of affairs deeply disturbing to him. *A Second Defence* was his first composition of any length since the loss of his eyesight; and it is not too much to assume that he undertook the task, in part at least, to persuade his superiors that he could continue to be of value to the Republic despite his handicap. If this was indeed his intent, it met with some success, for the number and scope of state papers he was called upon to execute increased significantly in the following years, which included a sudden burst of activity in the spring of 1655, when

Cromwell campaigned to unite the states of Europe in the cause of the Piedmontese.[13]

It is unclear how long it took Milton to write the tract. The first *Defence* occupied him for a full year, but at the time he was deeply involved in a variety of other duties as Latin Secretary. The second was his first major composition in three years, and the blind man had to dictate it. *A Second Defence* is half the length of the earlier work, so let us say conservatively that it took four or five months to compose.[14] It makes reference to the resignation of the Barebones Parliament and the inaugural of the Lord Protector; thus Milton in all likelihood began composition in January of a tract that was published at the end of May 1654.[15] The intervening months, significantly, were the first of the rule of Oliver Cromwell.

This chronology raises two questions: First, what did Cromwell do during these months to warrant Milton's admonition? And, second, did the poet disapprove of his assuming power in the first place? Cromwell did not meet his first Parliament until the following September, ruling in the interim by decree. During that time he ended the Dutch War, which both he and Milton deplored, signing peace treaties with the United Netherlands and Denmark in April; and he reopened negotiations with Portugal that resulted in a treaty the following July.[16] In the absence of a Parliament Cromwell issued decrees to set the Republic's internal affairs in order, ordinances such as those to enforce collection of the Excise and Customs, to repair roads and highways, to continue the draining of the Fens, to affirm the authority of the courts, and to pardon the Scots for their rebellion and confirm the union between the two nations promulgated in 1652.[17] As Milton wrote, then, the Lord Protector was laboring to rescue the nation from the disorder left by the previous governments, and it is unclear just what he might have been doing to cause the poet disquiet. It is too much to say that Milton was impatient with Cromwell for inaction on reforms of the church, education, and the law, which he urges in *A Second Defence,* inasmuch as the Protector had been in the office hardly long enough to warm the seat of power.

It has been suggested that Milton disapproved of Cromwell assuming the position of Lord Protector in the first place, with the all but absolute power it carried with it.[18] In *A Second Defence* the poet leaves no doubt as to his response to the events that led up to that elevation. He applauds Cromwell's dissolution of the Rump, a body in which, he complains, "every man [was] more attentive to his private interest than to that of the state," one that, he goes on, deluded the people "of their hopes" (YP 4:671). As for the Barebones Parliament, he dismisses it, not for abdicating its authority, but for squabbling and inaction; and his scorn is manifest in the stark brevity and abruptness of his dismissal: "The elected members came together. They did nothing" (YP 4:671). Having disposed of these inept bodies, Milton resumes his paean to the Lord Protector: "Cromwell, we are deserted! You alone remain"; and, as we have seen, he "admonishes" those who protest his elevation as men who are either envious of him or ignorant of the truth that nothing is more pleasing to God "than the rule of the man most fit to rule" (YP 4:671–72). Hardly "misgivings"!

Among the several digressions in *A Second Defence* are passages of praise for the founders of the Republic, chiefly for Cromwell, but also for John Bradshaw, Sir Thomas Fairfax, and Robert Overton; and scholars have detected in such praise a "coded criticism" of the Lord Protector, since the last three named, it is said, were out of government at the time for one reason or another and opposed the regime. Christopher Hill, among others, has suggested that since Bradshaw, Fairfax, and Overton were critical of Cromwell's rule, Milton intended his praise of them in *A Second Defence* to "admonish and warn" the Lord Protector, thereby reflecting the poet's own general disapproval of the Protectorate government.[19] This position must be examined on several counts. Those anxious to dissociate the poet from Oliver Cromwell are inclined to collapse time, attributing sentiments expressed in later years to the period in question, a practice that loses sight of a very practical consideration: At the time of the composition of *A Second Defence*, the winter and spring of 1654, did these men disapprove of Cromwell's assumption of power? And if so, outside of artfully interpreted words and phrases, is there any evidence, again at the time, that Milton shared the disapproval of Bradshaw, Fairfax, and Overton? On balance, it is only fair to ask why the poet did indeed pause to praise them. Might he have had purposes in mind other than to encode a criticism of the Protectorate?

An examination of the textual and historical context of Milton's passages of praise will cast a differently colored light on his meaning and intent. John Bradshaw, there can be no doubt, was highly critical of Oliver Cromwell. Bradshaw was one of the founders of the Republic, serving on the Rump's Council of State for the four years of its existence, half that time as president of the body, before members began to rotate the chair among themselves. When, in April 1653, Cromwell and his soldiers entered the council chamber to dissolve the body, Bradshaw challenged him brazenly: "Sir, you are mistaken to think that the Parliament is dissolved; for no power under heaven can dissolve them but themselves."[20] More to the point, however, Bradshaw had presided over the court that tried and condemned Charles I; and it is for this offense that *Cry* indicts him.

Milton pays tribute to Bradshaw, not because of his political stance in

1653, but because of his role in 1649.[21] The paragraph of praise comes at the point in his argument where he answers *Cry's* attack on the judges of the king's trial. In condemning the regicide the tract heaps scorn on Bradshaw; he is "an obscure and impudent knave," the "insolent" and "bragging, angry president" of a court of "gallows-slaves" (YP 4:1058–62). Milton comes to his defense, praising him as a man who brought to the task "a liberal frame of mind, a lofty spirit, and pure morals, subservient to no man" (YP 4:638), and his purpose clearly is to defend the president of the court against those who challenge its legitimacy. Bradshaw, we can be confident, opposed Cromwell's assumption of power; but Milton raises his name, not to endorse his opposition to the Protectorate, but to justify the regicide. To ignore the vilification of Bradshaw would be to leave open to question the legitimacy of the body over which he presided and the justice of the verdict it reached.

Milton pauses briefly in his long tribute to Cromwell to pay respects to Thomas Lord Fairfax (YP 4:669–70), and some have argued that he did so to subtly undercut the Protector.[22] An examination of the historical backdrop and textual environment of the passage casts doubt on this contention. Fairfax was named Commander-in-Chief of the Parliamentary armies in 1645, and Cromwell was appointed his Lieutenant General of Horse, effectively second-in-command of all forces. The two men served together in these capacities for the balance of the civil wars and during the first one and a half years of the new Republic. In 1650 Parliament ordered an invasion of Scotland, and Fairfax, who had serious reservations about a hostile intrusion upon a neighbor's sovereign territories, resigned his commission rather than carry out the order. Cromwell headed an embassy of distinguished leaders of the Republic who attempted to dissuade their Lord General from leaving the service, but to no avail; hence Cromwell was appointed to fill his place.[23] It is said that Fairfax regretted the trial and execution of Charles I and was therefore lukewarm in his allegiance to the new government; but if he had such reservations, they did not prevent him from remaining in command of the armies of Parliament for eighteen months after the event, nor was his loyalty in question when he put down the Leveller rebellion in 1649 and later applauded Cromwell's campaigns to subdue Ireland and Scotland. If Fairfax disapproved of Cromwell's assumption of power in 1653, he nowhere said so. Indeed, after the change of command the friendship and mutual respect of the two old comrades-in-arms, who had shared many trying campaigns, continued undiminished.[24] Fairfax retired to his country estate, Nun Appleton House, where he suffered from declining health. He died in 1665.

Why praise him, then? The brief digression on Fairfax comes at the point in Milton's chronology of Cromwell's achievements where he commends the soldiers of the New Model Army for their prowess in battle, sober behavior, devotion to duty, and obedience to their general's "command in all things" (YP 4:668–69); and he attributes these fine qualities to Cromwell's leadership. And then, almost as an afterthought, he recalls that for most of its existence the army had been under the command of Fairfax, so he pauses briefly to give credit where credit is due—"Nor should I pass you by, Fairfax"—before continuing his account of Cromwell's career. Conscious that in all fairness the quality of the New Model Army could not be attributed solely to Cromwell, Milton sets the record straight by adding a tribute to its retired Commander-in-Chief—hardly an affront to the Protector, who, we may safely assume, would have heartily agreed with the sentiments.

In assessing Milton's attitude toward the events of his day, scholars, as mentioned earlier, are prone to collapse time, bringing later events to bear on the period in question. Nowhere is this practice more evident than in the poet's praise of his close friend Robert Overton in *A Second Defence* (YP 4:676). Christopher Hill, for example, contends that Milton sought to "admonish and warn" Cromwell by expressing his warm regard for Overton, "an opponent of the Protectorate," and others have echoed his conjecture.[25] Colonel Robert Overton was a highly respected officer in the New Model Army, one who had distinguished himself in the civil wars. As Milton describes one of his exploits, "at the unforgettable Battle of Marston Moor, when our left wing had been routed, the leaders, looking behind them in flight, beheld you making a stand with your infantry and repelling the attacks of the enemy amid dense slaughter on both sides" (YP 4:676). Overton was sympathetic to the radical wing of the army, a Fifth Monarchist who supported the Leveller program of political and religious reform. He applauded Cromwell's dissolution of the Rump but was disappointed at the failure of the Barebones Parliament to enact legislation separating church and state; and, it appears, he had misgivings about the establishment of the Protectorate.

In the spring of 1654 Overton left Hull, where he was serving as governor, and traveled to London "in search of more active employment," as Samuel Rawson Gardiner puts it.[26] While there, he had an interview with Cromwell, who certainly knew the sentiments of his old comrade-in-arms. Overton assured the Lord General that if the time ever came when "conscience forbade him to render further service to him," he would resign his commission. Cromwell was satisfied, sent him back to resume his duties in Hull, and later gave him "more active employment" as second-in-command to George Monk, then head of English forces in Scotland.

Later that year, Overton became associated, either inadvertently or by design—it is not clear which—with a group of radical Army officers engaged on a conspiracy to overthrow the Protectorate.[27] He was arrested and in January 1655 sent to London, where he was consigned to the Tower, there to remain for the next five years. But this all came about months after the publication of *A Second Defence,* in which Milton recommends him to Cromwell as one of those to be admitted "to the first share of your counsels" (YP 4:674). Some have found Milton's mention of his friend, "who for many years have been linked to me with a more than fraternal harmony" (YP 4:676), as a subtle criticism of Cromwell. But at the time Overton was only one of many republican-minded army officers whose allegiance the Protector was anxious to retain in those early months of his rule, and it was not until later, when they openly conspired against him, that he was forced to repudiate them. In praising Overton, Masson suggests, Milton is encouraging the Lord Protector to "rather conciliate such men than alienate them further," to draw them into his confidence and include them in the work to be done. If this was indeed Milton's intent, he seems to have achieved some success, since shortly after *A Second Defence* appeared Overton was returned to service "in full favor," as Masson puts it, promoted to major-general, and entrusted with command of English forces in the north of Scotland.[28]

There is some question, therefore, whether Overton was "under a cloud" as Milton was composing *A Second Defence.*[29] He was admittedly radical in his religious views, which consorted well with Milton's on the question of church and state; but the ranks of the New Model Army were full of men with similar convictions, as the plot against the government later affirmed. Cromwell, who had served with these men for over a decade, was well aware of their sentiments; and, equally aware that his government had need of their allegiance, he took steps to enlist it. Overton represented not so much a threat as an opportunity to bring the radical elements of the army into the fold; thus in the spring of 1654 Milton could recommend him to Cromwell as a man to be admitted "to the first share of your counsels."

It is a premise of these several arguments that Milton endorsed the allegiances of the figures he praised, that in the case of Overton he embraced his Leveller and Fifth Monarchist sympathies and was critical of Cromwell for suppressing them. Milton was in full accord with the radical sects' proposals to separate church and state, but he was unequivocally opposed to their political agenda, in particular to their demands for manhood suffrage.[30] Milton was no friend of free and unfettered elections, which he warns contemptuously are likely to result in a body of "either inn-keepers and hucksters of the state from city taverns or from country districts ploughboys and veritable herdsmen." Who would think, he asks, "his own liberty enlarged one iota by such caretakers of the state" (YP 4:682–83). He favored political leaders of proven merit, a government of carefully chosen, "godly" men, a preference that explains his disappointment with the Nominated Parliament, which was just such a body and yet "did nothing." If, in praising Overton, Milton had anything more in mind than paying tribute to an old friend who had served honorably in the struggle for freedom, it was to recommend him to the Protector as a man who in the light of his loyal service was worthy of trust. If the poet was mistaken in his conviction, evidence of his error did not surface until well after he had penned his words of praise.

Perhaps the most questionable argument for Milton's disapproval of the Protectorate is that he failed to mention Sir Henry Vane in A *Second Defence.* The omission, it is said, constitutes an endorsement of Vane's opposition to the regime, an argument that asks us to accept silence as the author's accord with an unmentioned figure's sentiments, a position that is, to put the case charitably, disingenuous.[31] Cromwell certainly had no love for the man, who had vehemently objected to his dissolution of the Rump, prompting his exasperated outburst, "O Sir Henry Vane, Sir Henry Vane, the Lord deliver me from Sir Henry Vane!" An ardent advocate of the rule of Parliament, Vane was a close friend of Milton's, a man whom the poet had praised earlier in a sonnet for his balanced understanding of "both spiritual power and civil," and of "what severs each," in brief, his appreciation of the need to separate the two.[32] But any argument based on silence is weak, and here, however inventive, totally unconvincing. If Milton had really wanted to tweak the nose of "Old Noll," he could not have done better than to pay tribute to Vane; but the poet was realistically aware that Cromwell then held the destiny of England in his hands and it was his purpose to counsel, not alienate, the Lord Protector in his new office.

Milton's counsel comes in his peroration to A *Second Defence;* and it comes in two parts, the first addressed to the Protector himself, the second to the English people. William Kerrigan and Louis Martz have observed that in his political tracts Milton imagined himself in the role of an Old Testament prophet, warning his people of the danger of straying from their allegiance to the Almighty, of falling into idolatry and lascivious living.[33] The poet concluded his first *Defence* in this vein, counseling his countrymen to shun "self-seeking, greed, luxury, and the seductions of success" lest "you be as weak in peace as you have been strong in war" and lose the gift of freedom so dearly won (YP 4:535–36), and he takes up the theme again in the second.[34]

Milton's advice to Cromwell (YP 4:673–80) does not take this tone, however; it is rather a straightforward agenda for reform, counseling him to take action on measures left unfinished or neglected by Parliament during the first five years of the Republic. He urges the Protector to dedicate himself to preservation of the hard-won liberty of the English people and to surround himself with equally committed counselors, twelve of whom he goes on to name (including Robert Overton), among them a number of his fellow soldiers, the "comrades in your toils and dangers," in whom, the poet is confident, he can safely place his trust (YP 4:675–78). Prominent in this passage is the advice to "leave the church to the church," that is, to end state support of religion, a cause Milton championed from the beginning to the end of his career as public polemicist. Next he counsels reform of the law, support for education, and the elimination of censorship. Finally, he hopes Cromwell will always side with those who believe that "all citizens equally have an equal right to freedom in the state" (YP 4:678–80).

Commentary on this counsel begins with the assumption that Milton at the time felt Cromwell greatly in need of it, that the poet suspected him to be infirm of purpose in all these areas; or, as Arthur Barker put the case, "the weight of his advice is the measure of his doubts."[35] Milton goes out of his way to advise, surely, but he does so as would any loyal counselor who abhors the sycophant's parroting of his superior's sentiments. Honest advice is not criticism. Later developments may have disappointed Milton, especially the Protectorate church policy; but it is unreasonable to attribute subsequent sentiments to the time in question, the spring of 1654. Cromwell, as mentioned, ruled by decree during these months in an effort to set the Republic's affairs in order. The only ordinance that may have caused Milton concern was that of 20 March, which appointed "a Commission for the Approbation of all Public Preachers and Lecturers before their admission to Benefices," a signal that the government did not intend to withdraw state control of the church.[36] This decree may well have prompted Milton's rather pointed counsel to "leave the church to the church"; but this piece of advice cannot support speculation about the poet's blanket disapproval of the Protectorate, as some have implied.

Cromwell espoused tolerance toward all religious sects, except Catholics of course; and he took steps in March to ensure that ministers who received benefices were competent in their calling. In time it became evident that he could envision no method of sustaining religion in England except through state support of tithes for maintenance of the clergy, but he was not alone in this sentiment. In the mid seventeenth century there were few outside the radical sects who could conceive of a clergy exempt from state control. But, undeterred, Milton continued to hope for reform. With each dramatic change in government, he addressed the ruling body on the subject, here in 1654 the Protector with *A Second Defence*, later, in the winter of 1659, Richard Cromwell's Parliament with *A Treatise of Civil Power* and that summer the restored Rump with *Considerations Touching the Likeliest Means*. In the chaos of the following spring, in the absence of an effective ruling body for him to address, he urged the cause once again, this time to the

English people themselves in *The Readie and Easie Way* (YP 7:456–58).[37] They all, of course, disappointed him; but it cannot be concluded that at the time he composed his pleas he had lost faith in these institutions, simply because they eventually turned a deaf ear to him.

It is in his peroration to his "fellow countrymen" that Milton assumes the prophetic voice (YP 4:680–86). He urges them, as he had in his first *Defence*, to "expel avarice, ambition, and luxury" from their minds, else in time of peace they lose the liberty their courage had won in war and in consequence find themselves passing "through the fire only to perish in the smoke." He goes further, however, developing a theme to be repeated time and again in his great poetry—a people will be subject to the government they deserve: "a nation which cannot rule and govern itself, but has delivered itself into slavery to its own lusts, is enslaved also to other masters whom it does not choose" (YP 4:684).[38] One passage in this coda to his "fellow countrymen" has been cited as an admonition of Cromwell. In it Milton cautions that it would be a mistake for a people to consider foreign affairs more important than domestic reform, that is, to think that "the ability to devise the cleverest means of putting vast sums of money into the treasury, the power readily to equip land and sea forces," and to deal with ambassadors and contract treaties, are matters more important than the obligation to preserve liberty at home, "to administer incorrupt justice to the people, to help those cruelly harassed and oppressed, and to render to every man promptly his own deserts" (YP 4:681).

It has been suggested that, though Milton addressed the passage to his "fellow countrymen," he wrote it with a side glance at Cromwell, conveying his disapproval of Protectorate foreign policy.[39] One scholar, insisting that the poet was opposed to colonialism, finds in it a specific rejection of Cromwell's "Western Design," a proposal to send a naval expedition to prey on the Spanish silver fleet in the Caribbean, then under debate within the inner circle of the government. This conjecture is open to serious doubt, since there is no other evidence of the poet's opposition to this expedition against England's historic Catholic enemy.[40] Indeed, at the time Milton was writing, no clearly formulated Protectorate foreign policy had as yet emerged, aside from Cromwell's concerted effort to end England's wars, declared and undeclared, with its European neighbors, with which the poet was in full accord. Milton is not criticizing Cromwell's yet-to-be-revealed vision of England's role in the world; nor is he expressing discontent with his country's colonial expansion, which was in fact little contemplated at the time. He is simply expanding on the peroration of his first *Defence*, in which he urged those same "fellow citizens" to demonstrate "justice, restraint, and moderation in preserving your freedom" (YP 4:535).

In brief, it takes a highly inventive exercise of the imagination to construe this single passage as Milton's device to "put the Protector and his regime on probation" as has been suggested.[41] Milton does not argue that his country's fiscal and foreign policies are unimportant; he simply urges that they not be pursued to the neglect of domestic reform. Indeed, as Latin Secretary he served England in an office charged with the conduct of foreign policy, one in which the preparation of correspondence with other states, the dispatch of ambassadors, and the making of treaties had been and would continue to be among his principal duties. He would hardly demean these functions of his office in a public statement designed in part, as I have suggested, to persuade his superiors that he could remain useful in it. Milton is stating the obvious, that no nation can become great or remain free if it neglects the welfare of its own citizens.

◆❦

In the final analysis, one must question whether Milton composed *A Second Defence* as a "coded criticism" of the Protectorate, expressing his "misgivings," "reservations," or "dissatisfaction" with Cromwell's exercise of power. We may assume that statesmen of the time were as adept at reading between the lines as are modern scholars, who search out hidden meanings in those same lines some 350 years after their composition.[42] If we can detect such sentiments at this distance, those much closer to events most surely could have as well, and would have found the poet as antagonistic to his government as do we, which would have left him at a minimum without a job.

Something, surely, must be seen in Milton's uninterrupted service to the Protectorate, in terms both of his superiors' confidence in his loyalty and his own dedication to the English Republic. However Milton may have felt later about Cromwell, in the spring of 1654 the Lord General *was* the English government; and it was the poet's purpose to guide, not to alienate him. His later judgment of the Protectorate policies is not germane, though some scholars are confident that he found them "objectionable."[43] Did he regret the oppressive rule of the Major Generals in 1655–1656? We may assume he did, though he never said so. Did he disapprove of the mounting pomp and circumstance of the Cromwellian court? We may confidently conclude this of a man who railed against the profligacy of a royal retinue and warned his countrymen against "self-seeking, greed, luxury, and the seductions of success." Was he disappointed when the Protector failed to separate church and state? Every product of his pen would persuade us so. Was he concerned when Cromwell considered assuming the crown? Surely! Was he relieved when he refused it? Again, yes; and Milton remained in his office. Did he endorse Cromwell's foreign policy? Some of it perhaps he did, some not. Did he entertain doubts about Cromwell's "Western Design"? If he did, he never said so. Did he applaud the Protector's efforts to mount a Protestant League against Catholic powers and to succor the persecuted Piedmontese? Who can doubt it! Did he rejoice when Cromwell acquired Dunkirk as a haven for English trade? Most certainly, as did most Englishmen. These were all developments of later years, however: hence they cast no light one way or another on the poet's sentiments in the first months of the Protectorate.

We do little credit to Milton by scanning his poetry and prose for hints and obscure allusions, coded messages, and supposed ironies to construct a case for his dissatisfaction with the government he served. He may indeed have disapproved of some of its policies, but he did not desert it. One can sympathize with the desire of some scholars to dissociate the poet from a regime that by modern standards seems offensive, and with their sincere hope that he found Cromwell's ascendancy distasteful, but wishing does not make it so. He never voiced such discontent; and any argument that he did demeans Milton's dedication to his office and his fervent belief that the English Republic, whatever its configuration, was the last, best hope of freedom for his English countrymen. No artful reading of the silences in or reading between the lines of *A Second Defence* can disguise Milton's admiration for Cromwell at the time and his clear preference for the Protectorate over the bungling governments that preceded it. We do him a disservice to mine scattered words and phrases to depict him as conforming to this or that twentieth-century ideological stance. His poetry and prose are sources of wonder for all ages, and we do his words wrong by reducing them to fit the mold of fashionable modern causes.

However much a patchwork of concerns, *A Second Defence* represents a prodigious effort for a blind man, even one with Milton's formidable memory. In composing the tract, moreover, he gained the confidence and honed the skills that made *Paradise Lost* possible. In this first effort, this quiltwork of material pulled together from abandoned projects, it should not be surprising if some of the seams show in the abrupt changes of subject and digressions that are peripheral to his defense of the regicide. In later years, the seams in the cloth of his art would be all but invisible.

La Salle University

NOTES

I am indebted to Sharon Achinstein for her careful advice, and for taming my language.

1. For a more detailed analysis of Milton's office under the Protectorate, see Robert Thomas Fallon, *Milton in Government* (University Park, Pa., 1993), 123–39.

2. Ibid., 252–53.

3. A. N. Wilson, *The Life of John Milton* (Oxford, 1983), 180.

4. Austin Woolrych, "Milton and Cromwell: 'A Short but Scandalous Night of Interruption'?" in *Achievements of the Left Hand: Essays on the Prose of John Milton,* eds. Michael Lieb and John T. Shawcross (Amherst, 1974), 182.

5. Don M. Wolfe, in his introduction to vol. 4 of *Complete Prose Works of John Milton,* 8 vols., ed. Don M. Wolfe et al. (New Haven, 1953–82), vol. 4, 261–62. All quotations of Milton's prose are from this edition and are hereafter cited parenthetically in the text as YP, with volume and page number.

6. Don M. Wolfe, *Milton in the Puritan Revolution* (New York, 1941), 97.

7. Blair Worden, "Milton and Marchamont Nedham," in *Milton and Republicanism,* eds. David Armitage, Armand Himy, and Quentin Skinner (Cambridge, 1995), 178.

8. Christopher Hill, *Milton and the English Revolution* (New York, 1977), 193.

9. Sharon Achinstein, in *Milton and the Revolutionary Reader* (Princeton, 1994), observes that Milton "began to lose faith in the English rulers as early as February 1649" (205).

10. In *Writing the English Republic* (Cambridge, 1999), 331–37, David Norbrook offers an admirably even-handed analysis of *A Second Defence,* observing that Milton questioned the ability of the English people to sustain their liberty (336), but was "ready to place high hopes in Cromwell's semi-royal government" (18).

11. David Masson, *The Life of John Milton,* 6 vols., reprint (Gloucester, Mass, 1965), vol. 4, 608.

12. The long section on Cromwell is in two parts, the first a defense against *Cry's* spurious accusation that in 1648 he treacherously persuaded Charles I to take refuge on the Isle of Wight, which led to the king's subsequent imprisonment there by the army (YP 4:1054–57). Milton counters the claim effectively and then adds a much longer account of his life, yet another digression from his stated purpose to answer *Cry's* condemnation of the regicide, one far out of proportion to the brief attention Cromwell received in the tract (YP 4:1054–55).

13. These published state papers, which admittedly testify to only a fraction of his activity in office, record that he was responsible for eight in each of the years 1653 and 1654, thirteen in 1655, thirty-two in 1656, twenty-two in 1657, and twenty-two in 1658. See Fallon, *Milton in Government,* 124 and 251–58.

14. Kester Svendsen estimates that the following year Milton took four months to compose *His Defence of Himself,* exclusive of the reply to More's *Fides Publica* (YP 4:688n). It is 155 pages long, about 20 shorter than *A Second Defence.*

15. There are occasional hints of the length of his labors. The Treaty of Westminster ended the war with the United Netherlands on 5 April 1654. Early in *A Second Defence* Milton writes as if the war was still being waged (YP 4:591–92), and later in the tract as if it was over (YP 4:657). He neglected to resolve the contradiction before publication, leaving evidence that he composed some passages prior to that date and some thereafter.

16. That April, also, he successfully negotiated the Treaty of Uppsala, a commercial agreement with friendly Sweden.

17. Masson lists the eighty-two ordinances issued by Cromwell for December 1653 to September 1654 (*The Life of John Milton,* vol. 4, 558–62).

18. Blair Worden, "John Milton and Oliver Cromwell," *Soldiers, Writers, and Statesmen of the English Revolution* (Cambridge, 1998), 243–64. Worden is only the most recent scholar to suggest that Milton "may have been troubled by Cromwell's elevation" (155).

19. Hill, *Milton and the English Revolution,* 193–94.

20. *The Memoirs of Edmund Ludlow,* ed. C. H. Firth (London, 1894), 357.

21. Keith Stavely, *The Politics of Milton's Prose Style* (New Haven, 1974). Stavely suggests that the poet's praise of Bradshaw "qualified" his commitment to the Protectorate (93).

22. Perez Zagorin, in *Milton: Aristocrat and Rebel* (New York, 1992), suggests that Fairfax was "no longer active in government *because of* [his] opposition to Cromwell's one-person rule" (95, emphasis mine). As will be seen, Fairfax retired from service three and a half years before Cromwell assumed power. See also YP 4:263, where Wolfe remarks that the praise of Fairfax is "a pointed reminder" of Milton's objection to the Protectorate.

23. John Wilson, *Fairfax* (New York, 1985), 159.

24. Ibid., 163. The friendship apparently cooled somewhat in later years, especially when Fairfax's daughter, Mary, married the Royalist duke of buckingham in 1657, much to Cromwell's consternation (172).

25. Hill, *Milton and the English Revolution,* 193–94.

26. Samuel Rawson Gardiner, *History of the Commonwealth and Protectorate, 1649–1656,* 4 vols., reprint (Gloucester, England, 1989), vol. 3, 228. In this respect, see also Maurice Ashley, *Cromwell's Generals* (London, 1954), 138. It has been suggested that Overton was summoned to London to answer for his radical views, but there is no evidence one way or other on the matter.

27. Barbara Taft, " 'They that pursew perfaction on earth . . . ': the political progress of Robert Overton," *Soldiers, Writers, and Statesmen of the English Revolution* (Cambridge, 1998), 286–303. Taft questions Overton's complicity in the conspiracy (291–93).

28. Masson, *The Life of John Milton,* vol. 4, 607–8. This view has been echoed more recently by David Loewenstein in "Milton and the Poetics of Defense," *Politics, Poetics, and the Hermeneutics of Milton's Prose* (Cambridge, 1990), 171–92. Loewenstein observes that "Milton downplays differences" among those he names. His purpose, Loewenstein stresses, was to "reconcile" them, even those, like Overton, "discontented with recent events" (185).

29. Woolrych insists that Overton was "under a cloud when *A Second Defence* appeared" ("Milton and Cromwell," 193–94 and 214n). Others stress his opposition to the Protectorate and by implication Milton's as well, making much of the fact that Overton "was soon to be arrested" (Worden, "Milton and Marchamont Nedham," 178) or "soon to be imprisoned for plotting against the government" (Hill, *Milton and the English Revolution,* 194). But Overton's arrest came *seven months* after the publication of *A Second Defence* and hence could have had no influence on Milton's decision to express his affection for his old friend. See also Nicholas Von Maltzahn, *Milton's History of Britain* (Oxford, 1991), who errs in saying that Overton was "in prison at the time" (173).

30. Merritt Y. Hughes, in his introduction to vol. 3 of YP (32). As Hughes observes, Milton "was no egalitarian" (28). See also Austin Woolrych, "Political Theory and Political Practice," *The Age of Milton,* eds C. A. Patrides and Raymond B. Waddington (Manchester, 1980), 50.

31. Wolfe, writing on Milton's silence, observes that "no sophisticated reader would have overlooked its significance" (YP 4:264), but he fails to elaborate on just what it was sophisticates were to see. Zagorin goes only so far as to call the omission "ironic," but he, too, leaves it at that (95). Worden observes that Milton never mentions Cromwell again, a silence, he insists, that is "loud" ("John Milton and Oliver Cromwell," 155).

32. "To Sir Henry Vane the Younger," Merritt Y. Hughes, ed., *John Milton: Complete Poems and Major Prose* (New York, 1957), 161.

33. William Kerrigan, *The Prophetic Milton* (Charlottesville, 1974), esp. 176–77 and 183–84; Louis L. Martz, "Milton's Prophetic Voice: Moving toward Paradise," in *Of Poetry and Politics: New Essays on Milton and His World,* ed. Paul G. Stanwood (Binghamton, N.Y., 1995), 1–16.

34. Norbrook finds the passage a "denunciation" of the English people, which may be a bit harsh (336).

35. Arthur Barker, *Milton and the Puritan Dilemma, 1641–1660* (Toronto, 1942), 180.

More recently, Worden detects undertones of "doubt" and "warning" in Milton's praise ("John Milton and Oliver Cromwell," 244).

36. These commissioners were referred to as "Triers." In August, Cromwell followed up with an ordinance establishing another commission "for ejecting scandalous, ignorant, and insufficient Ministers and Schoolmasters," popularly called the "Ejectors" (Gardiner, *History of the Commonwealth and Protectorate,* vol. 4, 564). Milton would probably have approved of ejecting "insufficient" schoolmasters, though perhaps not ministers; but in any event the later decree had no influence on *A Second Defence,* which had been published three months earlier.

37. Milton did not raise the church issue in his letter to General Monk (YP 7:392–95).

38. See also *Paradise Lost,* 12.83–84 and 95–101; *Paradise Regained,* 3.403–40 and 4.143–45.

39. See David Armitage, "John Milton: Poet against Empire," in *Milton and Republicanism,* eds. David Armitage, Armand Himy, and Quentin Skinner (Cambridge, 1995), 214. Armitage quotes the passage, leaving the erroneous impression that it was addressed to Cromwell rather than Milton's "countrymen."

40. Ibid. But this project was barely in the talking stage in April–May 1654 and was but part of a much larger question the Council of State was considering—whether to enter the war between France and Spain or to remain neutral. Foreign policy was in the making at the time, to be sure, but no decision on the expedition was reached until mid-summer, and it did not embark until December. See Robert T. Fallon, "Milton, Cromwell, and the Western Design," in *Milton and the Imperial Vision,* eds. Balachandra Rajan and Elizabeth Sauer (Pittsburgh, 1999), 133–54.

41. Ibid. Worden echoes the sentiment in "John Milton and Oliver Cromwell," 252.

42. Worden, for example, is convinced that "in the early modern period, the most telling literary expressions of political opposition are to be found between the lines" ("Milton and Marchamont Nedham," 174).

43. Martin Dzelzainis, "Milton and the Protectorate in 1658," in *Milton and Republicanism,* eds. David Armitage, Armand Himy, and Quentin Skinner (Cambridge, 1995), 184.

THE REACH OF HUMAN SENSE: SURPLUS AND ABSENCE IN *SAMSON AGONISTES*

Thomas M. Gorman

SAMSON AGONISTES TANTALIZES its readers with an obscurity that both haunts its margins and opens a void in its midst: an ultimately incomprehensible and unattainable site which both stimulates and thwarts our desire for full meaning, for plenitude, for truth. In *Samson Agonistes* it is Milton's design, in other words, to restrict his readers (and frequently his characters) to a partial perspective on the events and the final meaning of his drama, and in executing that design he attests to what is for him the central fact, the governing limitation, of postlapsarian existence: the insufficiency of human language, knowledge, and consciousness before the impenetrable obscurity of divine truths. A reader closely attuned to this dimension of *Samson* will discern in the drama an epistemological position marked by a corresponding pair of tropes—the paradoxically synonymous terms of *surplus* and *absence*—that are the primary vehicles of the obscurity and indeterminacy with which readers of this drama have struggled.[1] Though a number of recent critical accounts of *Samson Agonistes* have emphasized its fundamental opacity, and others have stressed the drama's ominous character, the powerful atmosphere of terror and desolation it engenders,[2] none has yet accounted for the complex pattern of verbal effects, structural features, and intertextual dynamics by which Milton emphasizes both the impotence of human understanding in its attempt to grasp incomprehensible divine truths and the baleful qualities of divinity itself.

In this essay I mean to shed some light into these unexplored crevasses of Milton's text, and in doing so I will place *Samson* more emphatically than it has been heretofore within a post-Nietzschean theoretical context. For I will argue in what follows that moments of absence and surplus in *Samson Agonistes* encode or encrypt a conception of truth in its relation to human subjectivity that departs significantly from classical epistemology. A close examination of the function of these tropes in *Samson* enables one, in fact, to distinguish principles in Milton's epistemology that anticipate in important respects those propounded by key figures in the Nietzschean tradition informing (among other theoretical schools) poststructuralism and Lacanian psychoanalysis. The Miltonic position that I will describe below contains affinities with the theories of Nietzsche, Derrida, and Lacan not only in its predication of human culture and epistemology as structured around a central obscurity but also in its broad conception of metaphor as the horizon of human consciousness. As do the later theorists, Milton gives scope to a forceful critique of the visualism to which postlapsarian humanity is prone. All of the characters in *Samson*—with the signal exception of Samson himself—consistently behave as though our postlapsarian conceptual and representational economy were a closed and self-supporting totality. In so behaving they misrecognize that economy's true nature as a displacement from the realm of unknowable truth, as a material structure invested with the kind of overdetermination that characterizes metaphor, synecdoche, and metonymy. They behave, that is, as though truth were a property of the social, political, and cultural field when in fact, as Milton insists, truth lies wholly beyond its scope and thus remains inaccessible to postlapsarian knowledge and expression in any positive sense.

This overdetermination takes its most frequent and fundamental form in our predilection to construct truth through "the weak, and fallible office of the Senses,"[3] especially of the eyes. Absence and surplus emerge at times, as I have suggested, through the language of *Samson Agonistes,* at times through formal and structural properties involving the staging of specific incidents and the overall trajectory of its plot. At still other times they are evoked through the relationship the drama establishes both with its biblical source in the Book of Judges and with the literary form of classical tragedy. These tropes are significant even, as we shall see, in Milton's stated desire that the drama never be staged. On whatever level they emerge, in whatever context, they are the means by which Milton encodes and dramatizes the postlapsarian believer's arduous and ultimately impossible quest to know God's will, the "unsearchable dispose / Of highest wisdom" (1746–47)—to know the final truth which, as Raphael avers in *Paradise Lost,* "surmounts the reach / Of human sense" (5.571–72).

The first part of the essay attempts to establish the post-Nietzschean theoretical context in which I read *Samson Agonistes* by providing a sense of how Derridean and Lacanian concepts related to surplus and absence find analogues in Milton's work and thought. The next section, in which Milton's critique of visualism and metaphor comes into play, examines the operation of surplus and absence within the drama by focusing on language, scene, the function of riddling as a technique of characterization and as a means of illuminating the status of reason in Samson's story, and the drama's relation to its biblical source text, Judges 13–16. The intertextual relation between poem and biblical text also figures importantly in the last section, which comments on the poem's fluid relation to Greek drama, attempts to work out (again in terms of surplus and absence) the implications of *Samson*'s status as a closet drama, and finally finds in the kinetic relation between *Samson* and Judges another manifestation of Milton's critique of classical metaphor. By allowing surplus and absence to define these interweaving textual strategies, Milton offers a text that not only dramatizes its characters' confinement within the limitations of postlapsarian subjectivity but also shapes an experience for the reader that is mimetic of that confinement.

I

The dramatization in *Samson Agonistes* of the means by which the postlapsarian human subject constructs his perspective on the world around him and endeavors to know God's truth reveals an awareness on Milton's part of what Nietzsche, describing the fundamental role that metaphorization plays in human perception and cognition, would later call *gleich machen* (making equal).[4] *Samson Agonistes* reveals a more provocative and specific sensitivity —through the manipulation of surplus and absence as a verbal, structural, dramatic, and intertextual resource—to what Derrida would call *différance* and what Lacan would name the Real. To be sure, unlike Derridean *différance* and the Lacanian Real, the surplus and absence that govern Milton's universe constitute "no abyss of nothingness," as Harold Bloom puts it, "but rather a place of being that is already God."[5] Like the surplus and absence evoked by these later theoretical discourses, however, the God of *Samson Agonistes* is a truth that can neither be represented nor positively experienced, a fundamentally unknowable and ominous truth in relation to which the structures of human knowledge and consciousness function as tropic displacements. Indeed, even as one concedes Bloom's point, one surely must also recognize that, as a matter of epistemology, it is a far from easy task to distinguish the idea of a traumatic abyss of nothingness from the divine place of being as it is darkly shaped in *Samson Agonistes.*

Derrida and Lacan are useful both for their Nietzschean view of metaphor as the horizon of human consciousness and, in addition, for their emphasis upon an unrepresentable kernel or force that organizes the structures of language, knowledge, and consciousness even as this kernel maintains a radically exterior and even inimical relation to them.[6] Derrida is crucial to the present undertaking in light of his argument that all structures require surplus, that the fundamental paradox of any structure consists in its ambiguous relation to its own center.[7] "It has always been thought that the center, which is by definition unique, constituted that very thing within a structure which while governing the structure, escapes structurality," Derrida writes. "This is why classical thought concerning structure could say that the center is, paradoxically, *within* the structure and *outside* it. . . . The totality *has its cen-*

ter elsewhere. The center is not the center." To whatever extent classical thought had rendered the concept of the center problematic, the concept has remained at least "contradictorily coherent," Derrida notes; the "fundamental immobility" of the center was never doubted. But beginning with the Nietzschean critique of metaphysics, the center came to seem "not a fixed locus but a function, a sort of nonlocus in which an infinite number of sign-substitutions came into play. This was the moment when language invaded the universal problematic." Consciousness and signification are not structured, then, by any "present" and stable origin but by *différance*, Derrida's term for the limitless play of language, its lack of any controlling center or "full presence which is beyond the reach of play."[8] *Différance* functions as "the possibility of conceptuality . . . a conceptual process and system in general," without, however, serving as any sort of stable origin for conceptualization. "*Différance* is the non-full, non-simple, structured and differentiating origin of differences. Thus, the name 'origin' no longer suits it." Language, too, is a structure with a "nonlocus" for a center, a system of differences "which do not find their cause in a subject or substance, in a thing in general, a being that is somewhere present, thereby eluding the play of *différance*."[9]

In important respects Milton is attuned to these ideas. Remarking upon recent attempts to read Milton from a poststructuralist position, Annabel Patterson observes that "the philosophical critique of truth and guaranteed meaning is not only *applicable* to Milton's writings but was within his own range of pious yet daring response to the question of what he believed, and on whose authority."[10] The problem of which Patterson speaks is evident immediately upon turning to *On Christian Doctrine.*[11] Milton suggests in this work that Scripture is an indispensable but insufficient medium of divine truths. The believer comes nearest to knowledge of God's truth only through an interpretive encounter with "the external Scripture of the written word" that is mediated by the mysterious divine agency of the Holy Spirit, "the internal Scripture . . . engraved upon the hearts of believers" (YP 6:587). In consequence, Milton's God enters the consciousness of the postlapsarian subject only as a metaphorical—and therefore in some degree a dissimulated —conception, a verbal figure or image giving imperfect shape to the divine truths of which we can receive only the dimmest presentiment. "God, as he really is, is far beyond man's imagination, let alone his understanding," Milton writes. "It is safest for us to form an image of God in our minds which corresponds to his representation and description of himself in the sacred writings. Admittedly, God is always described or outlined not as he really is but in such a way as will make him conceivable to us" (YP 6:133). Milton's emphasis on the gaps and limitations that define postlapsarian consciousness and destabilize even scriptural texts establishes all representations of divine truths as incomplete, provisional, or *metaphorical* in something like a Nietz-schean sense. Although this conception of metaphor as the horizon of post-lapsarian consciousness has been noted in previous appraisals of Milton's work,[12] I would like to emphasize its signal departure from the classical tradition. Indeed Aristotle himself, as Derrida observes, ascribes "a certain original naturality" to metaphor—equating it with meaning itself[13]—while Milton appears to distinguish divine truths in their pristine unreadability from the postlapsarian verbal and symbolic structures which function as inexact metaphors for those truths.

Lacan is useful here chiefly on the basis of two formulations: first, the "mirror stage" of human development, which results in the subject's entry into the domain of language and symbolization; second, the cognitive register which he names the Real, the avenue through which one receives fleeting and murky presentiments of Freud's *das Ding* (the Thing). The Thing is the terrifying obscurity which, paradoxically, haunts the margins and opens a void at the center of human consciousness. It is a *traumatic* emptiness, an utterly unrepresentable "insistence without presence," as the Lacanian psycho-analyst and theorist Julia Kristeva puts it,[14] a buried psychic trace of the preorganic state from which human life arose and to which, through the death drive, human life seeks a return. The individual human subject gathers only dim and disturbing intimations of the Thing through the unconscious, for in the domain of the Real, "we are projected into something that is far beyond the domain of affectivity, something moving, obscure and without reference points," according to Lacan. Thus the Real, the "beyond-of-the-signified," marks the limit of what can be positively known.[15]

Standing forever apart from the truth of the Real, but representing a drive to possess or become one with it, is the "symbolic order," Lacan's name for domain of the signifier, the space of language and of the entire superstruc-ture of cultural, political, economic, religious, ideological, and philosophical systems—each claiming to have purchase on truth—that give shape and di-rection to human life. The symbolic order is really a fiction, however, because the Real, the truth that grounds and orients the symbolic network, is also irremediably hostile to it and forever out of its reach. Indeed, as Lacan asserts, the Real is "the first thing that separated itself from everything the subject began to name and articulate." The symbolic order is constrained to function, therefore, as a dissimulation of this obscure truth, as a kind of trope in relation to the Real, and the Real constitutes, in turn, both the absent center and unattainable surplus of the symbolic order—an "intimate exteri-ority or 'extimacy.' "[16]

For the subject, the Real is the realm of the unconscious, "the pre-historic Other that it is impossible to forget," as Lacan puts it, "something strange to me, although it is at the heart of me." The Real provides an intimation of what is "in you more than you," to which Lacan attributes the subject's sense of incompleteness, the innate yearning to recover the feeling of wholeness that disintegrates as a result of the "mirror stage," the moment when the infant, typically by apprehending his own reflection in a looking glass, first internalizes a unified body image, a *Gestalt* or "specular *I.*" This is, indeed, an exhilarating moment, one of self-discovery in the most fundamental sense, the moment when "the *I* is precipitated in a primordial form." But it is also the condition for the child's entry into the symbolic network, for almost immediately, as the discovery of self is followed by the discovery of the other, the child reaches his "alienating destination"—the *I* is "objectified in the dialectic of identification with the other"—and he experiences "the deflection of the specular *I* into the social *I.*"[17] And in thus acceding to the symbolic order in the mirror stage, the child has, in effect, bowed to the authority of the visual field, has adopted its parameters as the primary index of reality.[18] "It is obviously not for nothing," Lacan writes, "that we have referred to as a picture the function in which the subject has to map himself as such."[19] Out of the mirror stage the child's subjectivity is born—but at the price of the "primal lack" that he will forever feel owing to his expulsion from this originary plenitude, his impossible yearning for the maternal body. Freud connects this yearning to the preorganic origins of human life, and of course a return to those origins means the destruction of life. This is why the Real stands for what is "beyond the pleasure principle"—why it shadows forth the dimension of unpleasure, the realm of the death drive, why it stands for the mysterious and incomprehensible appeal that crime, abjection, and destruction can hold for us. "Neither pleasure nor the organizing, unifying, erotic instincts of life suffice in any way to make of the living organism, of the necessities and needs of life, the center of psychic development," Lacan writes.[20] The center of psychic development is instead something much more terrifying, a traumatic surplus, a force inimical to life itself.

In the context of his thinking on the Real, Lacan remarks on the nature of self-sacrifice, and I bring his comment forward here for the light it may shed on Milton's self-slaughtering hero Samson. Lacan describes the incomprehensible attraction to a force experienced as a dreadful transcendent power that threatens to consume the subject and argues that "the offering to obscure gods of an object of sacrifice is something to which few subjects can resist succumbing, as if under some monstrous spell. . . . The sacrifice signifies that, in the object of our desires, we try to find evidence for the presence of the desire of this Other that I call here *the dark God.*"[21] Michael Lieb has recently shown that an awareness of the inexplicable appeal, even authority, of dread or abjection is not at all foreign to the world of *Samson Agonistes.*

Lieb adduces Rudolf Otto in distinguishing between two conceptions of deity, and this distinction bears more than a passing resemblance to the Lacanian opposition between the Symbolic and the Real. The more familiar understanding of God, Lieb writes, emphasizes "the higher attributes of 'Spirit, Reason, Purpose, Good Will, Supreme Power, Unity, [and] Self-hood,'" and each of these we may readily associate with the Lacanian Symbolic, the province of the subject, of rationality, order, harmony, *telos*. An alternative conception of deity, however, expresses the "more archaic view of religion" which Lieb discerns in *Samson*, assigning to deity a host of terrifying attributes. One immediately notes a correspondence between Lacan's account of the Real and Lieb's description of this more primitive response to God's limitless power.

The product of a "creature-feeling" in response to a power totally beyond the realm of knowing, these attributes are what characterize the notion of God as a phenomenon replete with the quality of *numen*. This quality imbues deity with a sanctity, indeed, a power, that renders it "wholly other" (*"ganz andere"*). Otto defines "wholly other" as "that which exists quite beyond the sphere of the usual, the intelligible, and the familiar, which therefore falls quite outside the limits of the 'canny,' and is contrasted with it, filling the mind with blank wonder and astonishment."[22]

Julia Kristeva's description of the Lacanian Real as a "light without representation . . . an imagined sun, black and bright at the same time," and particularly of its function as "the center of repulsion and attraction" for the subject,[23] invests the Real with a paradoxical energy identical to that found in the conception of deity recorded, Lieb argues, in *Samson Agonistes*. Citing Kierkegaard's *The Concept of Dread*, Lieb contends that dread is "at once 'a *sympathetic antipathy* and an *antipathetic sympathy*.' The individual is simultaneously drawn to it and repelled by it, that is, attracted to that which repels him and repelled by that which attracts him. . . . Under this circumstance, dread becomes an 'alien power' that lays hold of him and consumes him, as he sinks in the dread which he loves even while he fears it." In *Samson*, Lieb argues, we encounter this paradoxical force "in its divinized form."[24]

Moving into the verbal, structural, characterological, and intertextual dimensions of Milton's drama, I hold on particularly to three ideas: the Derridean concept of an unstable center (the center as "nonlocus"); the related Lacanian concept whereby the Real haunts the subject with a presentiment of the Thing, a traumatic and incomprehensible internal energy, the "something strange to me, although it is at the heart of me," that which is "in you more than you"; and Lacan's contention that entering the symbolic order entails a submission to the authority of visual sensory impression. Each of these notions, as we shall see below, finds a striking analogue in *Samson Agonistes* as moments of surplus and absence are delineated on multiple levels throughout the drama's progression.

II

A concern with surplus and absence strongly informs not only the framing of the drama's central issues but also the setting of its single scene of action: the resting place outside the prison in Gaza to which Samson is led as the drama opens. Most of what follows upon this moment—everything up to the point of Samson's departure for the Philistine temple—takes place within a kind of margin defined both by Samson's physical position upon the "dark steps" of an "unfrequented place" as well as by his disposition toward the temporary reprieve he has been granted from the grinding toil that normally fills his days.[25] Samson condemns his captors not for putting him to hard labor but for imposing upon him this interval of rest: "This day a solemn Feast the people hold / To *Dagon* thir Sea-Idol, and forbid / Laborious works, unwillingly this rest / Thir Superstition yields me" (12–15). The impression of unwanted excess that attaches to Samson's brief respite is implicitly reinforced later in the drama when he remarks that his toil in the Philistine prison forms part of a just and equitable structure of exchange in which he contributes "labor / Honest and lawful to deserve my food / Of those who have me in thir civil power" (1365–67). Surplus also emerges in Samson's bemoaning of the inequity between his wisdom and his strength; indeed he ascribes his entire downfall to the discrepancy between these two faculties, which renders his strength an excessive liability: "O impotence of mind, in body strong! / But what is strength without a double share / of wisdom? Vast, unwieldy, burdensome" (52–54).

Samson's departure for the temple is also couched in the language of surplus. At first Samson refuses to accompany the Philistine officer to the feast, fearing that his participation will "add a greater sin" to his previous "great transgression" (1356–57). But he reconsiders, and his change of heart appears to commence at the point where he declares that "Commands are no constraints. If I obey them, / I do it freely" (1372–73). If Samson goes to the temple, in other words, he does so not in answer to a command but from a motivation which is entirely his own, wholly outside the equation of mastery and servitude. The Chorus, meanwhile, immediately voices an anxiety over Samson's fate in words—"How thou wilt here come off surmounts my reach" (1380)—that resonate strongly of Raphael's assertion in *Paradise Lost* that God's truth "surmounts the reach / Of human sense" (5.571–72). It is precisely at this moment that Samson begins "to feel / Some rousing motions in me which dispose / To something extraordinary my thoughts" (1381–83). He begins to come under the sway of irresistible and uncanny impulses emanating from the depths of his being and driving him to an act that had only moments before seemed, not merely *extra*ordinary, but quite beyond the range of the possible.

One finds Samson invoking surplus once again in the specific terms he employs early in the drama as he recollects the origin of his divine mission. Samson's was a "birth from Heaven *foretold* / *Twice* by an Angel," his "breeding order'd and *prescrib'd* / As of a person *separate* to God" (23–24, 30–31; emphasis mine). From the point of the doubled foretelling, that is, it is clear that Samson's divine calling will exceed the span of his life and the scope of even his prodigious abilities. His charge is waiting for him even before his birth, and it will remain unfinished at his death. For to "begin *Israel's* Deliverance" is "the work to which I was divinely call'd" (225–26), and to begin is not to complete.

The angel's visitation to Samson's parents provides an occasion for taking up the drama's critique of visualism, still another means by which Milton vexes the reader with surplus obscurity. For in *Samson* the field of visual sensory impression, notwithstanding its supreme authority among the characters of the drama, is a metaphorical reduction of and displacement from the unknowable truths that exceed its scope. As Stanley Fish argues in "Spectacle and Evidence in *Samson Agonistes*," the sense of sight emerges repeatedly as the primary index of "truth" for postlapsarian humanity; indeed, truth claims are shown continually in the drama to be heavily and fatally dependent upon specular configurations. Here it becomes possible—by closely attending to this component of Milton's agenda—to take issue with William Riley Parker, who praises Milton for omitting from *Samson Agonistes* certain irrelevant or otherwise (to Parker) objectionable material found in the biblical account, as in "the angel's instructions to the hero's mother, her story to Manoa, the description of the angel and his anonymity, Manoa's prayer for a second visit, the angel's encounter with the woman in the field, the hospitality offered the angel, the behavior of Manoa and his wife when the angel ascends."[26] It is true that Milton condenses all of this material into a few lines, but the manner of his doing so does not suggest that this material is irrelevant. Rather, Milton's compression of the transactions between the angel and Samson's parents has the effect of intensifying the motif of visualism and adding fuel to his critique of postlapsarian truth claims. Here is how, early on in Milton's drama, Samson describes the encounter with the angel:

> O wherefore was my birth from Heaven foretold
> Twice by an Angel, who at last in sight

> Of both my Parents all in flames ascended
> From off the Altar, where an Off'ring burn'd,
> As in a fiery column charioting
> His Godlike presence, and from some great act
> Or benefit reveal'd to Abraham's race?   (23–29)

"One is always wrong," Nietzsche writes with heavy irony in *The Gay Science,* "but with two, truth begins.—*One* cannot prove his case, but two are irrefutable."[27] The enjambment dividing "sight" and "Of both my Parents" (between lines 24 and 25) suggests that the visual field is the index of objective reality for Samson and is, as such, susceptible of independent corroboration. It suggests further that Samson, at this stage of the drama, is himself still beholden to the authority of the specular, that he is enclosed utterly within metaphor's reductive horizon. To Aristotle, as Derrida notes, metaphor becomes a theory of meaning, an instrument of truth, largely because of its mimetic function—that is, its visual dimension. In the *Poetics* Aristotle writes that "to use metaphor well is to discern similarities," from which Derrida concludes: "The condition for metaphor (for good and true metaphor) is the condition for truth. . . . In this sense, *mimesis* is therefore a 'natural' movement."[28] Milton would dissent, I believe, from the Aristotelian view as Derrida characterizes it. That he may not, at any rate, regard the visible as the unerring gauge of reality (and therefore as an instrument of good) is suggested by the passage that immediately follows, in which visualization functions as an instrument of Philistine oppression.

> Why was my breeding order'd and prescrib'd
> As of a person separate to God,
> Design'd for great exploits; if I must die
> Betray'd, Captiv'd, and both my Eyes put out,
> Made of my Enemies the scorn and gaze.
>
> . . . .
>
> Ask for this great Deliverer now, and find him
> Eyeless in *Gaza* at the Mill with slaves.   (30–34, 40–41)

One notes the homophonic relation between *gaze* and *Gaza,* perhaps suggesting that Samson's real prison is the gaze itself, a gaze that he is unable to return and that denies his spiritual calling. The lines cited above suggest that the visual field serves the Philistines as a jailhouse, but friends and enemies alike penalize Samson by means of a visualist construction of reality. As Anthony Low points out, Samson is persistently misunderstood and mischaracterized by those who constitute reality chiefly from specular evidence. Samson's ragged appearance, Low writes, prevents him from being recognized as "the cynosure of the Jews and a warning to the Philistines," and though the Chorus finds in Samson's appearance "a true indication of his inner state," the inner transformation he soon commences will estrange the visual from the actual. "Like the Messiah," Low writes, "there are those who cannot understand him even when his mission is most openly manifested to their eyes. . . . As he grows within, the physical sight of his visitors will reveal to them less and less accurately what kind of man he really is."[29] Thus through most of the drama, Samson is beleaguered by the seemingly unconquerable authority of the sense of sight—and yet how fragile a sovereign it turns out to be. Samson's lament, "why was the sight / To such a tender ball as th' eye confin'd? / So obvious and so easy to be quench't" (Low, 92–95), adumbrates Milton's progressively intensifying critique of visualism throughout the drama. Low observes that "Samson's inner sight grows" while "his visitors confirm themselves in blindness" (Low, 99), and he argues that Milton's concern with seeing and blindness also explains the "claustrophobic close-ness and frequent hypersensitivity" of the drama. "Milton gives us not the broad world of his visual imagination, as in *Paradise Lost*," Low writes, "but the narrow, tortured world of the blind Samson, a world where the other senses are magnified, where footsteps echo, where seeing is constantly spo-ken of, and sensed, and used metaphorically, yet little can be seen directly" (Low, 107). One might refine Low's point by saying that seeing functions metaphorically in *Samson Agonistes* in order to show *precisely* that little can be seen directly, that we see only metaphorically and therefore not "literally." For truth is precisely that surplus substance which cannot be apprehended by the eye.

Surplus and absence are also evoked in the drama's shifting and funda-mentally ambiguous treatment of Samson's blindness. Early on in the drama blindness seems to place Samson outside of Creation itself, excluding him from God's "first created Beam" and "prime decree" (83, 85). His lament is deeply felt: "Light the prime work of God to me is extinct, / And all her various objects of delight / Annull'd" (70–72). By the end of the poem, however, Samson's blindness is associated with the rousing motions that pre-cipitate him into the Philistine temple, the inner force that he and everyone else in the drama presume to have been divinely inspired. Both instances emphasize Samson's absence from the world of the seeing, his subsistence within an obscure margin of that world, but blindness functions as a disem-powering condition in the first instance and as a signifier of divine inspiration in the second. Whether one is to view the force behind Samson's departure for the temple as divine impulsion or mere delusion has long been the subject of critical debate, of course. It is, after all, the Chorus—a far from completely reliable source of information, as we shall see in due course—which asserts that Samson has acted "With inward eyes illuminated" (1689) in destroying the temple. But while one can say with some confidence that surplus and absence shape both the early and late references to Samson's blindness—different as these references are in import—one must recognize, finally, that the drama never settles on a clear position on the role that blindness plays in the events culminating in the destruction of the temple. By articulating two positions on Samson's blindness, proceeding to undercut both by enunciating them through figures whose perspicacity is highly questionable, and finally by associating Samson's blindness with the darkest of the drama's many dark spots (his motivations in entering the temple), Milton cloaks the meaning of Samson's blindness in an impermeable obscurity.

Stanley Fish effectively illuminates the indispensable role that visualization plays in grounding postlapsarian truth claims by describing each character's attempt to impose an intelligible narrative upon the events of Samson's life. Fish's assertion of the importance of visualization in *Samson* enables one to view Milton's depiction of truth claims in the fallen world as a form of metaphorical dissimulation, a vain attempt by postlapsarian man to possess a truth that exceeds his grasp. For all who encounter Samson during his imprisonment in Gaza find themselves struggling to reconcile their memory of the potent hero they once knew with the unkempt and subjugated figure they now see. They must, as Nietzsche would put it, *make* equal what is new, finding (or fabricating) the common principle uniting two seemingly incompatible notions. Manoa and the Chorus encounter the spectacle of the downtrodden Samson, a sight that deflects them from their conception of the former hero, and they know they must somehow reunite these two ideas; they must solve the riddle that confronts them, and they answer this challenge by making a metaphor of Samson, turning him "into an example of the wheel-of-fortune principle," Fish writes. "What is wonderful about this from the perspective of the choral anxiety," he adds, "is that it allows the chorus to look at Samson and to *not* look at him at the same time."[30] Fish characterizes this move as a "distancing of the present," the effect of which is "to make the present into something that has already happened, an event at once predicted and rendered intellectually manageable by formula ready and eager to account for it" (Fish, 560). In Nietzschean terms, the Chorus masters its initial disorientation in the face of this specular riddle by *making* the spectacle before them *equal* the reassuring formula they have prepared for it, discarding as unwanted surplus any aspects of the immediate reality that do not fit this formula. Put another way, the members of the Chorus respond to what they see by harnessing Samson, already shackled to the physical wheel of the millstone, to a second, metaphorical wheel, the "sphere of fortune" figure at line 172 that encodes their resignation to the bondage visited upon them and Samson by the Philistines. At its first glimpse of Samson, the Chorus notes his dejected countenance and soiled garb, finally registering its defamiliarization by saying: "Or do my eyes misrepresent? Can this be hee, / That Heroic, that Renown'd, / Irresistible *Samson?*" (124–26). Thus the riddle of Samson's fallen state poses itself as a visual phenomenon, and it is through manipulation of the visual field—what amounts to a denial of the obscure surplus that cannot be seen or known—that the riddle is finally "solved." The sense of sight is their ever-reliable instrument in this fabrication.

Visualism also plays an important role, Fish notes, in the "heroic act of interpretation" that Manoa must undertake to avert the dishonor he fears will follow the news that Samson has died, in effect, by his own hand. Manoa demands of the Messenger as detailed an account of the scene as possible. In enjoining the Messenger to "give us if thou canst, / Eye-witness of what first or last was done, / Relation more particular and distinct" (1593–95), he is really saying, argues Fish, "tell us the precise facts and nothing but the facts, order them in a sequence of inevitable cause and effect, and do not leave any blurred edges or imprecise characterizations." Fish writes that the Messenger "responds in the spirit of the request" and accedes to its underlying assumption: "that the true meaning of things can be derived from the configurations they present to the eye" (Fish, 566). This insistence on the authority of the visual field in determining the final meaning of Samson's fate suggests that Manoa and the Chorus are determined to discover "truth" strictly within the confines of the postlapsarian system of representation. Implicit in Manoa's instructions to the Messenger is a rejection of that which is not susceptible of representation by this symbolic network, and the rather nervous exactitude of those instructions—Manoa must surely strike the reader as exceptionally particular under the circumstances—seems to reveal an anxiety on his part toward some obscure force outside the field of the representable that is pressing uncomfortably onto the scene, some traumatic surplus of which he is anxious that the Messenger's report gives no intimation. Indeed, Manoa's request for information comes *after* he complains of a surplus of knowledge—"More than enough we know" (1592)—suggesting, one might say, that he hopes the Messenger will help him know less rather than more about what occurred in the temple, that he is relying upon the Messenger's account to pull his mind back into the familiar environs of his own symbolic system and out of the dire and traumatic regions to which Samson's cataclysmic demise has impelled it. In effect, Manoa is asking for the soothing blindness of postlapsarian vision.

Certainly the Chorus never overcomes its blindness. At the end of the drama we find it still busily manufacturing semblances of intelligibility—as Fish writes, "declaring God's ways to be 'unsearchable' (1.1746), and proceeding, in the very same breath, to search them" (Fish, 561). The Chorus declaims:

> All is best, though we oft doubt,
> What the unsearchable dispose
> Of highest wisdom brings about,
> And ever best found in the close.
> Oft he seems to hide his face,
> But unexpectedly returns
> And to his faithful Champion hath in place
> Bore witness gloriously.   (1745–52)

These lines strongly suggest the operation of metaphor, for the notion of searching corresponds to the metaphorical search for commonality between one term and another, and the unexpected return suggests the surprise of recognition that attends the discovery of a previously undiscerned similarity between two objects or ideas. Confused by what God has wrought, the Chorus must, again, find a way to harmonize the dissonant note. Fish's perception of a kind of riddle embedded within this scene is of interest here as well, in light of the similarity, as noted by Aristotle, between riddles and metaphors.[31] "Like any good storyteller," Fish writes, "God doesn't give his point away at the beginning but withholds it, calculating the moment at which its revelation will produce the maximum impact. At this moment—the moment of the 'close,' the end, the wrap-up—everything becomes clear, unmistakable, immediately readable" (Fish, 561). The members of the Chorus believe they have solved God's riddle; they believe they have overcome the riddle's "block element," the component intended to distract attention and postpone the moment of recognition.[32] But it is clear that the intelligibility finally found is illusory—a figure, an allegory, a metaphor that has been contrived to conceal the gap marking the incomprehensibility of God's movement. For this riddle is ultimately indecipherable; as Fish suggests, it evades the expected moment of readability, exceeds the reach of postlapsarian comprehension, and thereby refuses the role reserved for it by classical metaphysics.

The role played by riddling in the drama is one element of what some have seen as its lack of rationality and what I see as its dark evocation of the truth that lies beyond rationality and is experienced, in the manner of the Lacanian Real, as a traumatic surplus. "Be less abstruse, my riddling days are past," says Samson (1064) in one of only two explicit references to riddling in *Samson Agonistes*—and indeed at first blush the role played by riddling in Samson's fate, though featured quite prominently in the biblical account, may seem of only trifling interest to Milton. In fact, among the "irrelevant details" that Parker praises Milton for having "wisely omitted" from his drama are any specifics of the riddles that tripped Samson up in the Judges account. "There was no reason," Parker argues, "to mention the cause or the form of the riddle at the feast, no reason to mention the trivial part of Manoa and his wife in the affair."[33] I would suggest that riddling is much more important to Milton than Parker allows, and that Milton emphasizes the importance of the riddles precisely by omitting them, by drawing his readers' attention to details included in the biblical account but—in another telling instance of absence—excluded from his own text. For though Samson never speaks of riddling as such when, early on in the drama, he recalls for Manoa the circumstances of his consecutive betrayals at the hands of the woman of Timna and Dalila, a close examination of these lines suggests that riddling is anything but irrelevant to Milton's concerns. In speaking with his father, Samson mentions only the "secret" that the woman of Timna "wrested from me" (384) and revealed to his enemies, this secret being the answer to the riddle he had posed to the thirty Philistine groomsmen. Milton's rendering of this recollected encounter with Dalila makes clear that Samson himself is the true subject of the three riddles with which he seeks to deflect Dalila from discovering the source of his strength, and this is accomplished, I would suggest, precisely by Milton's exclusion of the three specific riddles themselves, his implicit invocation of elements in the biblical text that are absent from his own text. Trusting his audience to know riddles were involved, even if they did not necessarily remember the details of them, Milton more effectually arranges for Samson himself to supplant the original subjects, underscoring the fact that Dalila's purpose is not to discover the answer to the three riddles Samson poses but to solve the riddle of Samson himself. In this way, Milton also induces the reader to see Samson as a riddle—one whose resolution, because synonymous with the divine truth that surpasses the reach of the drama's system of signification, eludes us to the end. Samson's position as the sought-after "answer" in Milton's telescoped version of the riddling episode is unmistakable in the lines where he recalls Dalila's persistent entreaties. One also notes a metaphoric equation between dissimilar things in Samson's adumbration at line 401 of becoming "a Traitor to myself."

> Thrice assay'd with flattering prayers and sighs,
> And amorous reproaches to win from me
> My capital secret, in what part my strength
> Lay stor'd, in what part summ'd, that she might know:
> Thrice I deluded her, and turn'd to sport
> Her importunity, each time perceiving
> How openly, and with what impudence
> She purpos'd to betray me, and (which was worse
> Than undissembl'd hate) with what contempt
> She sought to make me Traitor to myself.   (392–401)

Daniel T. Lochman sees riddling as crucial to Milton's critique of post-lapsarian logic and consciousness. He argues that riddling helps facilitate Samson's development from confinement within a logocentric system of binary opposites to an understanding of "God's providential transcendence of the law" and of a "limitless potentiality" unprovided for in the realm of logic.[34] He cites the riddles found in the biblical narrative in support of his assertion that "Milton's Samson is given a nascently prophetic voice which, in the hero recorded in Judges, is concealed by riddles and verbal enigmas" (209). We find Samson at the beginning of the drama entirely beholden to "the limits of ordinary logic," by which reality is constructed as a series of "dualistic alternatives" (195, 196). Samson, in predicting that "This day will be remarkable in my life / By some great act, or of my days the last" (1388–89), reveals himself as the captive of binary logic, of mutually exclusive alternatives. "He fails to foresee that the day will be *both* remarkable *and* his last," Lochman argues. "Milton's audience, like Samson, must learn to see existence as mixed and ambiguous, irreducible to simple, absolute alternatives" (Lochman, 195–96).[35]

The indeterminacy that Milton's readers have always struggled with on the crucial question of Samson's motivations is another occasion of surplus and absence. Stanley Fish's response to the enduring mystery of *Samson's* meaning is to cut the Gordian knot and locate precisely in the fundamental unreadability of the drama—or at least of the protagonist—its chief source of power. The depiction of Samson as harboring a kernel of unintelligibility and of human life in general as an irreducibly ambiguous proposition is perfectly consistent with what Fish describes as "a theory of personality" discernible in Milton beginning with *Areopagitica.*[36] Fish notes that the early Milton of the tracts and poems written before 1644 admired all those who "hold themselves aloof and thereby avoid the pollution of alien contact," and Samson's initial refusal to accompany the Philistine officer to the temple appears "to signal his recovery of spirit and strength by once again claiming and demonstrating the inner consistency he had lost" (Fish, 575, 576). But when for unknown reasons Samson reconsiders and goes along to the temple after all, it is clear that he belongs in a different category. With the publication of *Areopagitica,* Milton had come to regard "fixity of mind and judgment . . . as the sign of spiritual sloth. Rather than being already complete, the true Christian self is imaged as 'wayfaring,' that is, as always being on the way and never having arrived. . . . In the context of such a life, constancy of mind is what one wants to avoid, while change, discontinuity, and endless transformation are what one avidly courts" (Fish, 576). Milton's conscientiously wayfaring Christian, in other words, resists the classical trajectory of metaphor and must accept a ceaseless deflection or displacement that issues in no authentic encounter with the truth. Such a believer, who refuses to be seduced by metaphor's claim of delivering truth or presence, intuitively rejects Aristotle's attribution of original naturality to metaphor. God's truth—not the laws of man, not even Scripture itself in the last analysis—is the only truth, and one must understand that this truth will be "always in excess of one's conceivings," as Fish puts it. "Paradoxically," he continues, "Samson will be able to maintain his relationship with God only when he is able to see that relationship as one always on the move, as a relationship 'anchored' by a conviction of its radical incompleteness" (Fish, 577). This radical incompleteness also structures the individual's relation to Scripture. Derek N. C. Wood reminds us of Milton's declaration in *Eikonoklastes:* "He, who without warrant but his own fantastic surmise, takes upon him perpetually to unfold the secret and unsearchable Mysteries of high Providence, is likely for the most part to mistake and slander them; and approaches to the madness of those reprobate thoughts, that would wrest the Sword of Justice out of Gods [own] hand, and imploy it more justly in thir own conceit."[37] Rejecting the idea of any single authoritative interpretation of God's mysteries, an interpretation to which others could be bound, Milton grants to the individual, insofar as he is guided by the Holy Spirit within him, complete freedom to interpret Scripture. "Every believer is entitled to interpret the Scriptures; and by that I mean interpret them for himself," he writes in *On Christian Doctrine* (YP 6:583). The essential inaccessibility of the truth or the being of God, in relation to which Scripture is a fallen remnant, authorizes the limitlessness of scriptural interpretation, Milton suggests.

This brings me to consider in more explicit terms *Samson's* relation to the Judges text, for the incompleteness that, in Milton's view, is a primary affliction of the postlapsarian world must define not only the believing subject but also Scripture, and it necessarily conditions each of Milton's poetic encounters with biblical material. This is why I consider the relation of *Samson Agonistes* to the Judges account indispensable to an understanding of Milton's drama— and why it seems to me that the most extraordinary aspect of Parker's analysis of the drama, his attempt to demonstrate its adherence to the model of classical tragedy, is his determination to read it as much as possible in isolation from its scriptural source. Not only, in my view, does this approach to *Samson* remove the drama from its true context; it also fails to take into account the considerable liberties Milton takes with the classical model, as we shall see in the next section. For these departures have a good deal to do with the drama's indeterminacy, its lack of a coherent final meaning.[38]

Though the relationship between Milton's drama and the Judges account is crucial, it becomes important largely in the breach, in the points where Milton departs from his biblical antecedent.[39] One of the most obvious points of departure is the characterological interiority that is present in *Samson Agonistes* and entirely absent from the Judges text. While Milton's drama provides an account of a soul in the throes of a profound moral, ethical, and spiritual agon, the biblical text never abandons a rigorously external perspective, which leaves unexamined the internal struggles of its characters. *Samson* seems therefore to supply what is "missing" from the biblical account, to function in relation to Judges as a surplus substance—what is in it more than itself, to paraphrase Lacan's description of the unconscious. The drama seems to call attention to the incompleteness of the scriptural text or perhaps its displacement from the true seat of the drama—the protagonist's soul, the stage from which the Holy Spirit, the mysterious force in Samson that is more than himself, impels the Nazarite toward the Philistine temple through the "rousing motions in me which dispose / To something extraordinary my thoughts" (1382–83).

One encounters this surplus and absence in a somewhat cryptic form when attempting, as though defining a geometrical pattern, to pinpoint the place along the surface of the Judges narrative where Milton has lodged *Samson Agonistes*—focusing, that is, on the incision that Milton makes into a seemingly flat, horizontal axis and opening a vertical dimension harboring a depth and interiority unauthorized by the biblical source text. For while the entire present action of Milton's drama is not, in fact, "present" at all within the Judges account in the sense that none of the dialogue we are permitted to witness appears in the anterior text, in another sense—essentially a chronological one—this material does find a place inside the biblical narrative. One may, indeed, assign a very precise location *within* the Judges account to the events in the drama leading up to Samson's departure for the temple. These events— that is, Samson's encounters with the Chorus, Manoa, Dalila, and Harapha, as distinct from the scenes and events from his past life that are recalled during his conversations with these figures—fall after 16:22 ("Howbeit the hair of his began to grow again after he was shaven") and before the Philistine lords order Samson delivered to the temple at 16:23. Chronologically, that is, Judges 13– 16 encompasses the events recounted in *Samson Agonistes* up to the point of Samson's departure for the temple. The result of this textual interplay is that one may now see the seemingly empty crevasse between 16:22 and 16:23 of Judges as an encrypted site of surplus and absence. For it is here, in this obscure gap which Milton circumscribes for us, that Samson's furious struggle to know the unknowable is staged. It is here that one encounters Samson's excruciating and finally self-destructive attempt to apprehend the divine truths which elude all systems of conception and representation. It is here that one discovers the biblical narrative's deepest *inside*, which is also its unreachable *outside*—the something that is strange to the Judges narrative although at the heart of it, as Lacan might have said.

It is precisely here, moreover—the moment of Samson's removal to the temple—when the drama's production of meaning seems to falter, when the motivations behind Samson's resolution to enter the temple emerge as the central indeterminacy of the work. This is also the moment when God's enigmatic influence over his subjects through the Holy Spirit is most directly at issue. Thus the relationship established between the representable machinery of the postlapsarian world and the unrepresentable movements of God anticipates Lacan's account of the relation between the symbolic order and the Real, between the pleasure principle and the death drive. Divine agency seems to emerge or erupt in *Samson,* bringing the events to their deadly climax at the very moment when the insufficiency of human linguistic and conceptual structures is most palpable. Like the Lacanian Real, divine truth functions here as an indigestible, inaccessible, impenetrable surplus defining the limits of the symbolic network, announcing from within its own midst the symbolic order's failure to deliver final truth. A presentiment of the Real, Lacan asserts, is an "impact with the obstacle" to one's desire. One might say that the Real is what enforces our submission to laws of signification, "the magic circle" foreclosing us from the impossible Thing. Lacan writes: "The Thing is that which in the real suffers from this fundamental, initial relation, which commits man to the ways of the signifier by reason of the fact that he is subjected to what Freud calls the pleasure principle, and which . . . is nothing else than the dominance of the signifier." Or as the Lacanian theorist Slavoj Žižek puts it, "the Real is the rock upon which every attempt at symbolization stumbles, the hard core which remains the same in all possible worlds (symbolic universes); but at the same time its status is thoroughly precarious; it is something that persists only as failed, missed, in a shadow, and dissolves itself as soon as we try to grasp it in its positive nature. . . . But it is precisely through this failure that we can in a way encircle, locate the empty place of the Real."[40]

III

Samson's removal to the temple marks a separation between two other important forms of absence operative in the drama—one consisting of past events recollected, the other consisting of the drama's climactic event, his destruction of the temple, which has not yet taken place when the drama begins and which, at the drama's conclusion, is reported to us only after the fact by a witness. This brief description of the singularly undramatic character of this drama brings me to Milton's prefatory remark that *Samson Ago-*

nistes was never intended for the stage. His interdiction is important in light of the nature of Samson's theatrical performance in the Philistine temple, and it also may be viewed as a strategy for keeping the dialogic interplay of poem and Scripture in the foreground, of emphasizing the textuality and therefore metaphoricity of both texts.

In many ways, Mary Ann Radzinowicz points out, *Samson Agonistes* resists conventions that typically are associated with dramatic effectiveness. She remarks, for example, the way motion is inhibited in the drama, resulting in a general absence of the sort of visual interest one is accustomed to expect. "A strong emphasis upon outward stillness and inward movement is created by Milton's disposition of events," she writes. "[Samson] cannot make even the simplest choices of moving or not moving. . . . The tragedy is stripped of spectacle. The only visual effect from movement available to the mind's eye lies in the approaches of the Chorus, their advance toward Samson and their accompaniment of the other limited number of characters a short distance away from him."[41] Elsewhere Radzinowicz describes Samson's off-stage performance and its recounting by the Messenger as a "play-within-a-play" that emphasizes "the artificial and representational quality of what they have been seeing"—or reading, if Milton's wishes are to be heeded.[42] The internal drama reminds audience members or readers of "the textuality of the whole play" and of their own responsibility to discover and apply whatever truth it holds. "The play metaphor, in short, hands over to the audience the playwright's thematic responsibility" (Radzinowicz 1983, 268–69). I would endorse Radzinowicz's point, as far as it goes, but I think something much more radical is at work here, and it has to do with the relation organized by the classical tradition between staged performance and written text. Again, surplus and absence are significant. Alain Robbe-Grillet writes, from a Heideggerian perspective: "The human condition . . . is *to be there*. Probably it is the theater, more than any other mode of representing reality, which reproduces this situation most naturally. The dramatic character *is on stage*, that is his primary quality: he is *there*."[43] But Samson, in a manner suggestive once again of his incompleteness and unreadability, is absent. He is *not* there. We are to know Samson, according to Milton's wishes, solely through the text—that is, through a tissue of absence. Milton's Samson is refused the sensory and physical immediacy of the stage—he is denied the presence it seems to conjure—and he seems to be removed from us still further precisely at the moment when his *being there*—his status as a physical presence—would have been most palpable. Samson's entrance *upon* the stage of the Philistine temple for his moment of violent action is simultaneous with his departure *from* the stage of Milton's drama, leaving Milton's readers in the hands of witnesses for an account of what happens in this temple that is situated on a margin or surplus region of the drama. Thus Milton seems to desire our sense of Samson to include the very problem, as Robbe-Grillet describes it, that Samuel Beckett was trying to overcome for "man" when he wrote the stage play *Waiting for Godot.* "At last we would see Beckett's man, we would see *Man*," Robbe-Grillet writes. "For the novelist, by carrying his explorations ever farther, managed only to reduce more on every page our possibilities of apprehending him" (111). Indeed it seems to me that *Samson Agonistes* could easily be read as a progressive reduction, as the drama marches toward its off-stage climax, in the possibility of apprehending Samson.

Anthony Low regards Milton's handling of the violent climax as perfectly consistent with Hellenistic tradition, noting that in Greek tragedy "all violent action takes place off stage and is recollected or reported to the audience by the characters, especially by that typically Greek personage, the Messenger."[44] And yet I think there is more to it than this. In the first place, to whatever extent the obscuring of violent action in ancient Greek theater was a concession to the limitations of stagecraft, it must be observed that Milton, who never intended his drama for theatrical performance, faced no such limitations in *Samson Agonistes*. It is true, as Low points out, that in the *Poetics* Aristotle asserts that "spectacle has little to do with the poet's art," but it is also true that in a dramatic poem intended to be read and not seen there is no spectacle even if the reader is allowed into the Philistine temple with Samson.[45] More to the point, however, we are dealing not simply with a violent action; we are dealing very specifically with a violent action that takes place in the context of a staged performance, an action for which Samson leaves the stage of Milton's drama and ascends a stage that remains unseen by most of the characters in the drama as well as Milton's audience. Partitions, veils, and thwarted expectations are the lot of Milton's readers because of both his refusal of a staging of the drama and the choices he makes about what his audience may and may not "see." This suggests to me at any rate that certain aspects of the classical tradition are under interrogation here, and I suggest that this interrogation is of a piece with the more general critique Milton undertakes of our postlapsarian condition and its classically enfranchised conceits.

This portion of Milton's agenda might be most effectively illuminated, strange as it may seem, by considering it alongside Antonin Artaud's prescriptions for the theater of cruelty, an upstart brand of theater that strives to emancipate itself from the text and indeed from the entire classical tradition. I would first point out the provocative similarities between Artaud's description of the type of theater he would like to see and Samson's performance at the Philistine temple. "The contemporary theater is decadent . . . because it has broken away from gravity, from effects that are immediate and painful—in a word, from Danger" Artaud writes. "The best way, it seems to me, to realize this idea of danger on the stage is by the *objective* unforeseen, the unforeseen not in situations but in things, the abrupt, untimely transition from an intellectual image to a true image . . . capable of reintroducing on the stage a little breath of that great metaphysical fear which is the root of all ancient theater."[46] Danger, metaphysical fear, the objective unforeseen: Samson's Philistine spectators would surely vouch for a surplus of each in the performance they witnessed. But beyond this, I would suggest that Milton and Artaud share a jaundiced view of the text, even if they act on that view in radically different ways: that is, while Artaud wants to dispense with the text altogether and erect a theater that is independent of the written word, the effect of Milton's engagement with the genre of drama is an assertion of the primacy of the text as a reminder of the limitations of human understanding. Derrida notes that Artaud's objections to the "theological" structure of the classical stage focus on the subservience of stage to text, to "the layout of a primary logos which does not belong to the theatrical site and governs it from a distance." Artaud's theater, Derrida writes, would "not operate as an addition, as the sensory illustration of a text already written, thought, or lived outside, which the stage would then only repeat but whose fabric it would not constitute. The stage will no longer operate as the repetition of a *present*, will no longer *re*-present a present that would exist elsewhere and prior to it, a present whose plenitude would be older than it, absent from it, and rightfully capable of doing without it: the being-present-to-itself of the absolute Logos, the living present of God." But Milton, abjuring the stage, allows his text to remain a text, to remain visible and unambiguously material—for as Artaud and Derrida imply, classical theater renders the governing text invisible, imparting to it the illusion of originary plenitude, the being present to itself of absolute Logos, the living present of God. Milton's position on postlapsarian signification in all its forms, even the scriptural, allows no such association of the text with divine presence, and perhaps this is behind Milton's wariness toward a staging—or, as Derrida might say, a "spatio-temporalization"—of his drama. It is interesting that Derrida is writing not of theater but of metaphor when he remarks: "How are we to know what the temporalization and spatialization of meaning, of an ideal object, of an intelligible tenor, are, if we have not clarified what 'space' and 'time' mean? But how are we to do this before knowing what might be a logos or a meaning that in and of themselves spatio-temporalize everything they state? What logos as metaphor might be?" It seems, then, quite plausible to suggest that Milton would have seen a theatrical production of *Samson Agonistes* as tending to dematerialize, etherealize—perhaps *spiritualize* is the most apt term—his written text, thereby obscuring the problematical interplay he has set in motion between his text and its scriptural source.[47]

That interplay engenders a kind of kinesis, and I believe this kinesis is the real experience of reading *Samson Agonistes*. Stanley Fish attempts to illustrate the logic of textual kinesis by exposing as a "dangerous illusion" our habit of regarding a text as a self-sufficient, complete, and objective vessel "of whatever value and meaning we associate with it." We should instead interact with a text as with a piece of kinetic art, which "forces you to be aware of 'it' as a changing object—and therefore no 'object' at all—and also to be aware of yourself as correspondingly changing. Kinetic art does not lend itself to a static interpretation because it refuses to stay still and does not let you stay still either. In its operation it makes inescapable the actualizing role of the observer. Literature is a kinetic art, but the physical form it assumes prevents us from seeing its essential nature, even though we experience it."[48] Milton's poetry, as I have tried to show, similarly precipitates a dissolution of Scripture as stable object by confronting the reader with an interpretation of Scripture that foregrounds the actualizing role of the observer-reader-believer. The reader of *Samson Agonistes* is projected in a ceaseless orbit between the drama and the Judges narrative, a process that dissolves the objectivity of both texts and refers the believer to the Holy Spirit within, the "something in you more than yourself," which obscurely presages the divine truths that elude symbolization. The notion of kinesis suggests that the "meaning" lies somewhere between—and therefore necessarily apart from—the two texts. It is for the believer to decide upon this meaning, but of course neither is Milton's "wayfaring" Christian a stable entity; rather, recalling Fish's earlier remarks, he is one who seeks "change, discontinuity, and endless transformation." Everything is in motion here: instability marks Milton's reading of Judges 13–16 and his creation of *Samson Agonistes,* and it conditions the reader's encounter with both texts. The idea that it may all be definitively resolved into stability is an illusion, for static interpretation is impossible and, as Fish has suggested, Milton considered fixity of mind and judgment a sign of spiritual sloth. Thus the relationship between the biblical text and Milton's poetic transformation of it becomes subject to the fundamentally human process of making equal what is new. We cannot speak of a truth that is simply there to be recognized, for Milton's interpretation testifies to the possibility of numberless others. The riddle he confronts his readers with is one that will engender endless interpretations but no conclusive solution.

It is with this incessant and unstable intercommunication between poem and Scripture in mind that I return to metaphor. I adduce Derrida's account of the grammatical constitution of the trope as Aristotle conceived it and find that, like Fish's discussion of kinesis, Derrida's argument also subverts normative assumptions about stable substances and provides us with another angle of vision into Milton's critique of classical metaphor. Derrida's analysis of metaphor involves a distinction between the "categorematic" and "syncategorematic"—essentially, that is, between the nominal or substantive parts of speech and those performing connective or syntactical functions. "True metaphor . . . keeps within the limits of the Aristotelian 'noun,'" Derrida writes; indeed the noun (*epiphora onomatos*) is the component of *lexis* under which Aristotle discusses metaphor. Aristotelian metaphor, Derrida argues, can make use only of words which claim to have "a complete and independent signification, that which is intelligible by itself." And yet there are

whole "words" which play an indispensable role in the organization of discourse, but still remain, from Aristotle's point of view, totally without meaning. The conjunction . . . is a *phone asemos*. This holds equally well for the article, for articulation in general . . . and for everything that functions *between* signifying members, between nouns, substantives, or verbs. Articulation has no meaning because it makes no reference by means of a categorematic unity, to an independent unity, the unity of a substance or a being. Thus, it is excluded from the metaphorical field as the onomastic field.[49]

In the metaphorical horizon delimited by Judges 13–16 and *Samson Agonistes,* the meaning subsists precisely where Aristotle would deny the possibility of meaning; it is in neither of the two substantives or nominals (the texts) but in the article or copula running between them. We have seen in these pages how Milton's critique of visualism, his use of language, structure, the laying of scene, even his specification that *Samson Agonistes* should be read and not seen, evoke surplus and absence to encode the believer's experience of the obscurity of divine truths. And here again, in locating the meaning of his drama in an illegible nonlocus that simultaneously subtends and escapes the reach of both *Samson* and Judges 13–16, surplus and absence play a determining role in the reader's experience of Milton's text. Here again Milton finds a cryptic means of encoding the necessary exclusion of divine truth from the sensory, perceptual, representational, and conceptual economy of the postlapsarian world. The Real is "distinguished . . . by its separation from the field of the pleasure principle," Lacan writes, "by the fact that its economy . . . admits something new, which is precisely the impossible." Indeed, it seems that *Samson Agonistes* invites us to view the obscure truth of God not only as impossible for postlapsarian existence but as distinctly hostile to it, though this may merely be two ways of saying the same thing. "What one finds at the level of *das Ding* once it is revealed," Lacan argues, "is the place of the *Trieb,* the drives. And I mean by that the drives that, as Freud showed, have nothing at all to do with something that may be satisfied by moderation —that moderation which soberly regulates a human being's relations with his fellow man at the different hierarchical levels of society in a harmonious order, from the couple to the State with a capital S."[50] In *Samson Agonistes* divine truth emerges as just such an excessive, dreadful, and senseless force, one that threatens the postlapsarian order, just as the Real threatens the symbolic order, with disruption and even destruction. Samson destroys his enemies as well as himself in the staggering violence issuing from his apparent belief that he has stepped outside of the metaphorical horizon of human consciousness and entered the realm of the truth of God—nor should we fail to recognize that this all-consuming violence, which Milton makes such a point of veiling from his readers' gaze, brings the drama's conception of God into close conjunction with the notion of the *mysterium tremendum,* the singularly awe-striking dread proper to divinity.[51]

I conclude by calling attention to Lacan's contention that any work of art is an evocation of the Thing, an encounter with the vanishing point of the Real. The work of art "is really a signifier . . . of nothing other than signifying as such or, in other words, of no particular signified"—and by "no particular signified" Lacan means, of course, a signified that is not amenable to particularization, to representation in a positive sense. The artisan who fashions a vase, for example, creates

an object made to represent the existence of the emptiness at the center of the real that is called the Thing, this emptiness as represented in the representation presents itself as a *nihil,* as nothing. And that is why the potter . . . creates the vase with his hand around this emptiness, creates it, just like the mythical creator, *ex nihilo,* starting with a hole. . . . the fashioning of the signifier and the introduction of a gap or a hole in the real is identical.[52]

Samson Agonistes, too, is a work of art that ultimately has "no particular signified," and if it shares this characteristic with all works of art, it may yet be distinguished from many others by the seemingly precise awareness of this fact, which it signals through its use of language, structure, and the construction of scene, as well as its relationship with its biblical source text. For if it is possible to assign a final meaning to *Samson Agonistes,* I propose that this meaning consists in nothing other than the drama's fundamental and distinctly ominous *unreadability*—in its invitation to the reader, first, to recognize its necessary failure to assimilate within its verbal, conceptual, and structural resources the final truth that is its true subject and, second, to share in the ambiguity or indeterminacy that conditions the lives of the drama's characters. For like the potter's vase, Milton's drama—which emphasizes not simply the incomprehensibility but the radical externality of the divine truths fervently and paradoxically believed to reside at the center of postlapsarian human life—is fashioned around a traumatic emptiness, the *mysterium tremendum,* which is its essential substance. Moreover, the drama's very existence—attesting as it does to the interpretive procedure undertaken by the believer in reading Scripture—calls attention to the biblical narrative's own obscure extrinsic center, the indeterminate space that stages the believer's interpretive activity and engages the Holy Spirit within him.

In his analysis of *Paradise Lost,* Stanley Fish asserts that Milton combines "the ontology of monism—there is only one thing real—with the epistemology of antinomianism—the real is only known perspectively, according to the lights of individual believers."[53] By recasting this idea slightly, I believe one begins to glimpse what is to be gained by reading *Samson Agonistes* in the manner I have outlined above. For I have tried to show that in *Samson* Milton combines a monistic ontology predicated on one (unknowable) real thing with an epistemology that anticipates two major expressions of post-Nietzschean theory (Derridean poststructuralism and Lacanian psychoanalysis), and I believe this reading does more than simply credit Milton with precocious thinking on epistemology. I would argue that it also illuminates the post-Nietzschean theorists, whose radically negative ontology, built upon an unrepresentable and traumatic surplus, begins itself to look like a kind of monism that posits, behind the phenomenal façade of ceaselessly proliferating difference, its one true thing, the terrifying nothingness of surplus and absence. Milton accomplishes this, as we have seen, in a text replete with obscure margins and occluded crevasses that function to intensify our awareness of the obscurity shrouding divine truths and their enigmatic role in Samson's resolution to act. These concealed spaces and dark interstices enable Milton to put the Lacanian dictum "reality is marginal" into dramatic and poetic form, to invoke an ominously unreadable meaning, one that refuses to *make* the materials of the drama *equal* any clearly defined truth claim, one that short-circuits the *telos* of metaphor by withholding the terminal point of recognition that closes off the metaphoric loop. They give us a meaning that negates the entire conceptual apparatus by which "meaning" is produced in the postlapsarian world. It is a meaning which, finally, coincides with nothing except an irreducible flux, a stubborn indeterminacy that defines the place of being that is always already God.

University of Illinois at Chicago

NOTES

1. A lively debate has been in progress for many years, of course, on the fundamental question of whether *Samson Agonistes* makes complete sense. In *Milton's Debt to Greek Tragedy in "Samson Agonistes"* (New York, 1969), William Riley Parker finds—rather too simply, I believe—the drama's coherence in its relationship to Greek tragedy (later I examine Parker's views in more detail). Mary Ann Radzinowicz, meanwhile, in *Toward "Samson Agonistes": The Growth of Milton's Mind* (Princeton, 1978), contends that there is a point in the drama, a different point for every reader, where one "will see a pattern of significance subsuming and arranging within it all the materials of the drama experienced at first one by one. The tragedy is then recognized as a pattern or design which mirrors and organizes a number of converging designs" (3). I differ with Radzinowicz's view that reason finally synthesizes all of the violent and puzzling events of Milton's drama. I am more inclined to agree with William Kerrigan, who in "The Irrational Coherence of *Samson Agonistes*," in *Milton Studies* 22, ed. James D. Simmonds (Pittsburgh, 1986), asserts as a positive virtue the drama's seeming lack of closure and the stubborn opacity of its protagonist's motivations. To Radzinowicz's argument that *Samson Agonistes* reflects Milton's belief that Christian liberty derives "from the free following of the spirit of truth and reason in the individual" (169; cited in Kerrigan, 222), Kerrigan retorts that "a good deal of special pleading" is required "to discover this exalted vision of rational license" in *Samson Agonistes,* a drama whose movement within a system of binary alternatives is "destined to collapse into the both/and of the climax, as Samson's capitulation to Dagon becomes the fulfillment of his glorious mission" (222, 225).

2. Examples of readings that stress ambiguity or indeterminacy in *Samson* include Kerrigan, "The Irrational Coherence"; Anthony Low, *The Blaze of Noon: A Reading of "Samson Agonistes"* (New York, 1974), 62–89; Daniel T. Lochman, "'If There Be Aught of Presage': Milton's Samson as Riddler and Prophet," in *Milton Studies* 22, ed. James D. Simmonds (Pittsburgh, 1986), 195–216; John C. Ulreich Jr., "'Beyond the Fifth Act': *Samson Agonistes* as Prophecy," in *Milton Studies* 17, ed. James D. Simmonds (Pittsburgh, 1983), 281–318; John Rogers, "The Secret of *Samson Agonistes*," in *Milton Studies* 33, ed. Albert C. Labriola and Michael Lieb (Pittsburgh, 1996), 111–32; Derek N. C. Wood, "Intertextuality, Indirection, and Indeterminacy in Milton's *Samson Agonistes*," *English Studies in Canada* 18 (1992): 261–71; and especially Stanley Fish, "Spectacle and Evidence in *Samson Agonistes*," *Critical Inquiry* 15 (1989): 556–86. Meanwhile, the more unsettling aspects of Milton's vision are developed by Michael Lieb in *Milton and the Culture of Violence* (Ithaca, 1994). In this work Lieb examines the function of violence as a religious category and attempts to delineate in Milton a "sparagmatic" sensibility wherein bodily dismemberment, paradoxically both an experience of destruction and a harbinger of renewal, encodes Milton's understanding of the irreparable dismemberment of truth in the postlapsarian world. "In no other work of Milton is the sparagmatic experience more germane than in *Samson Agonistes.*" (237). As we shall see in more detail below, Lieb also focuses attention on the dark and terrifying dimensions of *Samson Agonistes* in "'Our Living Dread': The God of *Samson Agonistes*," in *Milton Studies* 33, ed. Albert C. Labriola and Michael Lieb (Pittsburgh, 1996), 3–25.

3. John Milton, *Of Reformation in England,* in *The Riverside Milton,* ed. Roy Flannagan (Boston, 1998), 875.

4. Metaphorization, or making equal, is for Nietzsche "the originary process of what the intellect presents as 'truth,'" as Gayatri Chakravorty Spivak puts it in her introduction to Jacques Derrida's *Of Grammatology* (Baltimore, 1976), xxii. Nietzsche's belief in the primary role played within human cognition by the metaphorical process of making equal is evident throughout his body of work. In *The Will to Power,* trans. Walter Kauffmann and R. J. Hollingdale (New York, 1976), he writes: "All thought, judgment, perception, considered as comparison, has as its

precondition a *'positing* of equality,' and earlier still a *'making* equal.' The process of making equal is the same as the process of incorporation of appropriated material in the amoeba" (273– 74). This same perspective informs Nietzsche's attempt to delineate the speaking subject's relation to truth. In "On Truth and Lies in a Nonmoral Sense," in *The Rhetorical Tradition: Readings From Classical Times to the Present,* ed. Patricia Bizzell and Bruce Herzberg (Boston, 1990), Nietzsche writes: "The 'thing in itself' (which is precisely what the pure truth, apart from any of its consequences, would be) is likewise something quite incomprehensible to the creator of language. . . . This creator only designates the relations of things to men, and for expressing these relations he lays hold of the boldest metaphors. To begin with, a nerve stimulus is transferred into an image: first metaphor. The image, in turn, is imitated in a sound: second metaphor. And each time there is a complete overleaping of one sphere, right into the middle of an entirely new and different one" (890).

5. Harold Bloom, *Ruin the Sacred Truths: Poetry and Belief from the Bible to the Present* (Cambridge, 1989), 97.

6. In making a connection with Derrida I am preceded by William Myers, whose reading of *On Christian Doctrine* and *Paradise Lost* finds Milton surprisingly attuned to the Derridean critique of the metaphysics of presence. In "The Spirit of *Différance,*" in *John Milton,* ed. Annabel Patterson (London, 1992), Myers writes: "There is abundant evidence that Milton himself was aware of *différance* (without, of course, knowing the word) and that he understood presence and so the classical subject in its light" (106). Myers's reading of *Paradise Lost* leads him to the conclusion that Milton conceives God as "a necessarily non-functioning presence, a non-functioning centre, a non-functioning author" while at the same time being "the beginning and the end of all things" (113).

7. Derrida's meditation, apropos of Artaud's theater of cruelty, on the canons and conventions of the classical stage will be significant later, when I consider Milton's disavowal of the staging of his drama.

8. Jacques Derrida, "Structure, Sign and Play in the Discourse of the Human Sciences," in *Writing and Difference,* trans. Alan Bass (Chicago, 1978), 279, 280, 279.

9. Jacques Derrida, "*Différance,*" in *Margins of Philosophy,* trans. Alan Bass (Chicago, 1982), 11.

10. Annabel Patterson, "Introduction," in *John Milton,* ed. Annabel Patterson (London, 1992), 7.

11. See *On Christian Doctrine,* in *Complete Prose Works of John Milton,* 8 vols., gen. ed. Don M. Wolfe. (New Haven, 1953–82), vol. 6, ed. by Maurice Kelley. This edition is hereafter cited parenthetically in the text as YP, with volume and page number. The present study provisionally accepts Milton as the author of *On Christian Doctrine.* William B. Hunter has of course in recent years brought the authorship of the treatise into question, first in "The Provenance of the *Christian Doctrine,*" *Studies in English Literature* 32 (1992), 129–66, and more recently in *Visitation Unimplor'd: Milton and the Authorship of "De Doctrina Christiana"* (Pittsburgh, 1998). Hunter's argument against ascribing the treatise to Milton's pen is intriguing but, as he acknowledges, circumstantial.

12. One example of Milton's sense of the metaphorical grounding of postlapsarian existence is discussed by John Leonard in his meticulous study of *Paradise Lost.* In *Naming in Paradise: Milton and the Language of Adam and Eve* (Oxford, 1990), Leonard notes how Milton laboriously postpones, over long stretches of his epic poem, any clear identification of "Lucifer" as Satan. It is only in Book Seven, Leonard reminds us, that the angel Raphael seems at last to pronounce them one and the same (and even here the matter is not as clear as we would wish). Yet, Leonard argues, the deferral effectively captures the qualified sense in which Milton would have us understand "Lucifer" as the name borne by Satan as an angel in heaven prior to his

rebellion —for Satan's angelic name, in common with all of prelapsarian language, is necessarily inaccessible to the postlapsarian world, and therefore "Lucifer" must be understood as a retroactive inscription which simply marks the absence of the lost name. Even Milton's early editors, Leonard writes, knew that Satan was "'Lucifer' by metaphor, not by name"—that "someone called 'Lucifer . . . in the Dialect of men' (5.761) could not have been called 'Lucifer' in the dialect of angels. . . . 'Lucifer' is an *interpretation* of Satan's 'other glorious Name'; it is not itself that name which is now 'razed out, and lost in everlasting oblivion'" (98). William Myers, meanwhile, finds a similarity between Milton's view of metaphor and that elaborated by Nietzsche. Myers provides an analysis of proto-Derridean motifs in *Paradise Lost* and *On Christian Doctrine,* ascribing the believer's inability to comprehend the truth of God to "the great gulf fixed between all signification and the Divine Referent"—a gulf to which Raphael gives voice in *Paradise Lost* when he attempts to evoke "what / Surmounts the reach of human sense" (5.571– 72). God's encounter with postlapsarian verbal language necessarily reduces him, Myers writes, to "a Nietzschean metaphor . . . a series of signs with no claim to 'truth', but invested none the less with a legitimate effectiveness in the human imagination sufficient to generate a sense of real and specific obligations in our minds" (Patterson, 106–7).

13. Jacques Derrida, "White Mythology: Metaphor in the Text of Philosophy," in *Margins of Philosophy,* trans. Alan Bass (Chicago, 1982), 233.

14. Julia Kristeva, *Black Sun: Depression and Melancholia,* trans. Leon S. Roudiez (New York, 1989), 13.

15. Jacques Lacan, *Seminar VII: The Ethics of Psychoanalysis, 1959–1960,* trans. Dennis Potter (New York, 1992), 103, 54.

16. Lacan, *Seminar VII,* 83, 139.

17. Lacan, *Seminar VII,* 71; "The Mirror-Stage as Formative of the Function of the I as Revealed in Psychoanalytic Experience," in *Écrits: A Selection,* trans. Alan Sheridan (New York, 1977), 2, 5.

18. Derrida, too, though less explicitly than Lacan, acknowledges the primacy of the visual field when he declares it a *"speculary* dispossession" which the human subject experiences at his accession to the "law of language." See Jacques Derrida, *Of Grammatology,* trans. Gayatri Chakravorty Spivak (Baltimore, 1976), 141 (italics mine).

19. Lacan, *The Four Fundamental Concepts of Psycho-Analysis,* trans. Alan Sheridan (New York, 1978), 100. The Lacanian theorist Luce Irigaray, in *Speculum of the Other Woman,* trans. Gillian C. Gill (Ithaca, 1985), describes, in the context of gender difference and the Freudian castration complex, the role played by visualization in the construction of self and of truth: *"The gaze is at stake from the outset. . . .* Woman's castration is defined as her having nothing you can see, as her *having* nothing. . . . *Nothing to be seen is equivalent to having no thing. No being and no truth"* (47, 48; italics in the original). Noteworthy readings of Milton's work involving Lacanian ideas, and particularly his theory of the mirror stage of human development, include Claudia M. Champagne, "Adam and His 'Other Self' in *Paradise Lost:* A Lacanian Study in Psychic Development," *Milton Quarterly* 25 (1991): 48–59, and James W. Earl, "Eve's Narcissism," *Milton Quarterly* 19 (1985): 13–16. Other critics, meanwhile, have noted the visualist critique in Milton's work. Stanley Fish's discussion, in "Spectacle and Evidence in *Samson Agonistes,"* of the function of visualization in *Samson* will be considered in some detail below. Also of interest is Regina M. Schwartz's observation, in *Remembering and Repeating: On Milton's Theology and Poetics* (Chicago, 1993), that "Milton joins Augustine in associating knowledge with sight—curiosity was the lust of the *eye*—and both anticipate much later psychoanalytic discussions of knowledge-seeking as a form of scopophilia" (54).

20. Lacan, *Seminar VII,* 104.

21. Lacan, *The Four Fundamental Concepts of Psycho-Analysis,* 275.

22. Lieb, " 'Our Living Dread': The God of *Samson Agonistes*," 6–7.

23. Kristeva, *Black Sun,* 13.

24. Lieb, " 'Our Living Dread': The God of *Samson Agonistes*," 13.

25. *Samson Agonistes* 2.17, in *John Milton: Complete Poems and Major Prose,* ed. Merritt Y. Hughes (New York, 1957). Unless otherwise noted, all further citations to Milton are from this edition.

26. Parker, *Milton's Debt to Greek Tragedy in "Samson Agonistes,"* 5.

27. Nietzsche, *The Gay Science,* trans. Walter Kaufmann (New York, 1974), section 260.

28. Aristotle, *Poetics,* trans. Stephen Halliwell (Cambridge, Mass., 1995), 115; Derrida, "*Différance*," 237.

29. Low, *The Blaze of Noon,* 95–96.

30. Fish, "Spectacle and Evidence in *Samson Agonistes*," 559.

31. In the *Rhetoric,* trans. George A. Kennedy (New York, 1991), Aristotle writes: "From good riddling it is generally possible to derive appropriate metaphors; for metaphors are made like riddles; thus, clearly, [a metaphor from a good riddle] is an apt transference of words" (3.2.11).

32. W. J. Pepicello and Thomas A. Green, *The Language of Riddles: New Perspectives* (Columbus, 1984), 8.

33. Parker, *Milton's Debt to Greek Tragedy in "Samson Agonistes,"* 5.

34. Lochman, " 'If There Be Aught of Presage': Milton's Samson as Riddler and Prophet," 209, 211.

35. Anthony Low's *The Blaze of Noon* makes essentially the same point in the chapter titled "Irony: Reversal and Synthesis" (62–89). John C. Ulreich, Jr. also finds riddling to be germane to the concerns of *Samson Agonistes*. In " 'Beyond the Fifth Act,' " Ulreich argues that the riddle Samson poses in the Judges account—"Out of the eater came forth meat, and out of the strong came forth sweetness"—is the key to understanding how the drama's "prophetic" or parabolic dimension reconciles the seeming incompatibility between its classical form and its Hebraic argument. "The apparent impossibility of reconciling drama and argument suggests that we should explore the possibility of a third, figurative line of development," Ulreich writes (284). Noting the similarities between parables and riddles, Ulreich finds in Samson's riddle a larger parabolic significance, for the solution to Samson's riddle—"What is sweeter than honey? and what is stronger than a lion?"—itself poses a question or a riddle that "begins to unfold its figurative possibilities" by suggesting that Samson, assuming the place of the eater, is himself consumed (producing meat) by perishing in the temple. At the same time he "nourishes his people with the honey of deliverance" (284). He concludes: "In this way the ancient riddle is transformed into a religious paradox, and the primitive fable of Samson the Destroyer becomes a parable of deliverance. . . . By juxtaposing classical action and Hebraic argument, Milton insists on their radical incongruity; he renders the literal surface of his play 'inexcusable' in order to crystallize its figurative meaning" (284). For a related discussion, also see Ulreich's " 'This Great Deliverer': *Samson Agonistes* as Parable," *Milton Quarterly* 13 (1979): 79–84.

36. Fish, "Spectacle and Evidence in *Samson Agonistes*," 559.

37. Cited in Derek N. C. Wood, "Aristotle, the Italian Commentators, and Some Aspects of Milton's Christian Tragedy," in *Milton Studies* 29, ed. Albert C. Labriola (Pittsburgh, 1992), 99.

38. Even where Parker does see fit to discuss *Samson's* relation to Judges, he does so only in order to absorb that relation into a supposedly more overarching and defining debt to the Greeks; thus he manages to estrange Milton's drama from its biblical source text even when discussing a point of connection between them. "In the entire fifth century," Parker notes, "so far as we have any record, there were only four plays which did not take their material from sacred legends. . . . Milton did not, to be sure, go to the sacred legends of Greece for the subject matter

of *Samson*. But the fact that, unlike so many other 'classical' dramatists, he refused to do so, persuades me that his debt to classical drama was therefore the greater" (Parker, 77). It is true, as Parker notes, that Milton's preface to *Samson* specifies only the Greeks as his source of inspiration and guidance, but many scholars, notably Mary Ann Radzinowicz in *Toward "Samson Agonistes"* (9, 10–11, 12), have remarked the important ways in which *Samson Agonistes* departs from the classical standard that Milton appears to invoke in the preface when he adduces Aristotle and speaks of "Tragedy . . . as it was antiently composed" (Hughes, 549). One may even wonder if Milton's awareness of the dialogic interplay between his drama and the biblical account in Judges prompts him to phrase the acknowledgment in precisely the way he does. Of those who would appraise his dramatic poem, Milton declares, "they only will best *judge* [my italics] who are not unacquainted with *Aeschylus, Sophocles,* and *Euripides*" (Milton 1957, 550). While there is certainly nothing strained about Milton's use of the word *judge* here, perhaps it is nuanced all the same. Perhaps there is an allusion to the biblical narrative in this piece of advice to the reader, a hint of this textual interdependency, an adumbration of the discrepancies one is to find between classical prescriptions for tragedy and the form of the drama one is about to read.

39. Here I should perhaps say a word to distinguish my project from that of Joseph Wittreich in those parts of his *Interpreting "Samson Agonistes"* (Princeton, 1986) that attempt to define the relationship of Milton's drama to the Judges narrative. Wittreich argues that the liberties Milton took with the Judges text in *Samson Agonistes* reflect the poet's desire to correct the misinterpretations of the scriptural account that had gained such widespread currency during the Renaissance. Milton's aim, Wittreich argues, is to restore to his fellow believers a true understanding of the Samson narrative—therefore Milton's drama "is not an encoding but a decoding of the Samson story" (57). Wittreich goes on to assert that, in its encounter with the scriptural narrative, *Samson Agonistes* "*condenses* by including some events and excluding others; it *displaces* by foregrounding this and backgrounding that; it *encodes* some events as causes, others as effects" (61), and of course one recognizes in the words that Wittreich italicizes the same effects wrought by tropes. In contrast, my attempt here is to argue that, precisely by condensing, displacing, and encoding the Judges text, *Samson Agonistes* also condenses, displaces, and encodes its true subject—God's truth—and declares that Judges 13–16 performs this same procedure itself. For no true *de*coding of divine truths is possible.

40. Lacan, *The Four Fundamental Concepts of Psycho-Analysis*, 167; Lacan, *Seminar VII*, 134; Slavoj Žižek, *The Sublime Object of Ideology* (London, 1989), 169, 172.

41. Radzinowicz, *Toward "Samson Agonistes": The Growth of Milton's Mind*, 15–16.

42. Mary Ann Radzinowicz, "The Distinctive Tragedy of *Samson Agonistes*," in *Milton Studies* 17, ed. James D. Simmonds (Pittsburgh, 1983), 268.

43. Alain Robbe-Grillet, *For a New Novel*, trans. Richard Howard (Evanston, 1989), 111. Robbe-Grillet alludes here to Heidegger's famous conception of *Da-sein* ("being there"), which receives its most extensive elaboration in *Being and Time*.

44. Low, *The Blaze of Noon*, 6.

45. *Poetics*, 75. Milton evidently had considered writing another biblical drama in which the climactic scene would be handled in similar fashion, as Norman T. Burns observes in " 'Then Stood Up Phinehas': Milton's Antinomianism, and Samson's," in *Milton Studies* 33, ed. Albert C. Labriola and Michael Lieb (Pittsburgh, 1996). Burns calls attention to Milton's notes in the Trinity College manuscript concerning a projected drama about Abraham—notes that give one ample reason to wonder whether Milton was doing more than simply acceding to dramatic convention when, in *Samson Agonistes,* he screened the violent climax from view. Burns writes: "To capture in [the projected drama about Abraham] this sense that the divine command could not be rationally comprehended, Milton planned to keep Abraham and the sacrificial scene offstage while he focused on the responses of the people in Abraham's household to reports

about what Abraham was doing at the scene of sacrifice." By configuring the drama's climax in this way, Milton would be suggesting that "the faithful hero is 'justified in the sight of God rather than in the sight of man' " (33). It is worth pointing out, apropos of the notion that classical drama moved the violent action off stage, that in the case of Abraham the climactic scene would contain no actual violence in any event, since God stops the sacrifice of Isaac once he is satisfied that Abraham had been prepared to go through with it in deference to divine command. Thus Milton would have been obscuring not the sensational and horrifying commission of a violent act but its rather unspectacular (in terms of visual interest) prevention.

46. Antonin Artaud, *The Theater and Its Double,* trans. Mary Caroline Richards (New York, 1958), 42, 43–44.

47. Jacques Derrida, "The Theater of Cruelty and the Closure of Representation," in *Writing and Difference,* trans. Alan Bass (Chicago, 1978), 235.

48. Stanley Fish, *Is There a Text in This Class? The Authority of Interpretive Communities* (Cambridge, 1980), 43.

49. Derrida, "The Theater of Cruelty and the Closure of Representation," 233, 235, 233; Derrida, "White Mythology," 240.

50. Lacan, *The Four Fundamental Concepts of Psycho-Analysis,* 167; Lacan, *Seminar VII,* 100.

51. Lieb, *Milton and the Culture of Violence,* 7. "If the Thing were not fundamentally veiled," Lacan argues, "we wouldn't be in the kind of relationship to it that obliges us, as the whole of psychic life is obliged, to encircle it or bypass it in order to conceive it. Wherever it affirms itself, it does so in domesticated spheres. That is why the spheres are defined thus; it always presents itself as a veiled entity" (*Seminar VII,* 118).

52. Lacan, *Seminar VII,* 120, 121.

53. Stanley Fish, *Surprised by Sin: The Reader in "Paradise Lost,"* 2nd ed. (Cambridge, 1997), xliv.